HOW TO DRAW MANGA WITH BATMAN, SUPERMAN, AND OTHER DC SUPER HEROES AND VILLAINS!

by Christopher Harbo

illustrated by Haining, Giulia Campobello,
and Mel Joy San Juan

Batman created by Bob Kane with Bill Finger

Superman created by Jerry Siegel and Joe Shuster
by special arrangement with the Jerry Siegel family

Wonder Woman created by William Moulton Marston

CAPSTONE PRESS
a capstone imprint

TABLE OF CONTENTS

POWER UP WITH MANGA!

When the forces of evil are at work, DC Super Heroes leap into action! Batman battles to keep the mean streets of Gotham City clean. Superman shines bright as a beacon of truth and justice for the city of Metropolis. Wonder Woman fearlessly faces mythical gods to protect humanity. And Super-Pets fight alongside their Super Hero pals to curb crime, making the world a little friendlier and furrier! With these mighty champions, there's no shortage of heart-pounding thrills.

How can YOU power things up even more? By uniting the heroes, and their friends and foes, with MANGA!

What is manga? Simply put, it's comics and graphic novels from Japan. While the manga art style dates back more than 800 years, its popularity in books and magazines exploded in the late 1940s. Since then, manga mania has spread all over the world! Manga is famous for its awesome art. Cool characters have large eyes, small noses and mouths, and pointed chins. And when it comes to dynamic action, few comics match manga's electric look.

SO WHAT ARE YOU WAITING FOR? TAP INTO YOUR CREATIVE POWERS AND BRING THE MARVELS OF MANGA TO THE DC UNIVERSE. DRAW DC SUPER HEROES AND VILLAINS IN MANGA STYLE!

THE MANGAKA'S TOOLKIT

All manga artists—or mangaka—need the right tools to make amazing art. Gather the following supplies before you begin drawing:

PAPER

Art supply and hobby stores have many types of special drawing paper. But any blank, unlined paper will work well too.

PENCILS

Sketch in pencil first. That way, if you make a mistake or need to change a detail, it's easy to erase and redraw.

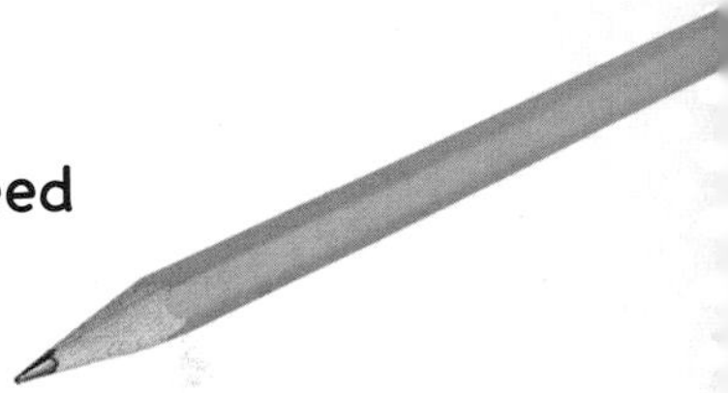

PENCIL SHARPENER

Keep a good pencil sharpener within reach. Sharp pencils will help you draw clean lines.

ERASERS

Making mistakes is a normal part of drawing. Regular pencil erasers work in a pinch. But high-quality rubber or kneaded erasers last longer and won't damage your paper.

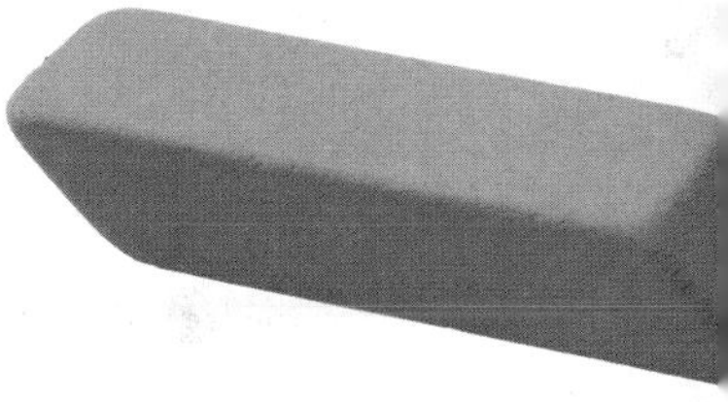

BLACK MARKER PENS

When your sketch is done, trace over the final lines with a black marker pen. By "inking" the lines, your characters will practically leap off the page!

COLORED PENCILS AND MARKERS

While manga stories are usually created in black and white, they often have full-color covers. Feel free to complete your manga masterpiece with colored pencils and markers. There's nothing like a pop of color to bring characters to life!

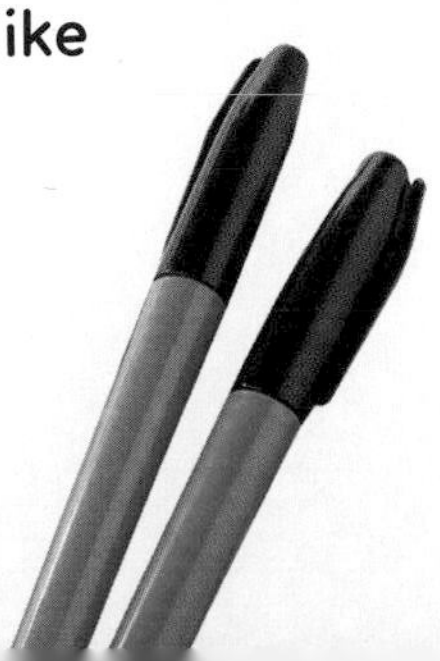

BATMAN

When the Bat-Signal blazes over Gotham City, the Dark Knight always answers the call. Leaping into action, he follows the clues to track down the world's worst Super-Villains. And when he finds his foes, the Caped Crusader grabs a Batarang from his Utility Belt, then lets it fly with a flick of the wrist!

MANGA FACT

In 1966, the Dark Knight leaped into the pages of manga! *Batman* by Jiro Kuwata featured original adventures and ran for more than a year.

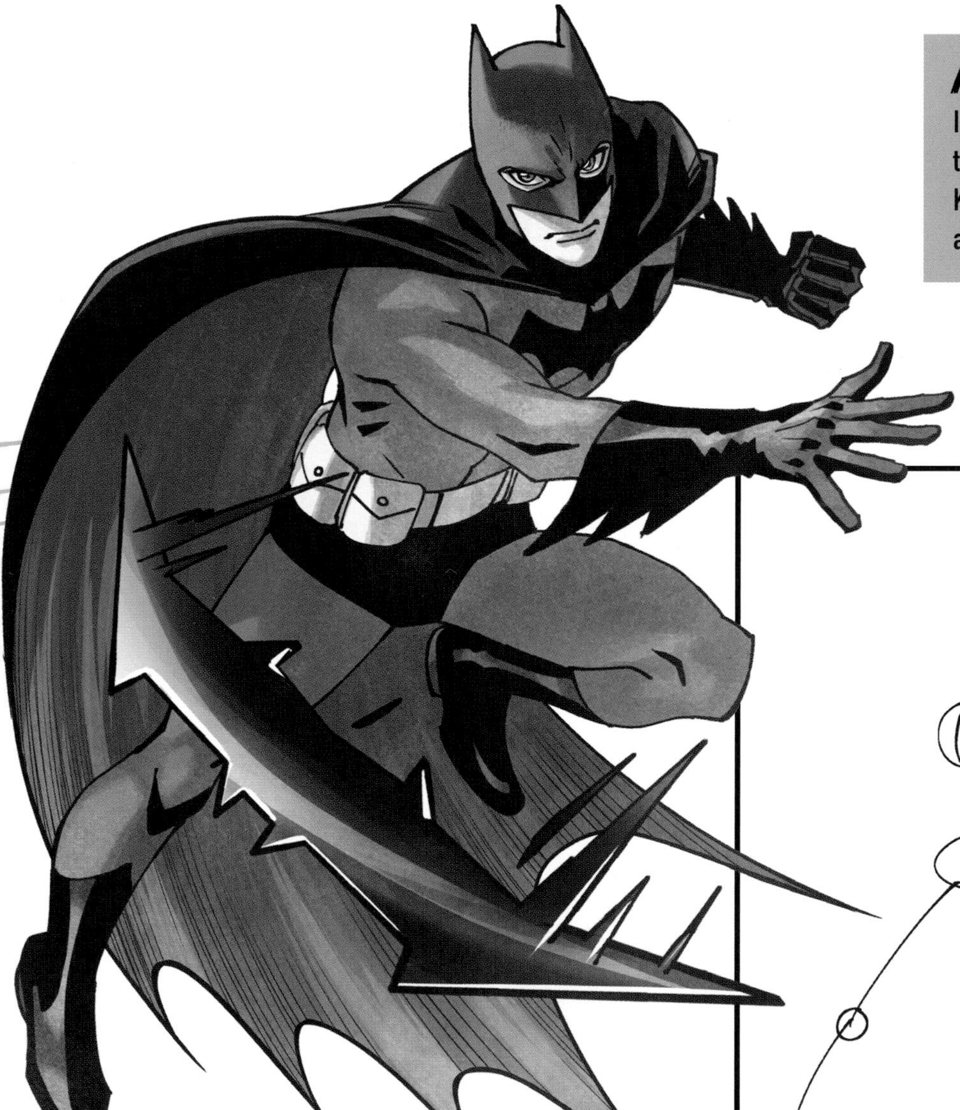

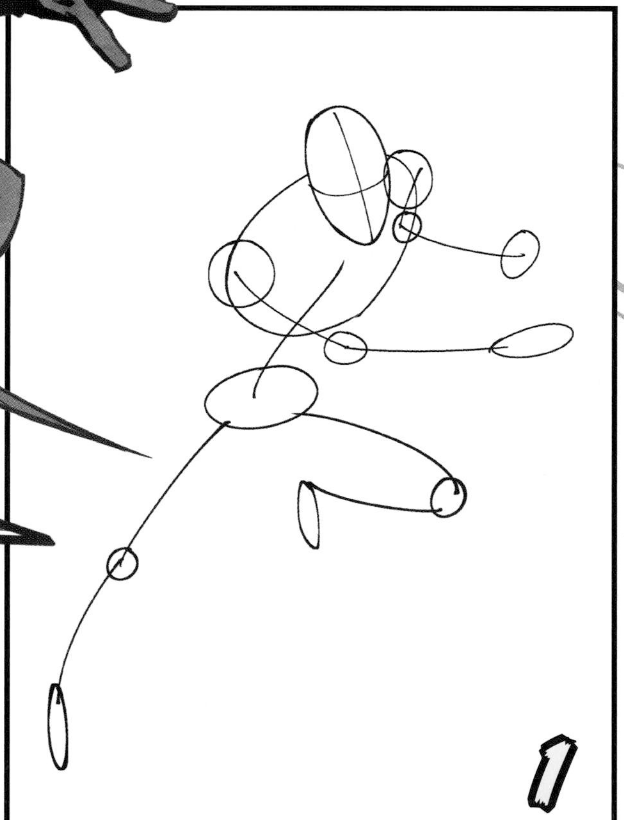
1

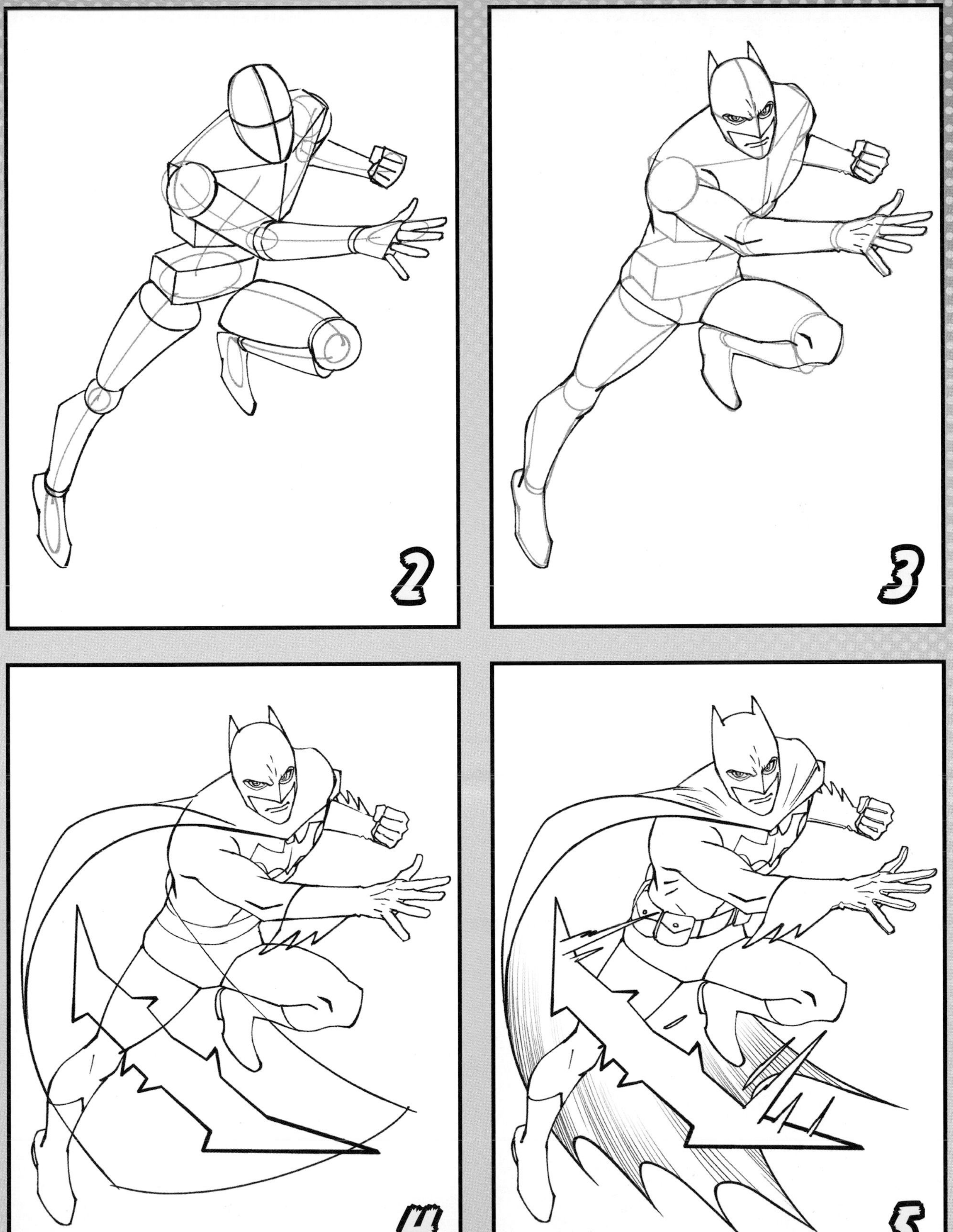
2
3
4
5

ROBIN

Few Super Hero sidekicks compare to Robin. His lightning-fast reflexes and quick wit are more than a match for any of Batman's baddies. Best of all, Robin is loyal and true. Whenever the Caped Crusader gets in a bind, he can count on the Boy Wonder to swoop down on a Batrope in the nick of time!

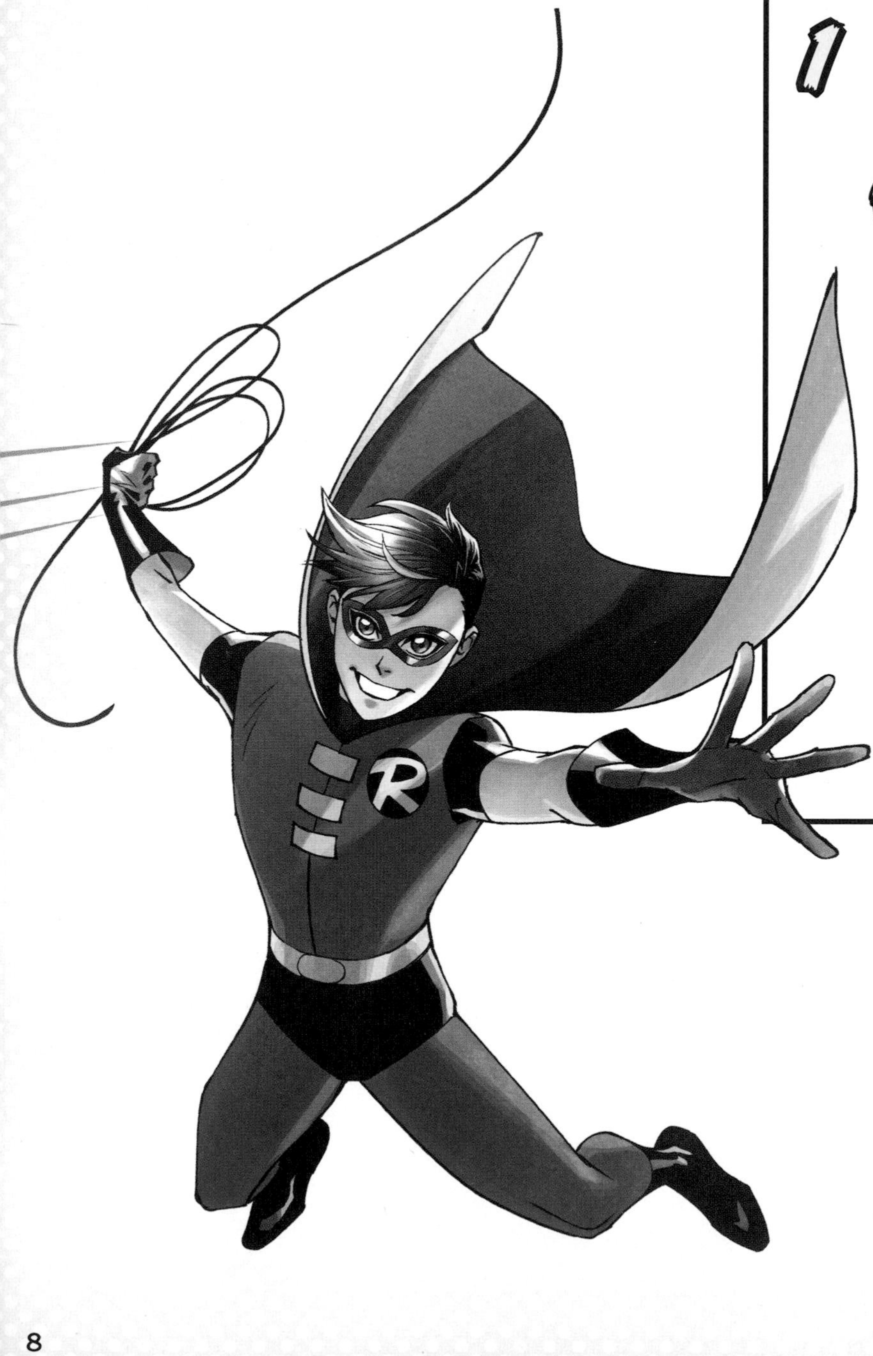

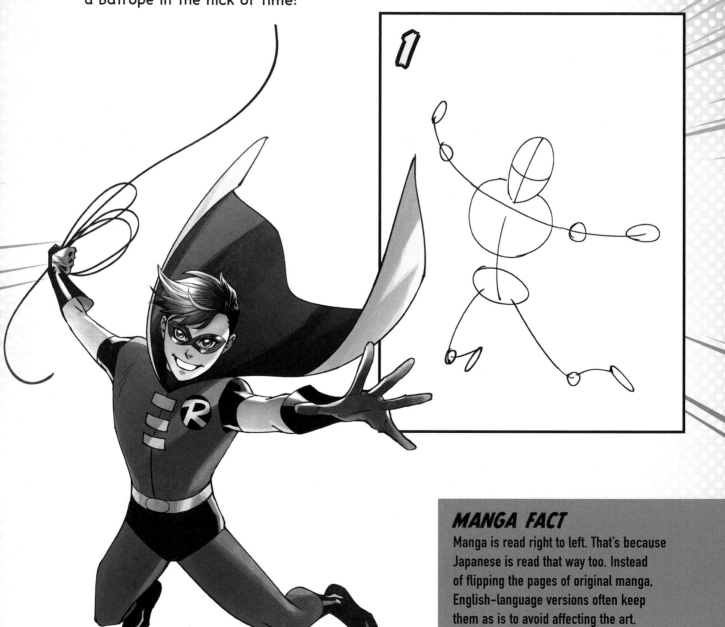

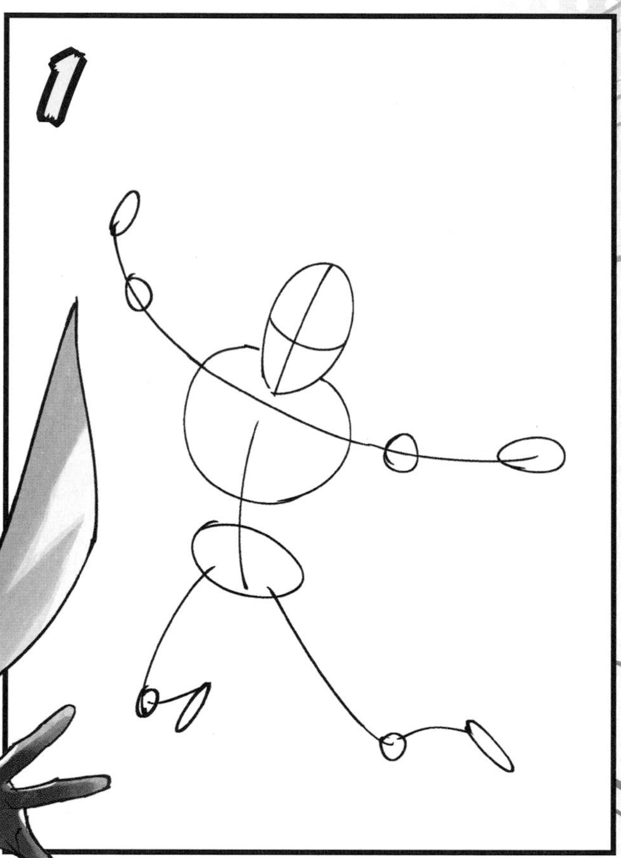
1

MANGA FACT

Manga is read right to left. That's because Japanese is read that way too. Instead of flipping the pages of original manga, English-language versions often keep them as is to avoid affecting the art.

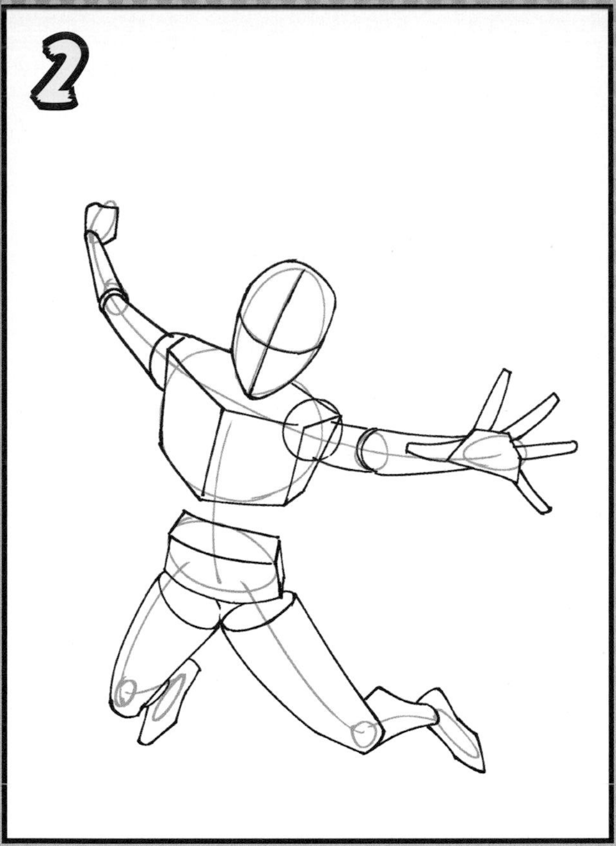
2
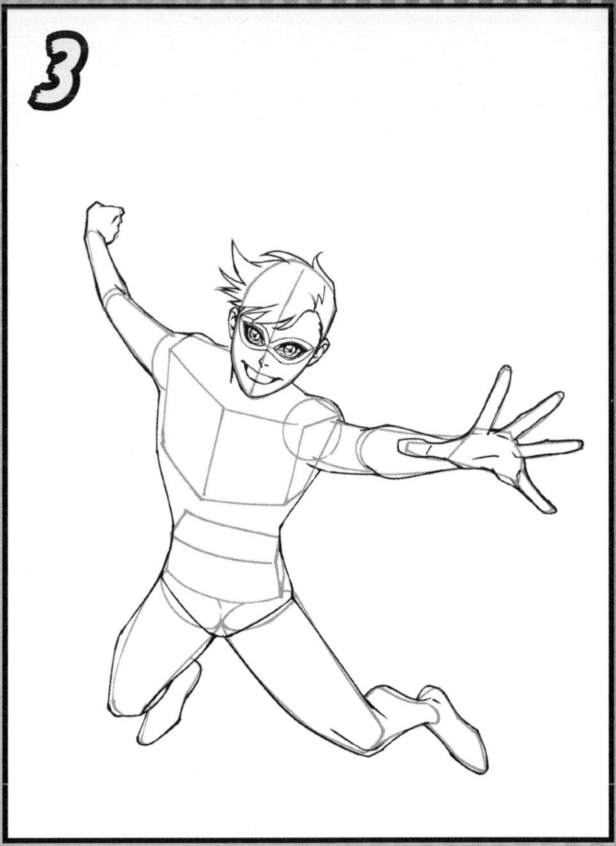
3
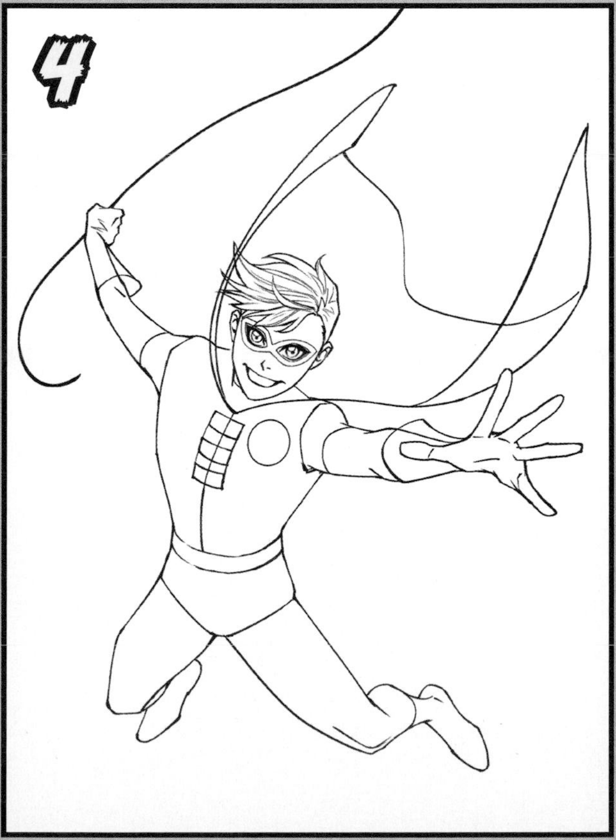
4
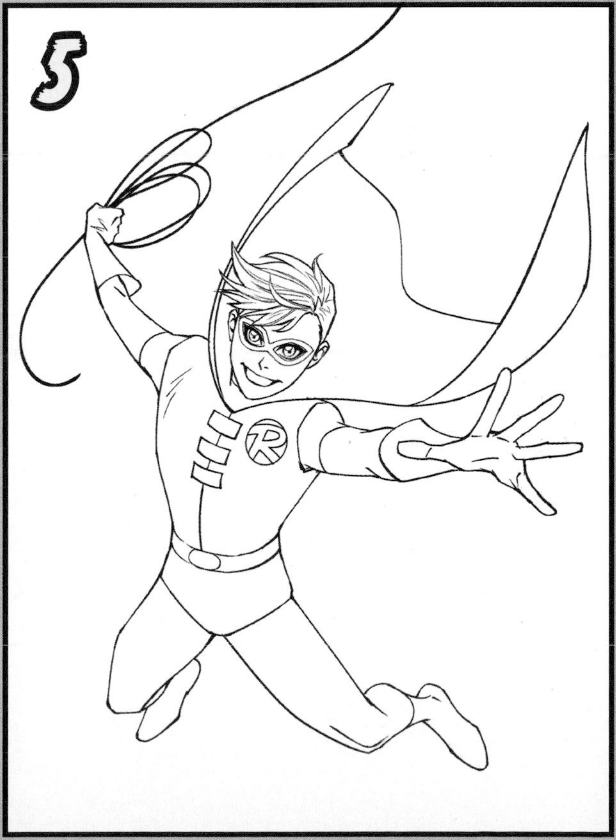
5

BATGIRL

Batgirl isn't about to let the Dynamic Duo have all the fun. Each night, this tech-savvy teen patrols Gotham City for coldhearted criminals. Will tonight be the night she hunts down Harley Quinn or rounds up the Riddler? Either way, this martial arts master is bound to have a blast kicking crime to the curb!

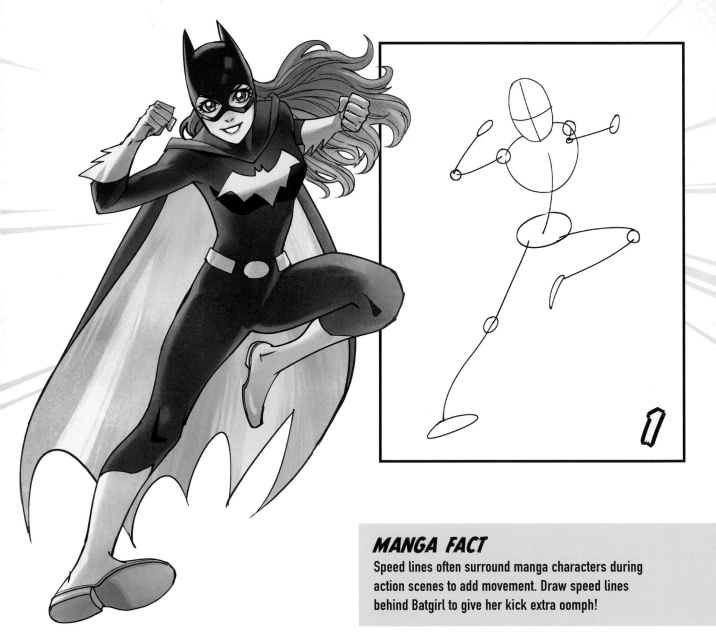

MANGA FACT
Speed lines often surround manga characters during action scenes to add movement. Draw speed lines behind Batgirl to give her kick extra oomph!

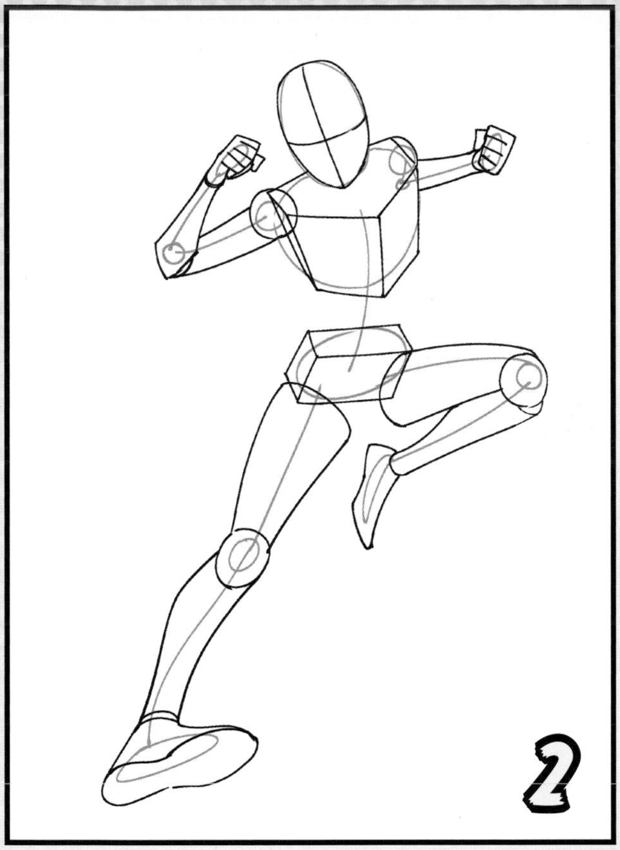
2
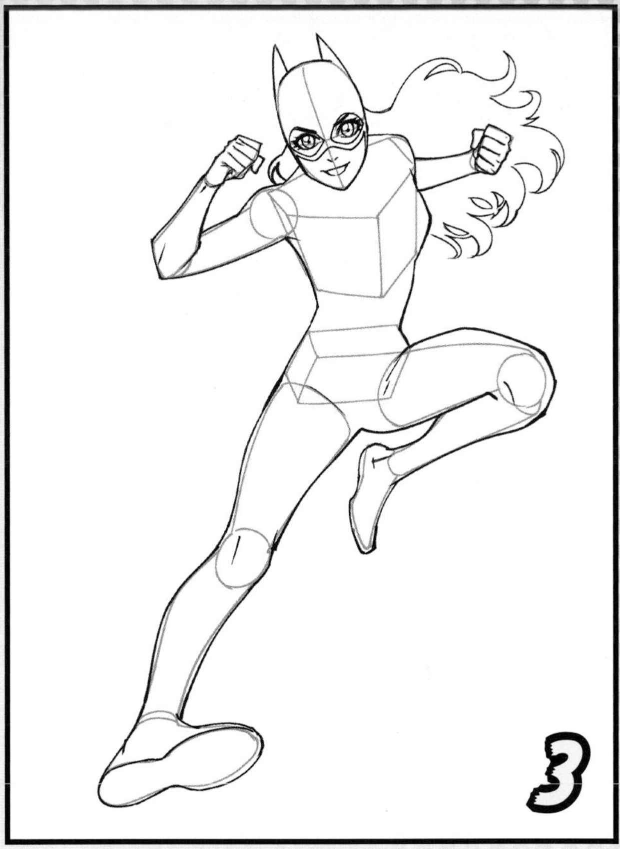
3
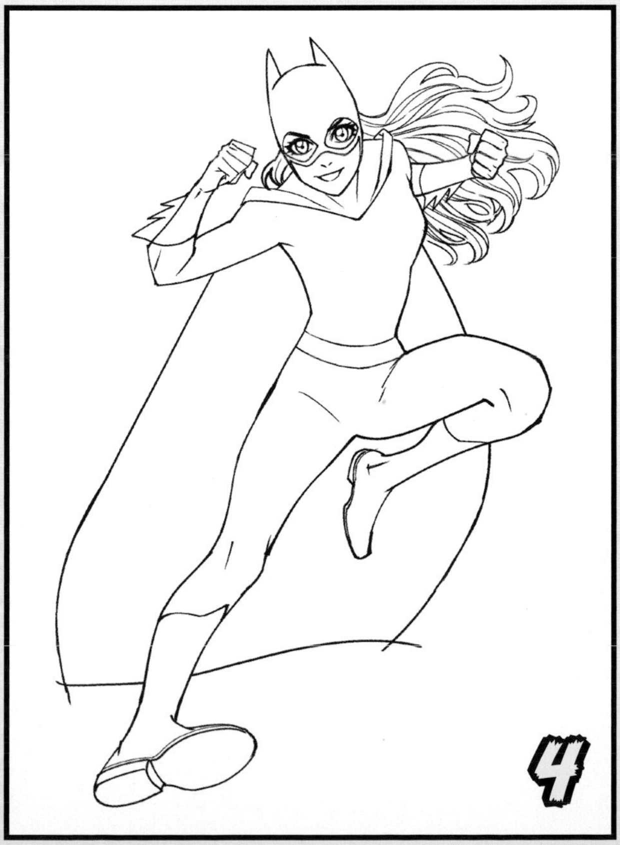
4
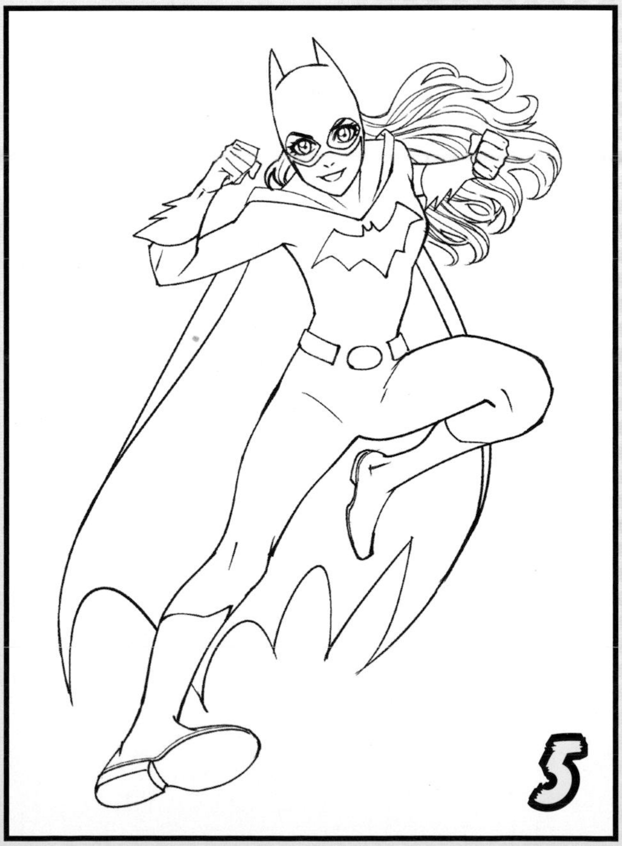
5

BATWING

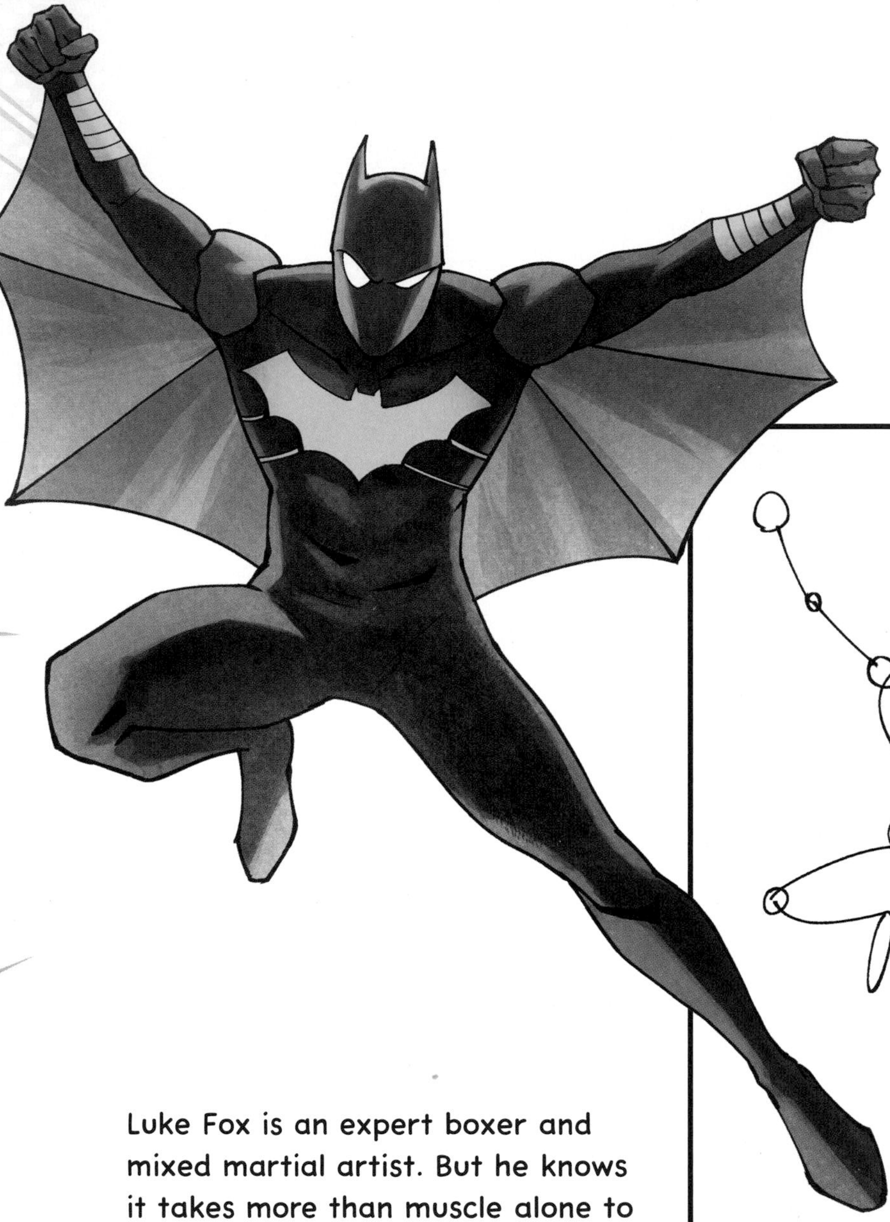

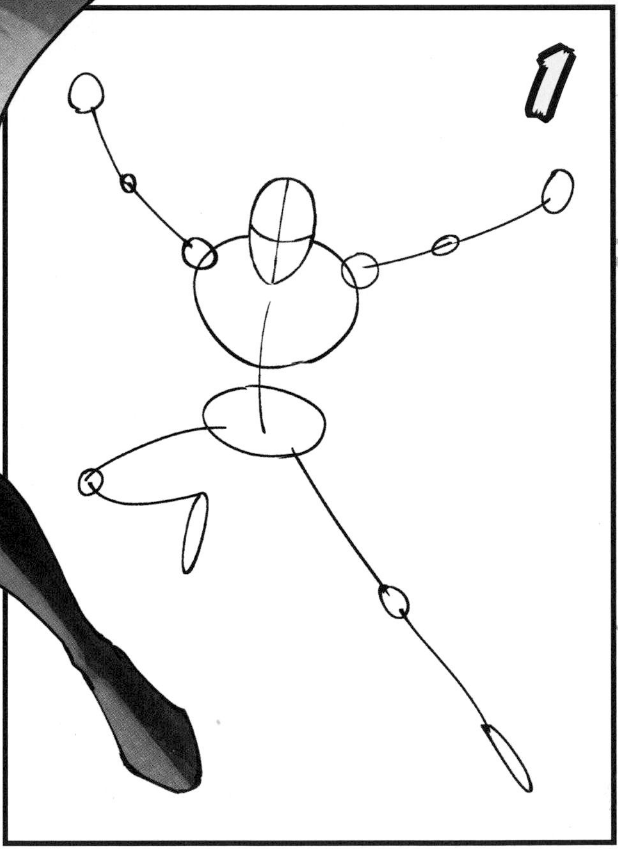
1

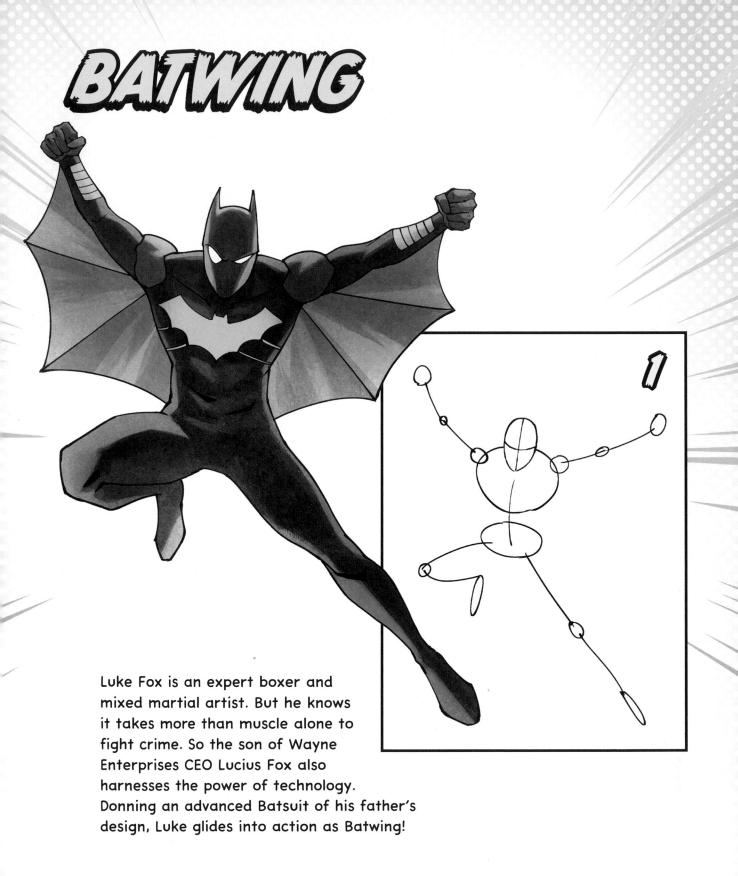

Luke Fox is an expert boxer and mixed martial artist. But he knows it takes more than muscle alone to fight crime. So the son of Wayne Enterprises CEO Lucius Fox also harnesses the power of technology. Donning an advanced Batsuit of his father's design, Luke glides into action as Batwing!

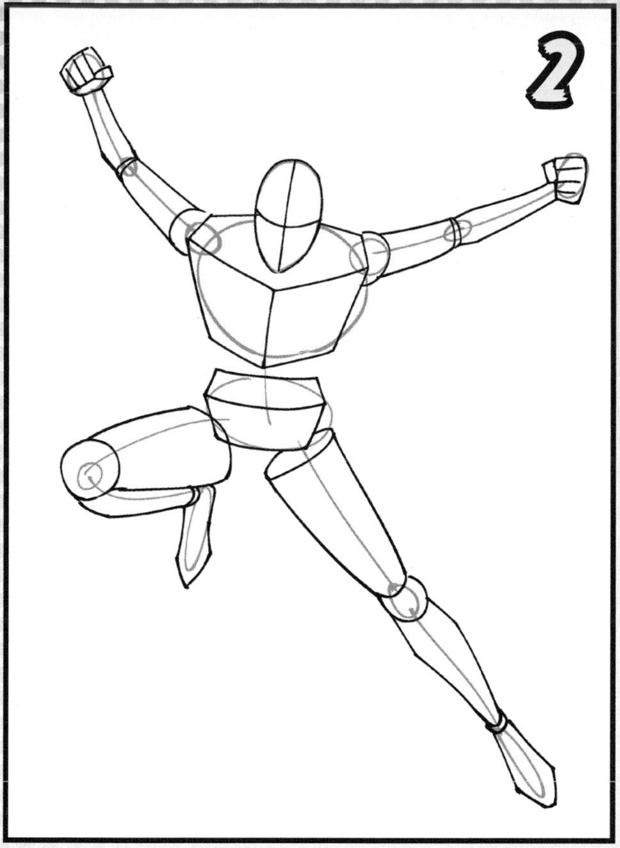
2
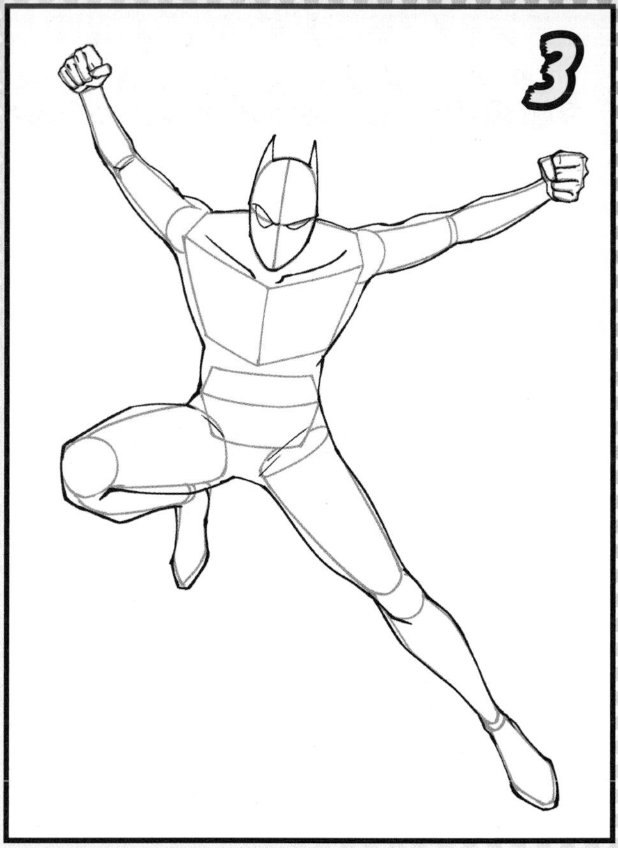
3
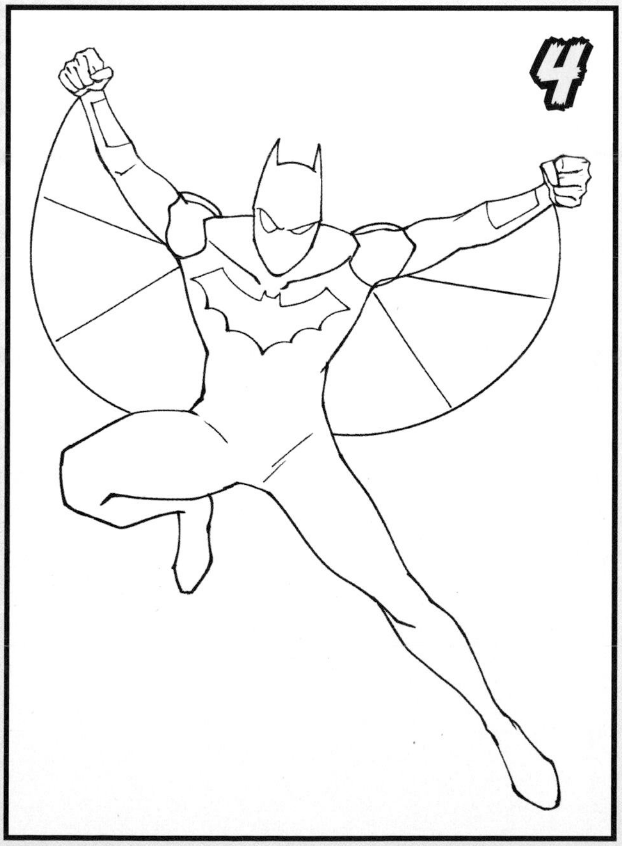
4
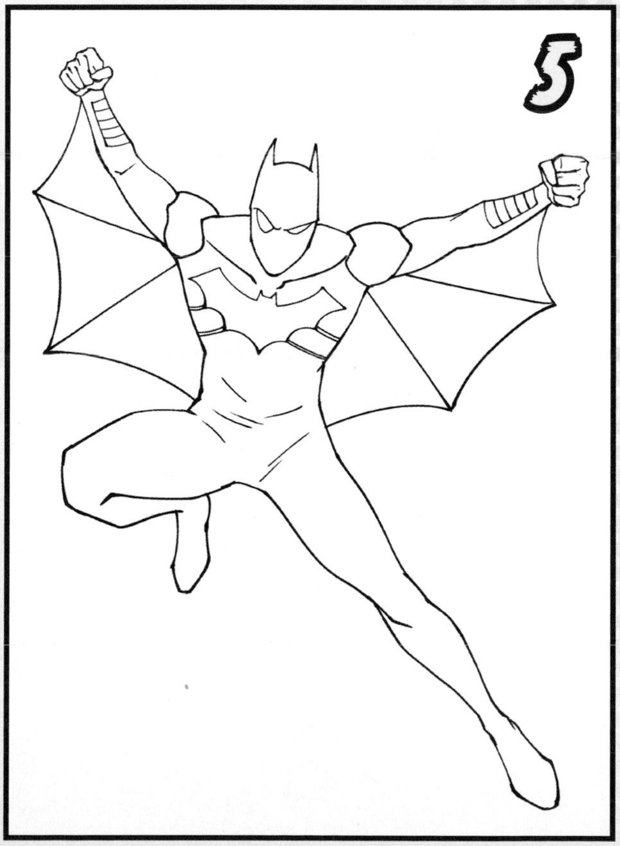
5

BATWOMAN

Kate Kane proves crime fighting runs in the family—the Bat Family. She's a cousin of Bruce Wayne, aka Batman. She's also a dedicated defender of Gotham City. Disguised as Batwoman, she relies on her keen mind and superior combat skills every time she charges fearlessly into a fight!

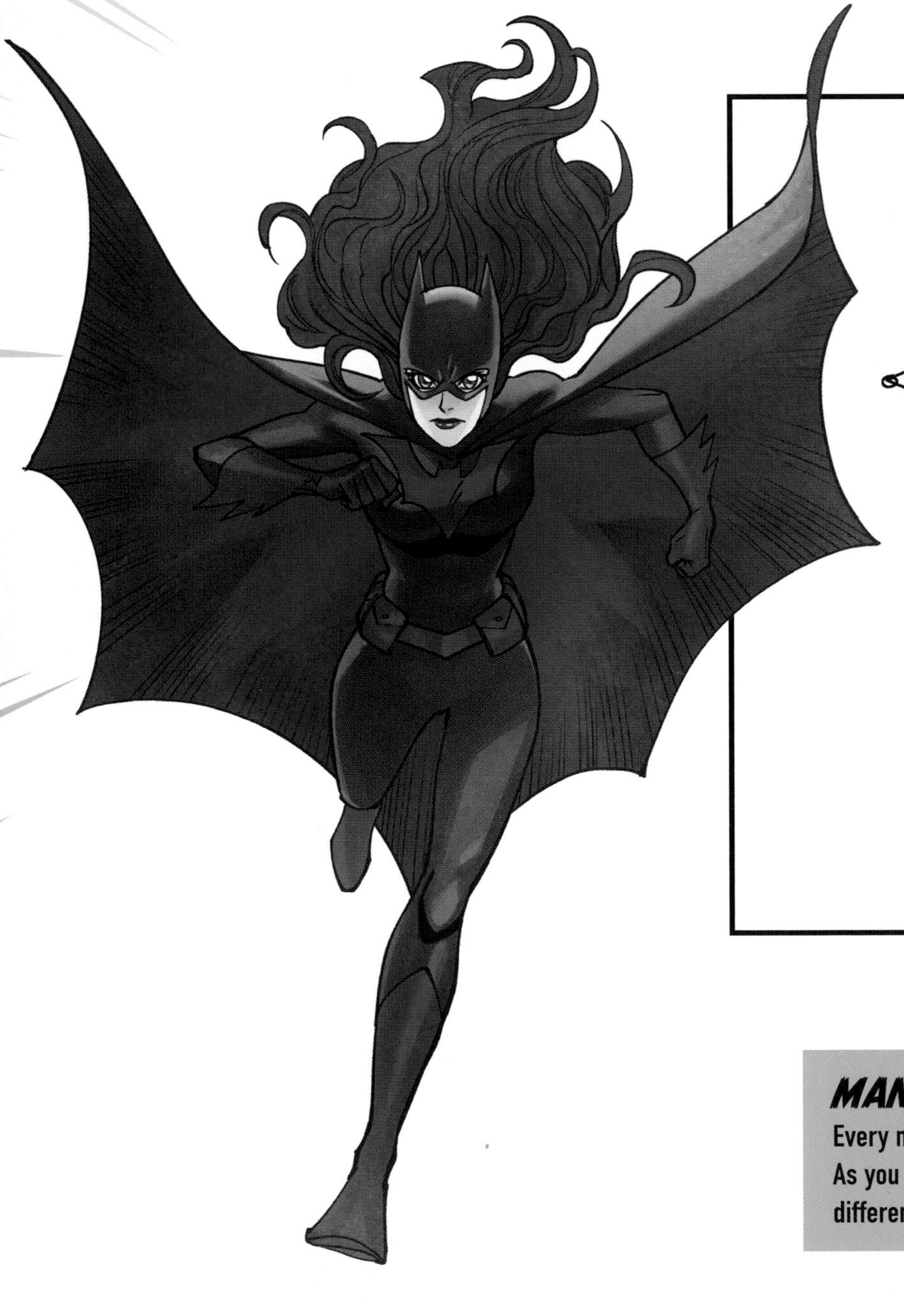

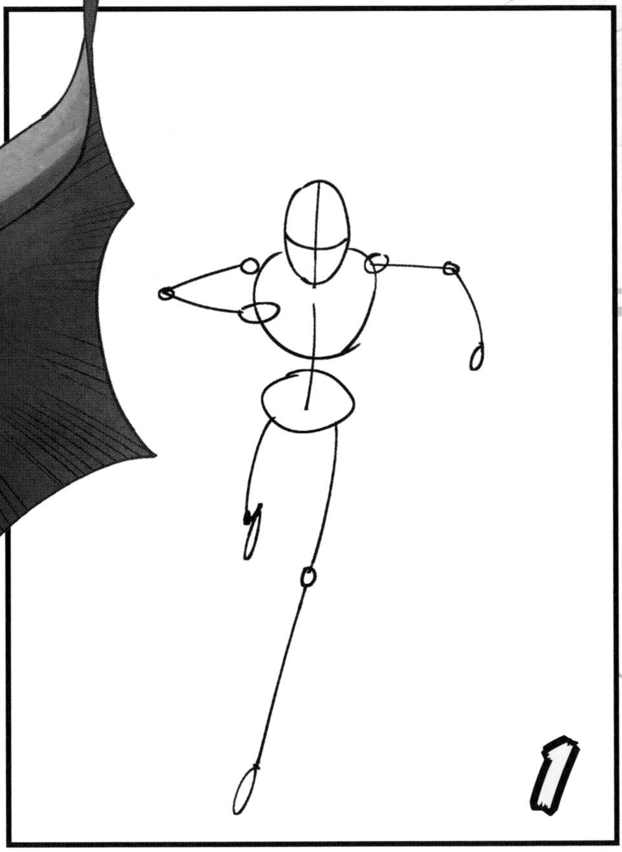
1

MANGA FACT

Every mangaka has their own unique style. As you practice your drawing skills, explore different styles to see which one suits you best.

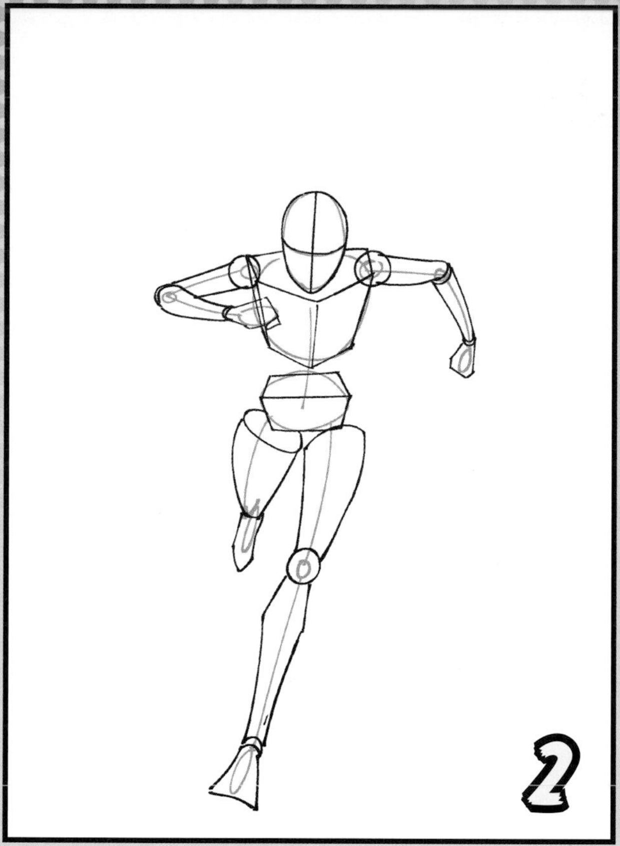
2

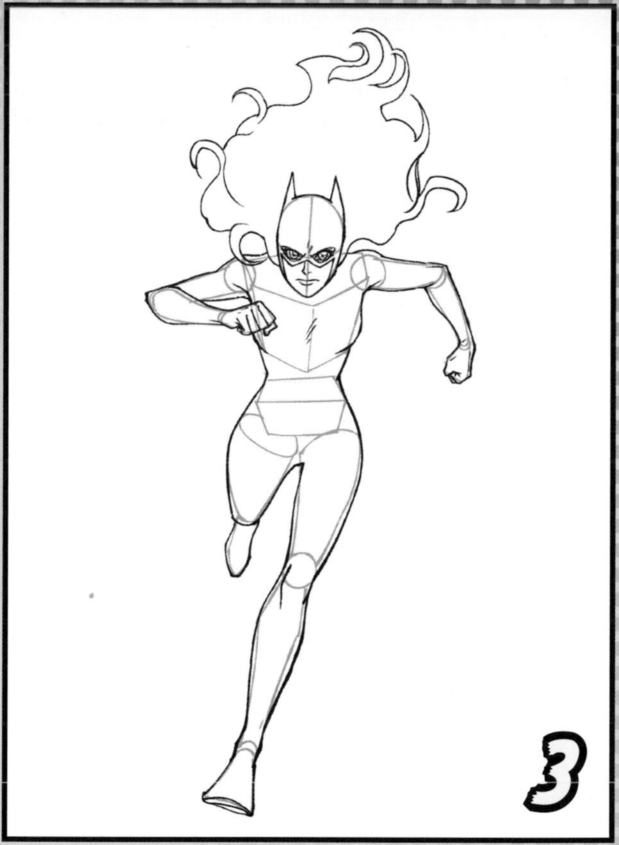
3

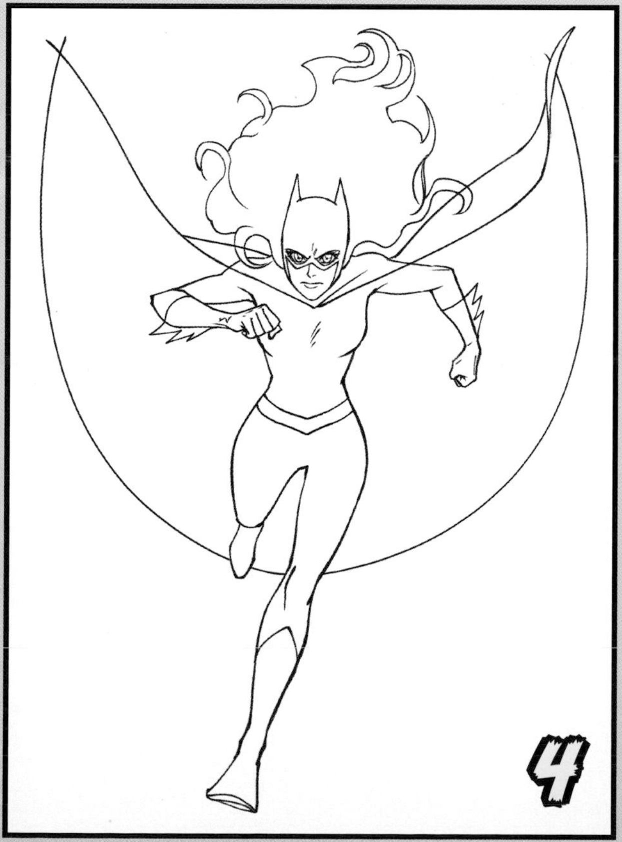
4

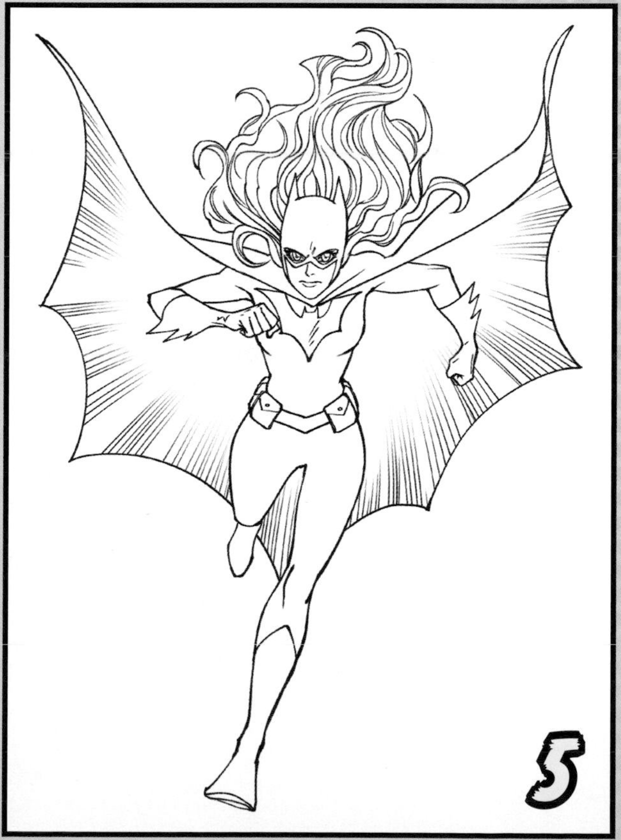
5

CATWOMAN

This professional thief is a bit of a *purr*-fectionist. With feline grace and agility, Catwoman can slink her way into just about any museum gallery or bank vault. But don't think that cracking safes is her only skill. She's also a cunning fighter who isn't afraid to crack her whip!

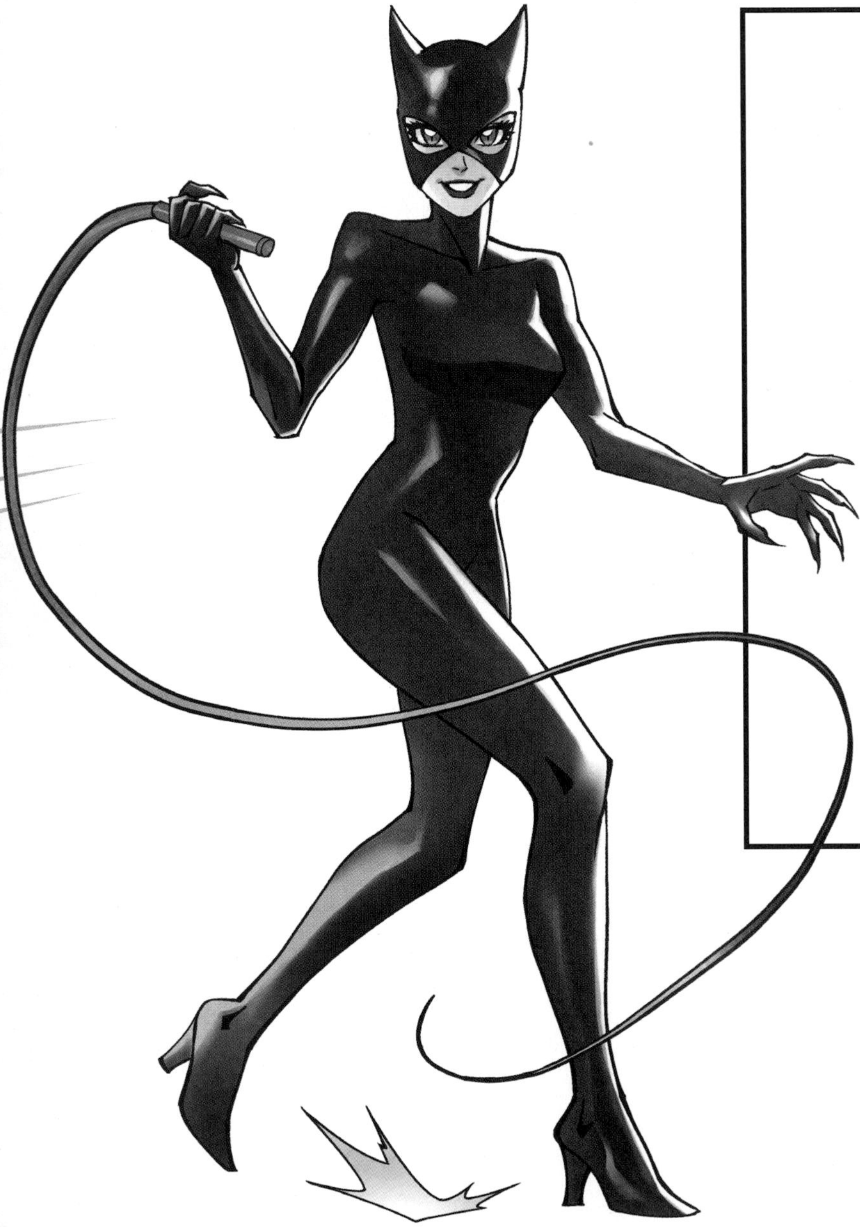

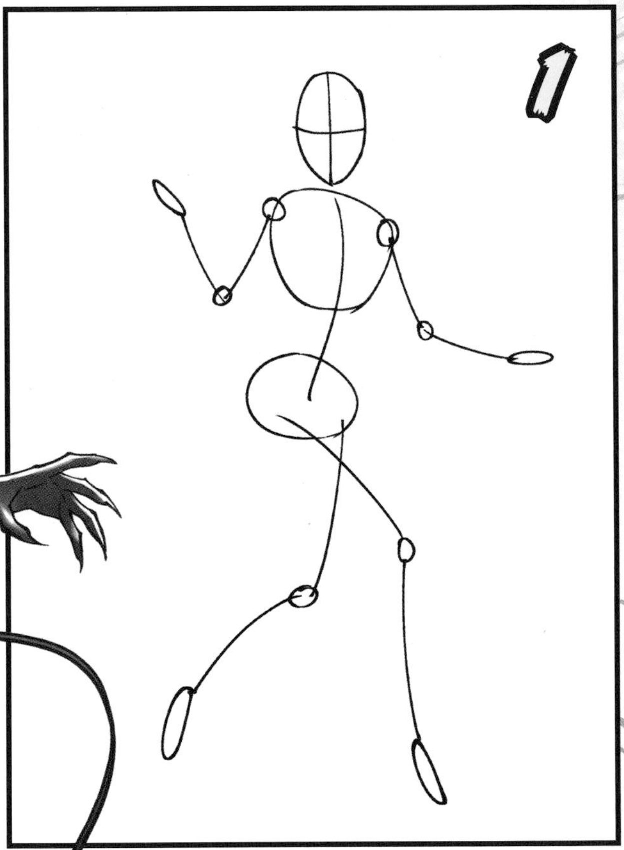
1

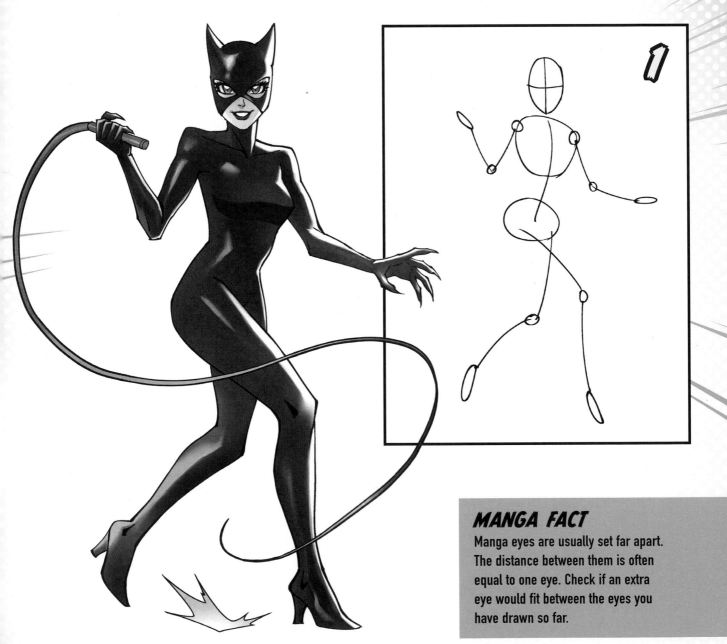

MANGA FACT

Manga eyes are usually set far apart. The distance between them is often equal to one eye. Check if an extra eye would fit between the eyes you have drawn so far.

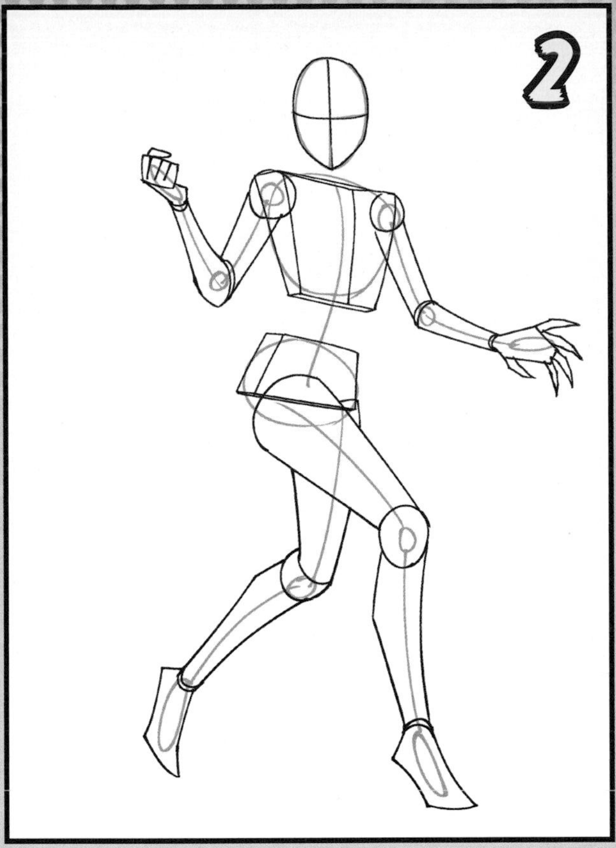
2

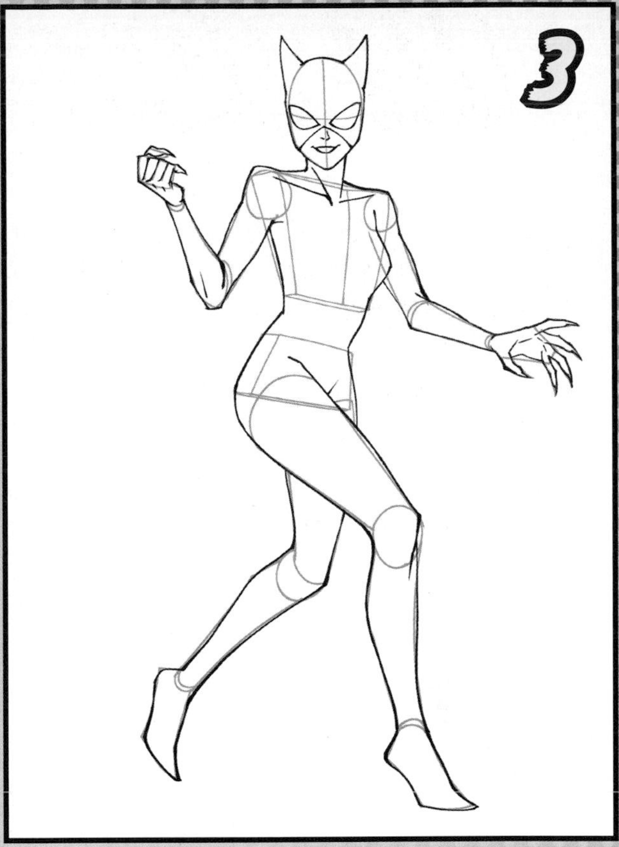
3

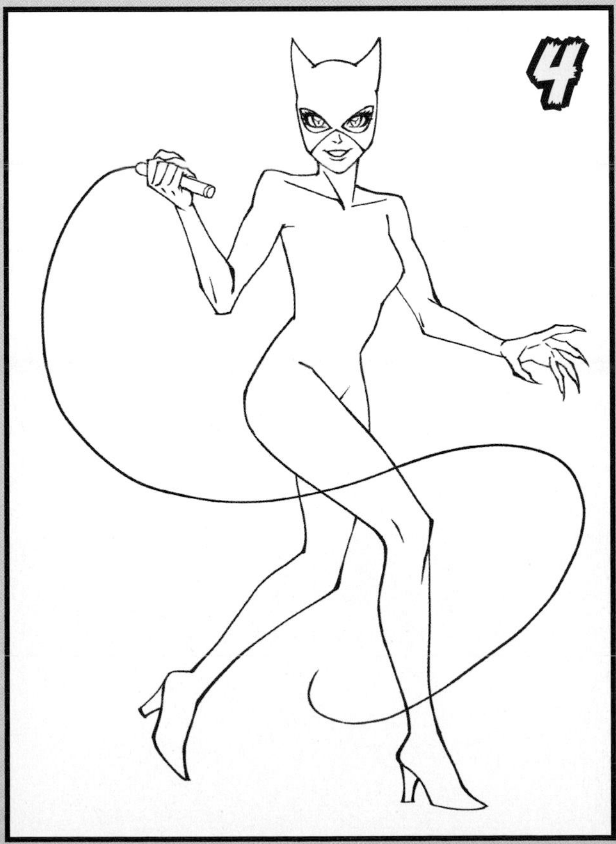
4

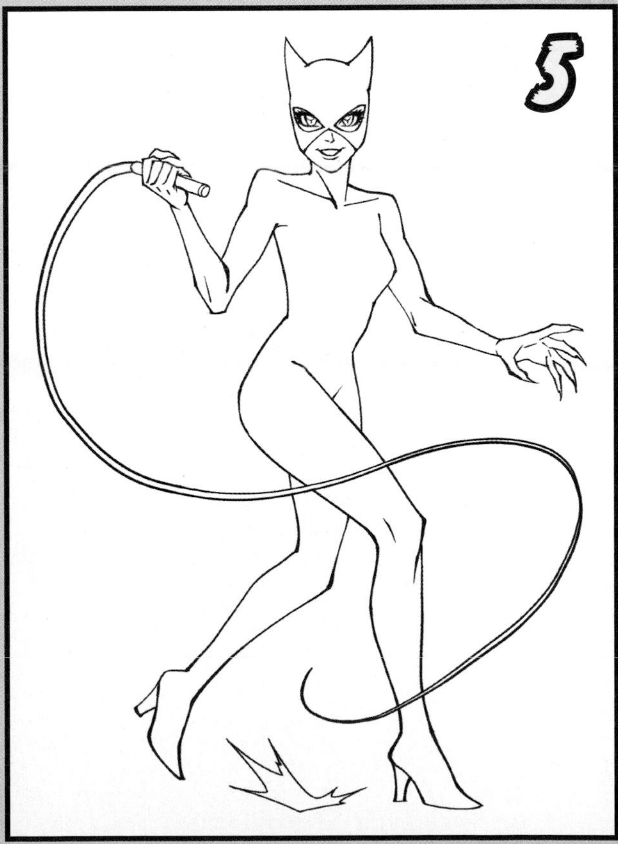
5

THE JOKER

The Joker is Batman's greatest enemy—and a treacherous trickster. From Joker Toxin in his lapel flower to a shocking hand buzzer, the Clown Prince of Crime always has a trick up his sleeve. So look out! Those playing cards are as razor-sharp as his criminal mind!

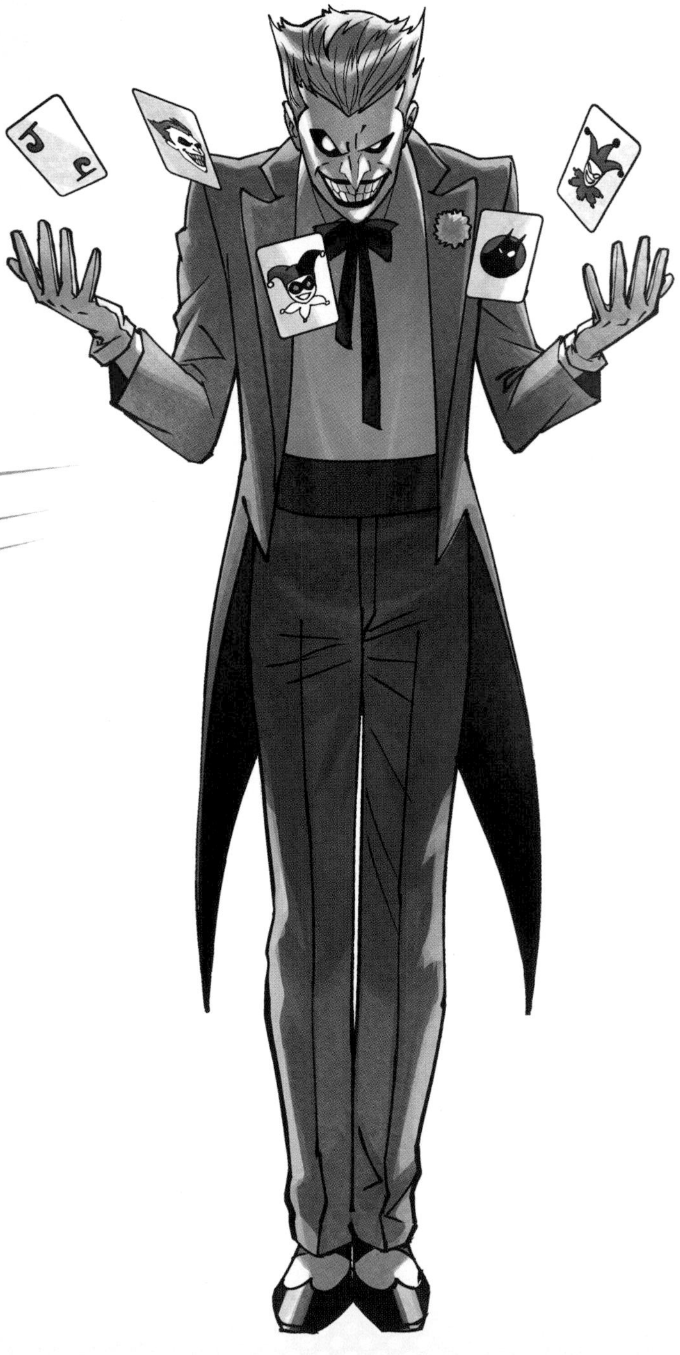

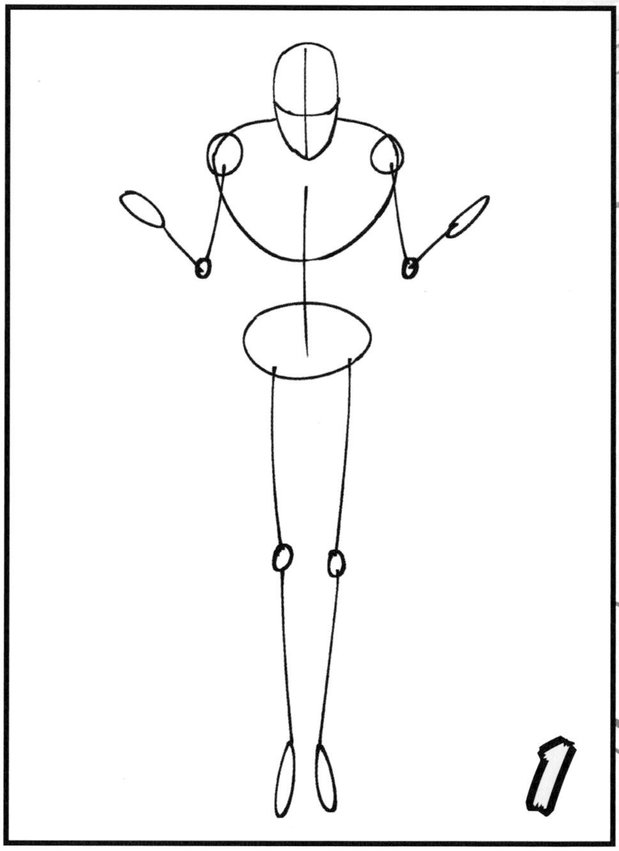
1

MANGA FACT

In Japan, shōnen manga is geared toward boys. Shōjo manga is aimed at girls. But boys and girls often read both.

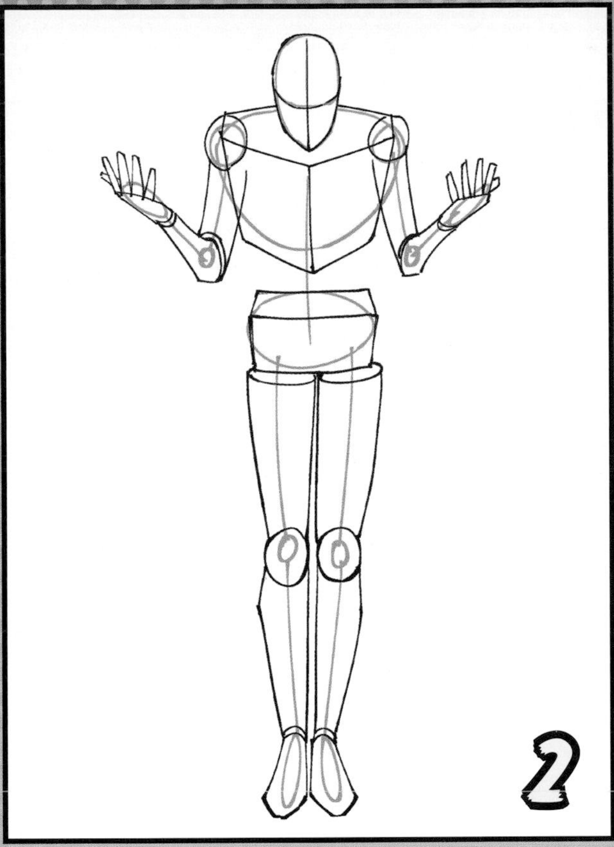
2
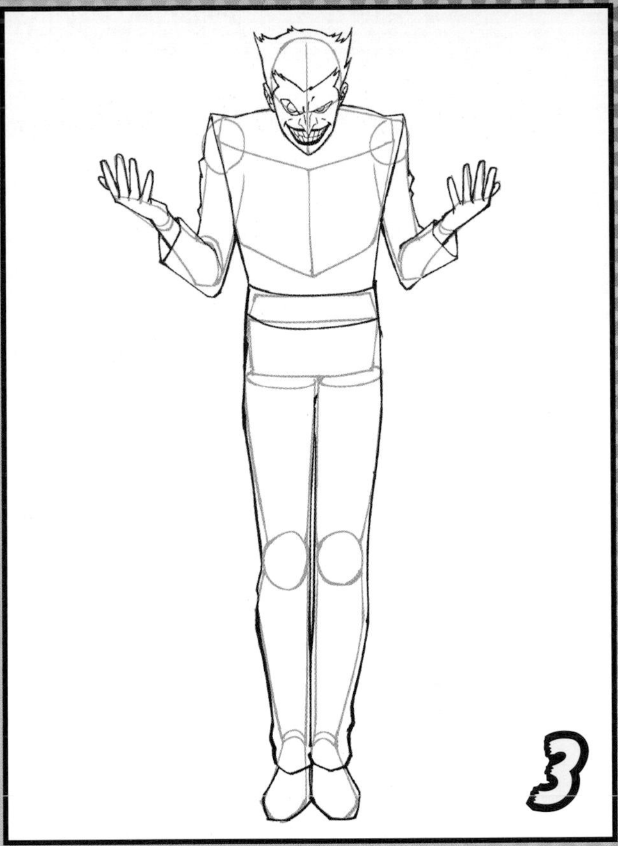
3
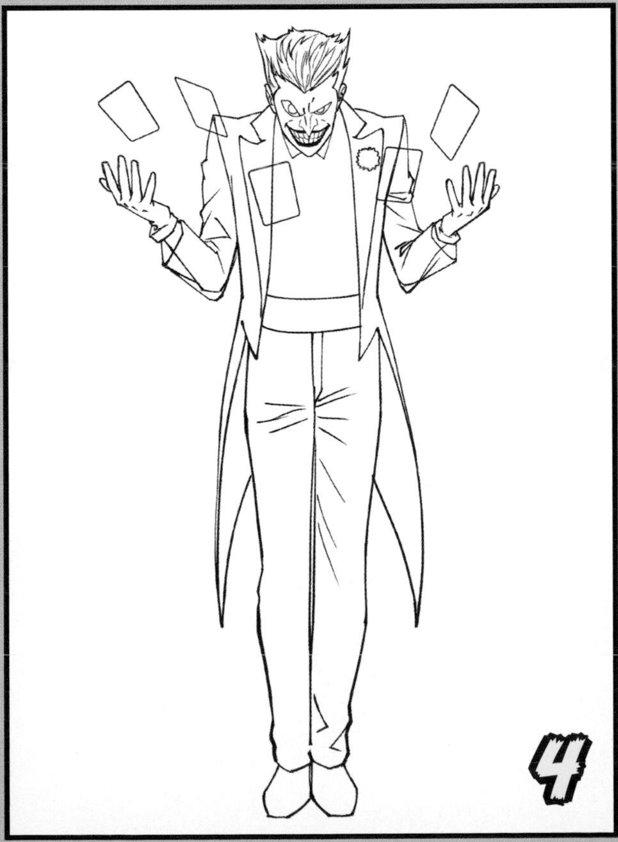
4
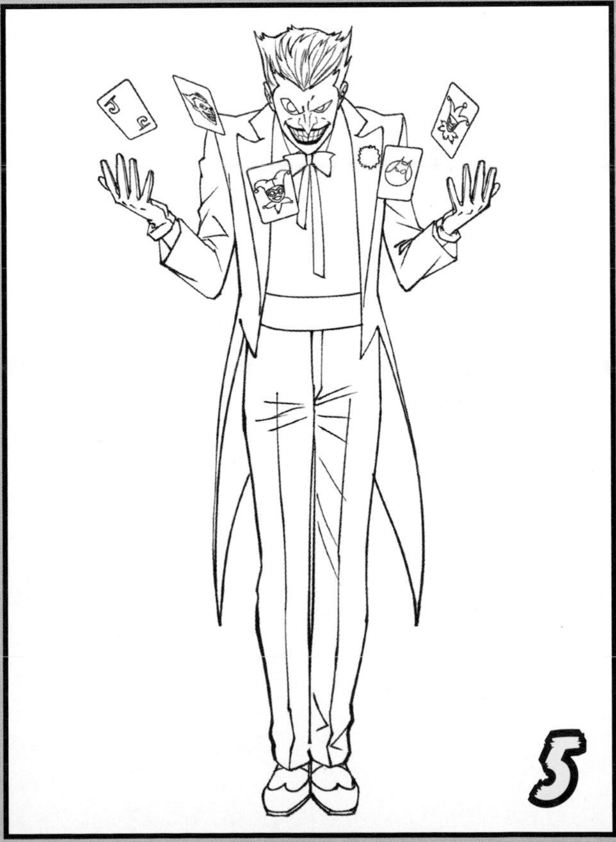
5

HARLEY QUINN

Harley Quinn may be a jester, but she's nobody's fool. The Clown Princess of Crime knows what she wants—lots and lots of moolah! And you can bet she's going to have a hoot while grabbing the loot. With her huge mallet in hand, Harley has a smashing good time!

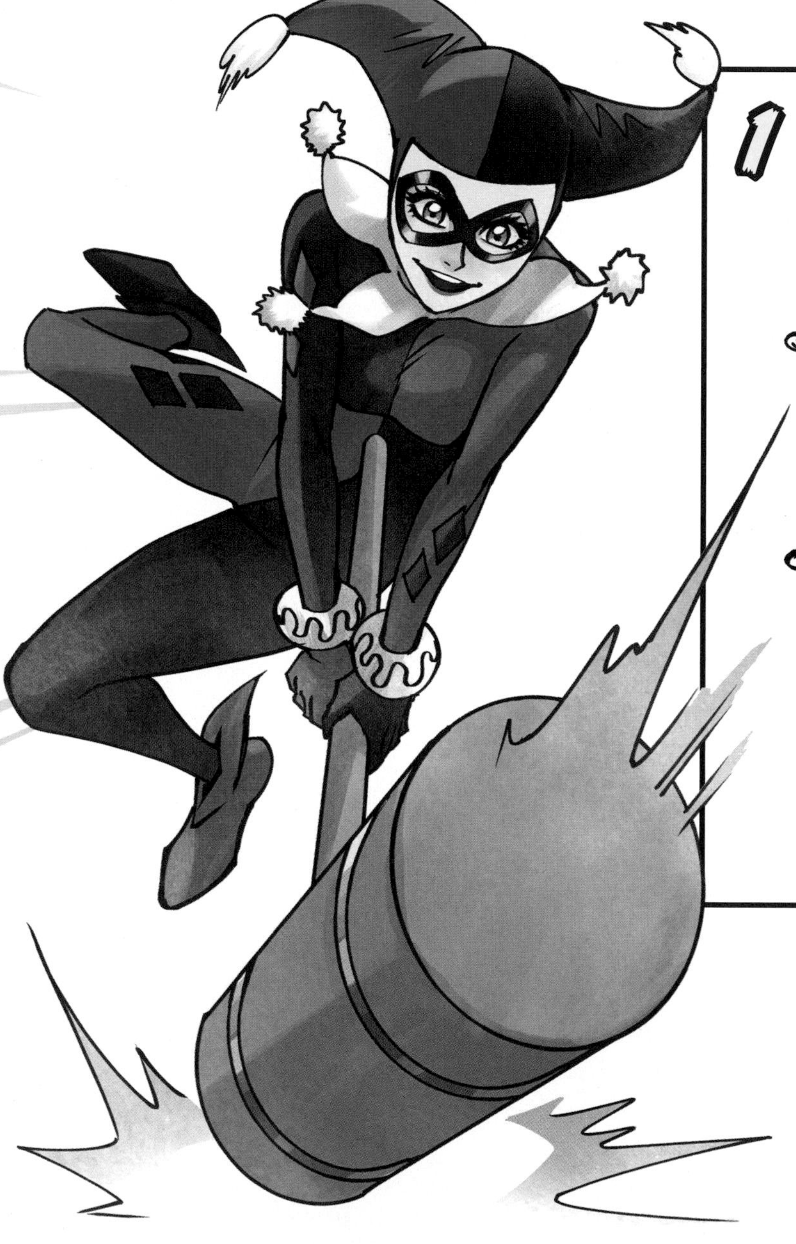

1

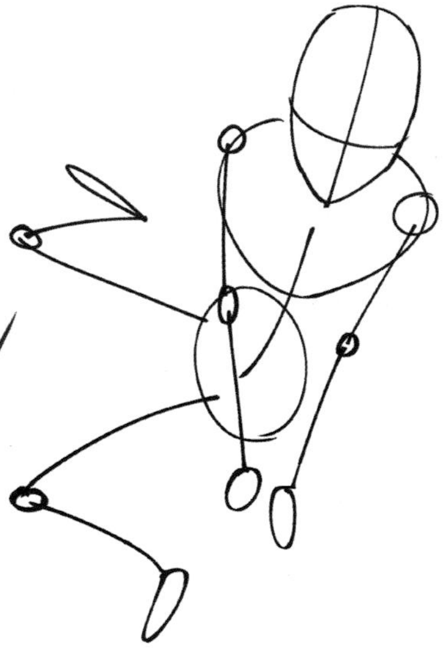

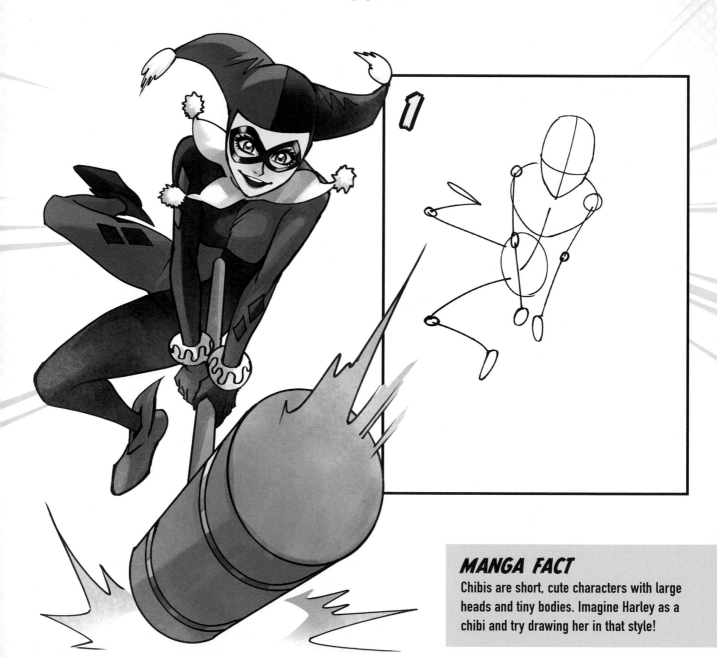

MANGA FACT

Chibis are short, cute characters with large heads and tiny bodies. Imagine Harley as a chibi and try drawing her in that style!

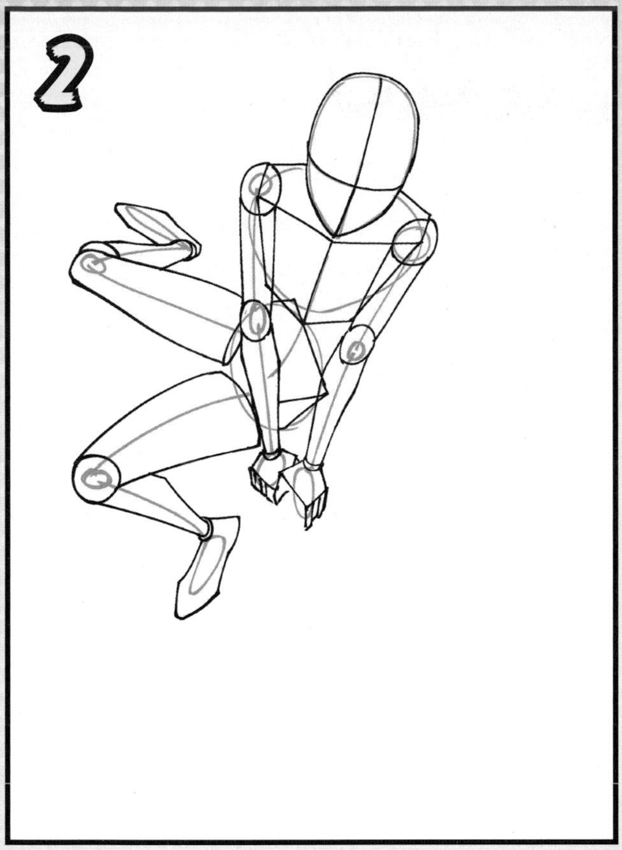
2
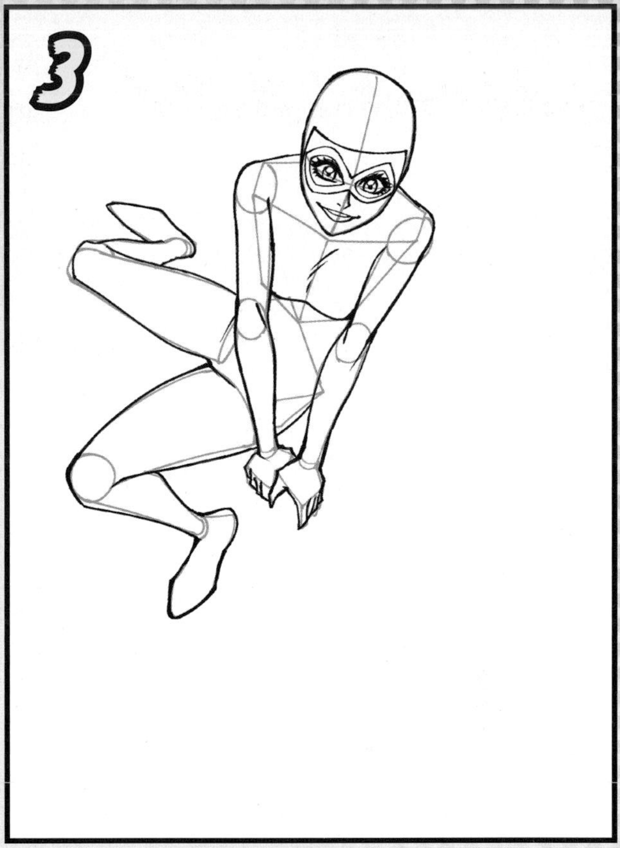
3
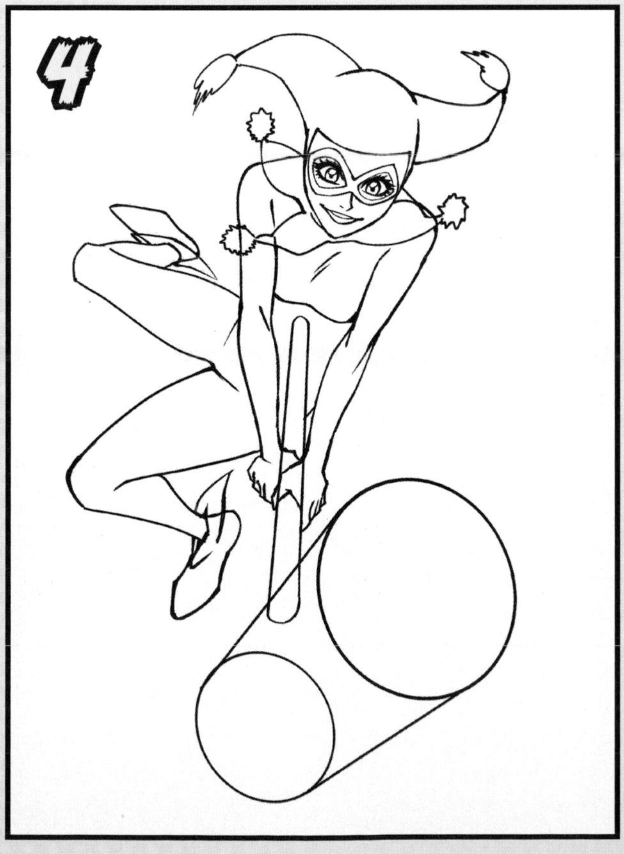
4
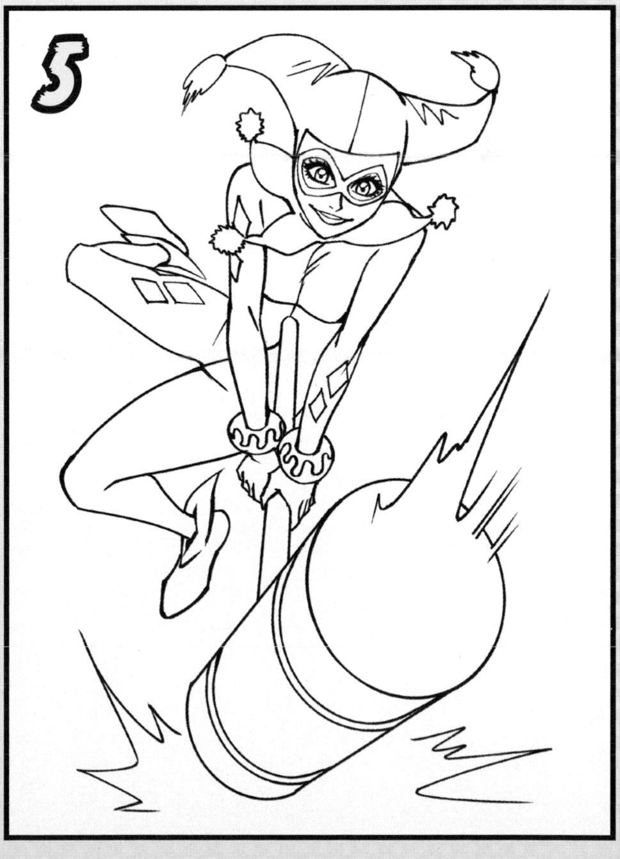
5

THE RIDDLER

Why would a cunning criminal leave clever clues for a caped crime fighter to crack? For this rascal of riddles, the answer is elementary: Why not? Armed with his question mark cane and a wily wit, the Riddler loves nothing more than to baffle Batman!

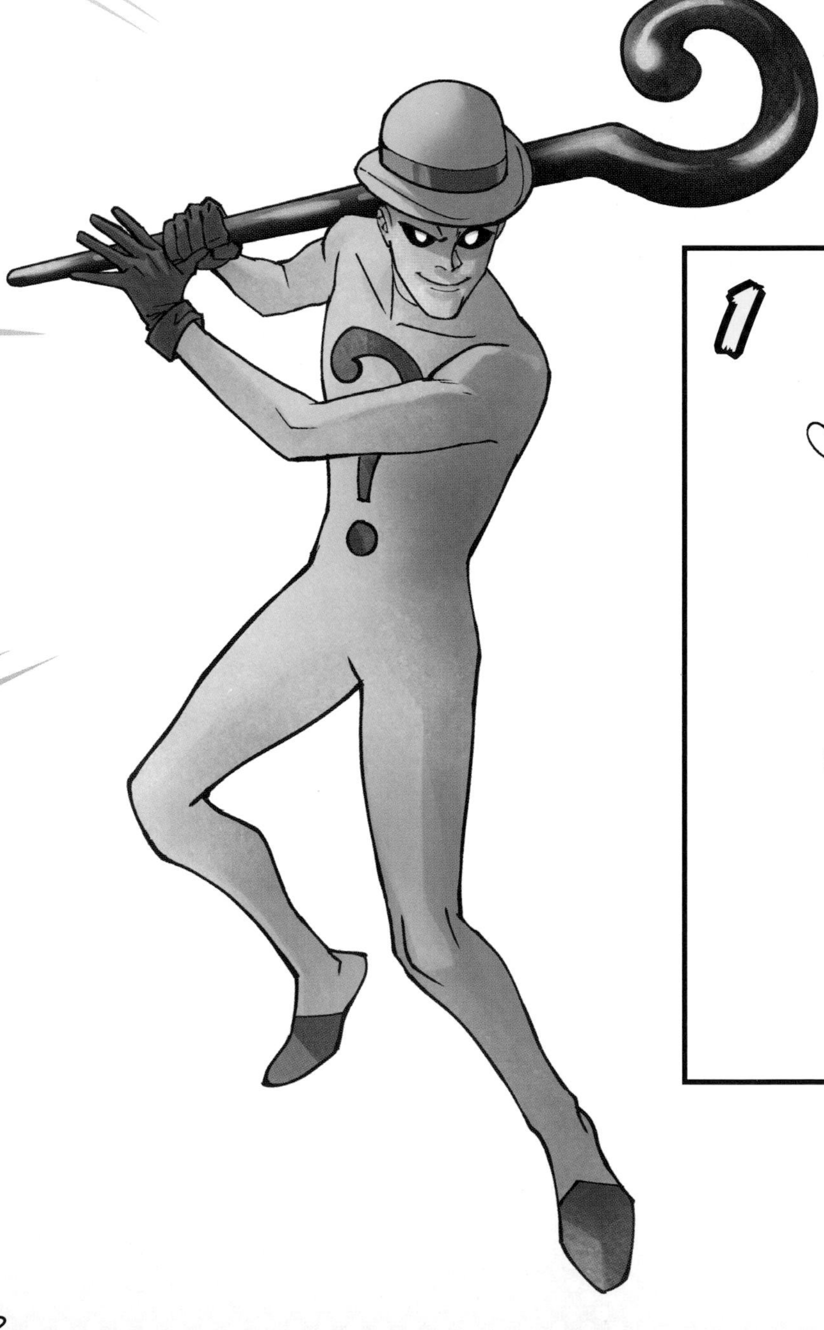

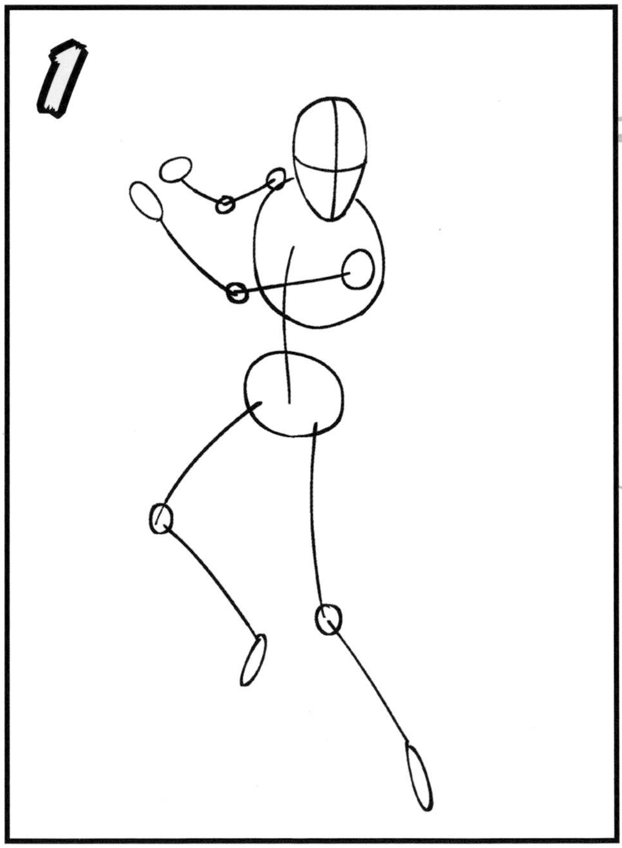
1

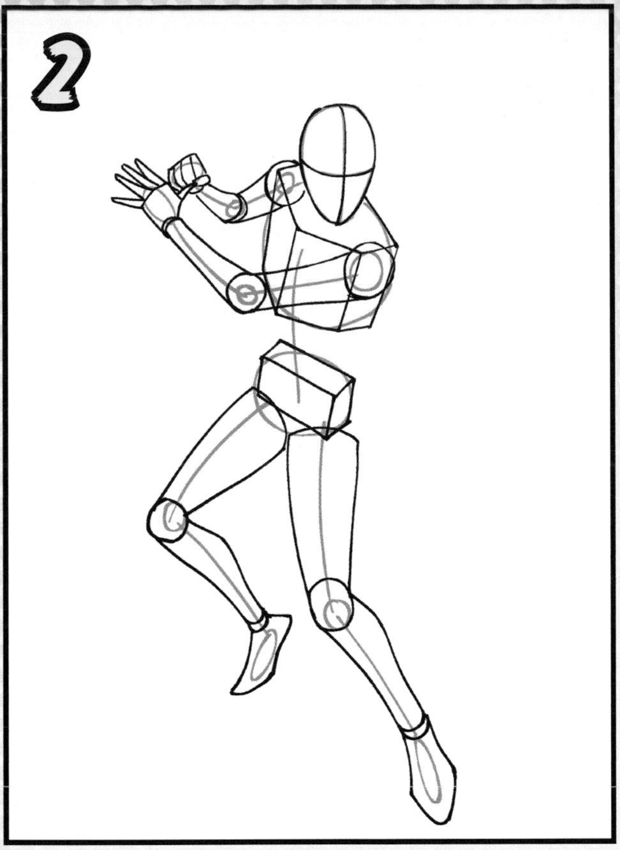
2
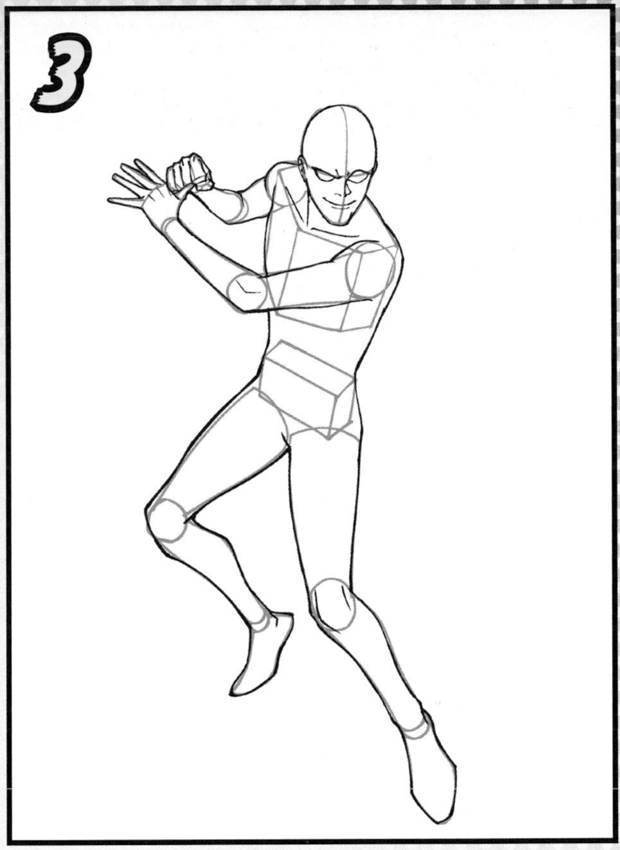
3
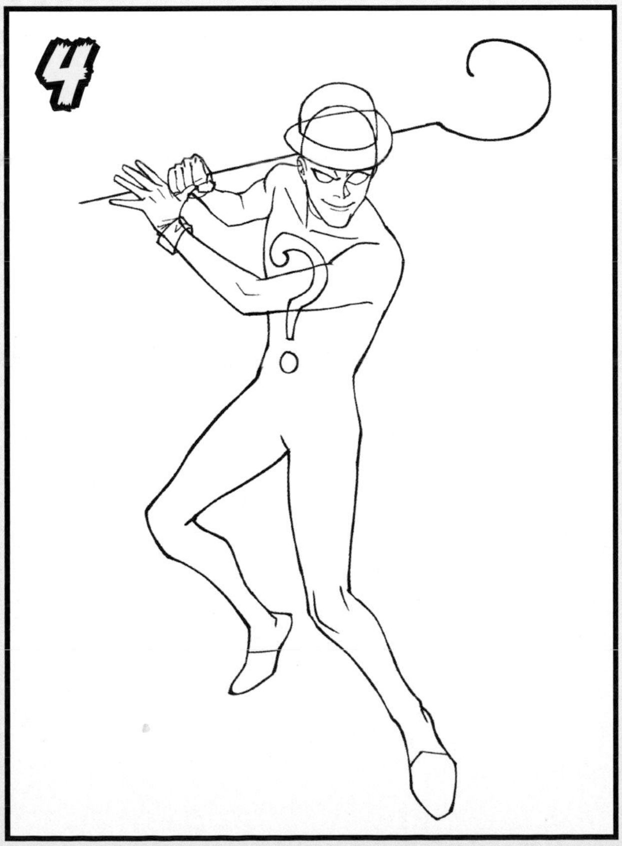
4
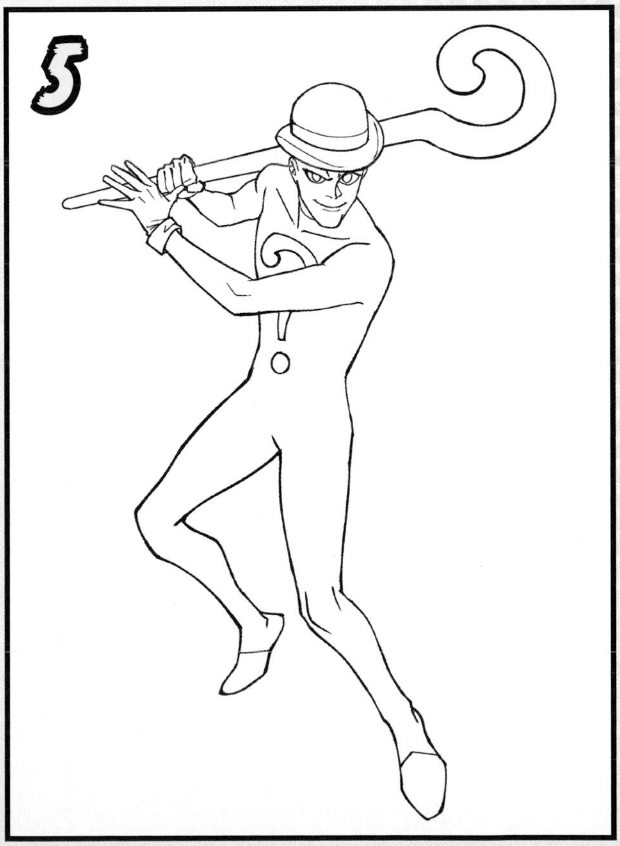
5

POISON IVY

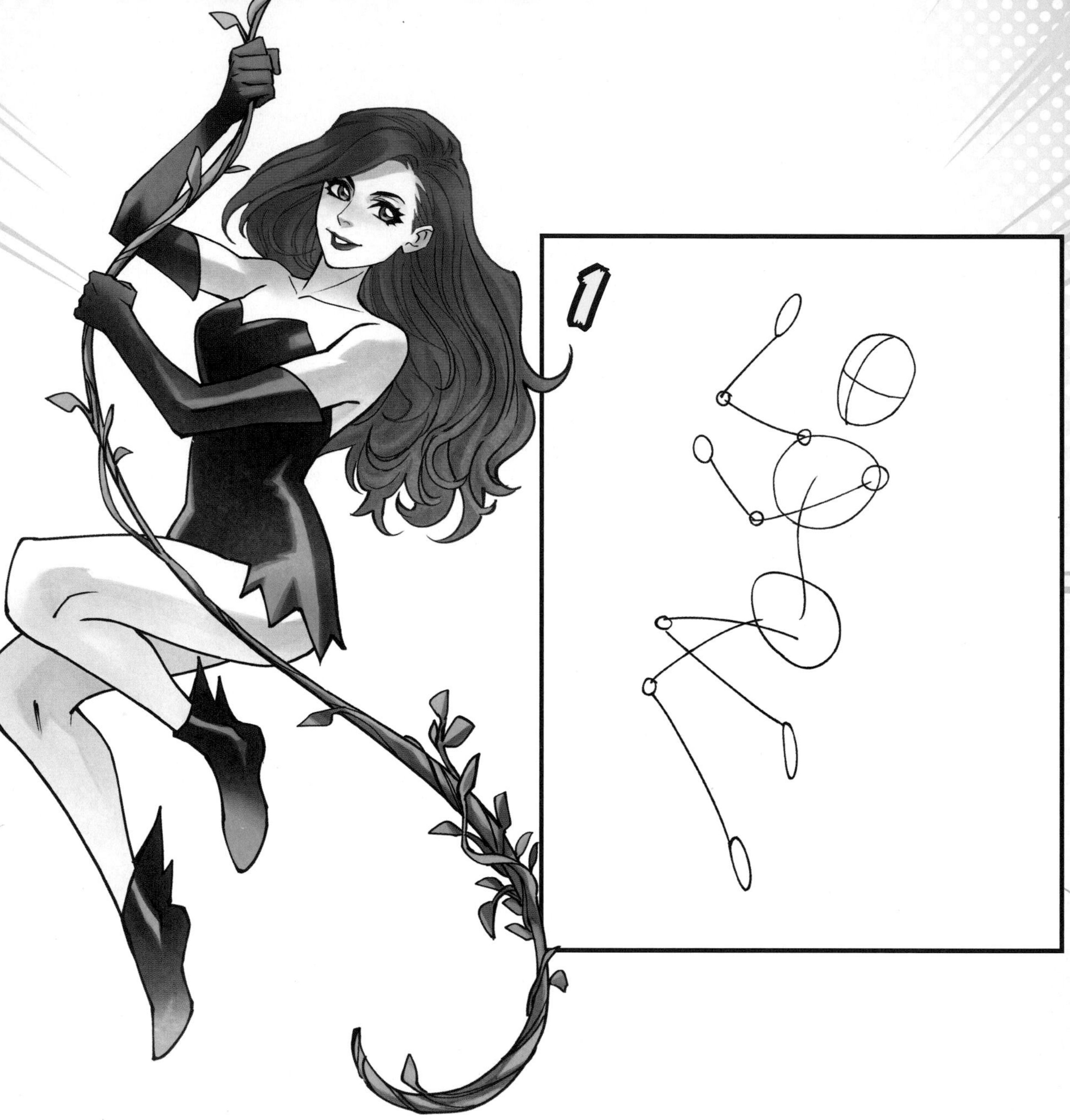
1

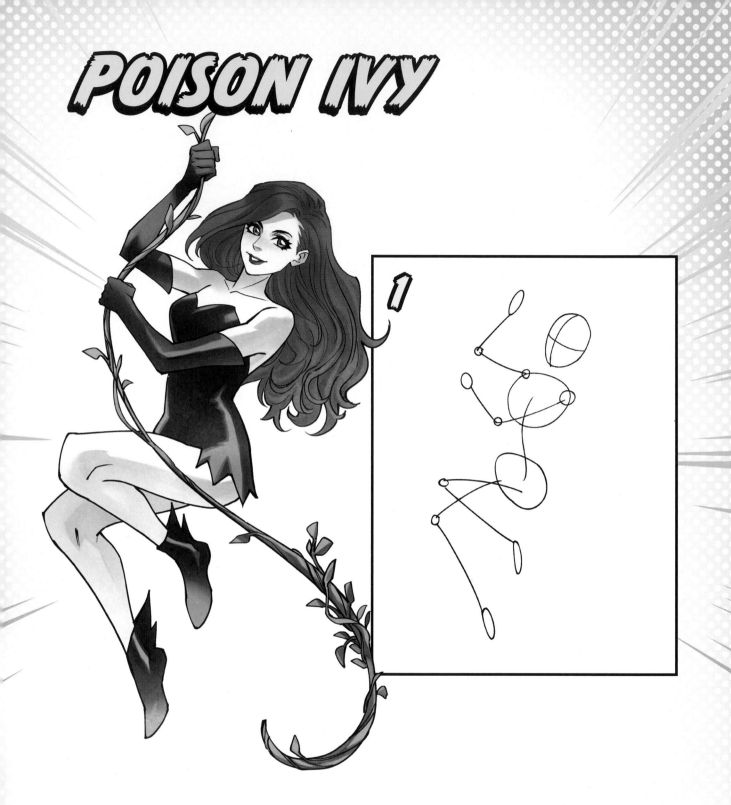

Make way for the Queen of Green! Using just her mind, Poison Ivy commands plants to carry out her wicked whims. From venomous Venus flytraps to vicious vines, this villain's fearsome flora can ensnare even the most daring do-gooders!

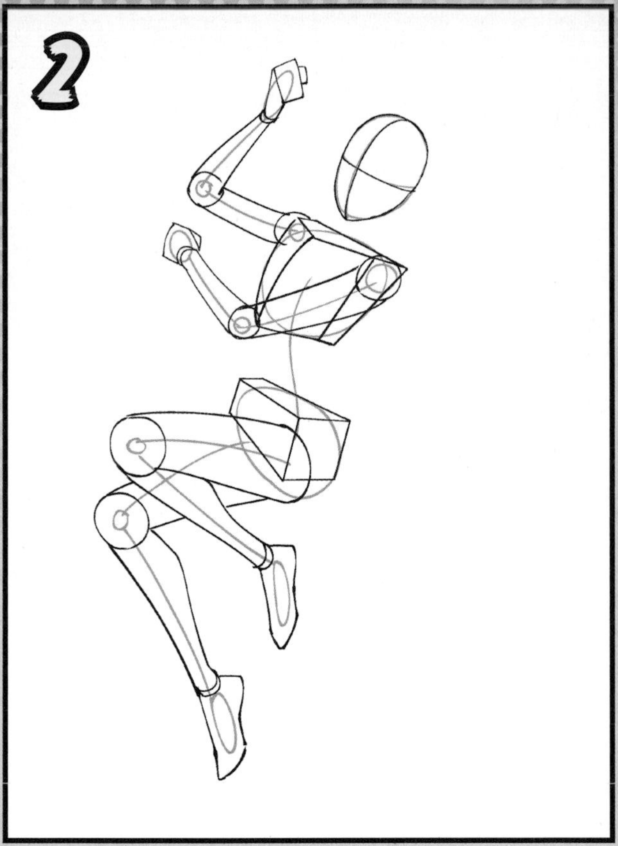
2
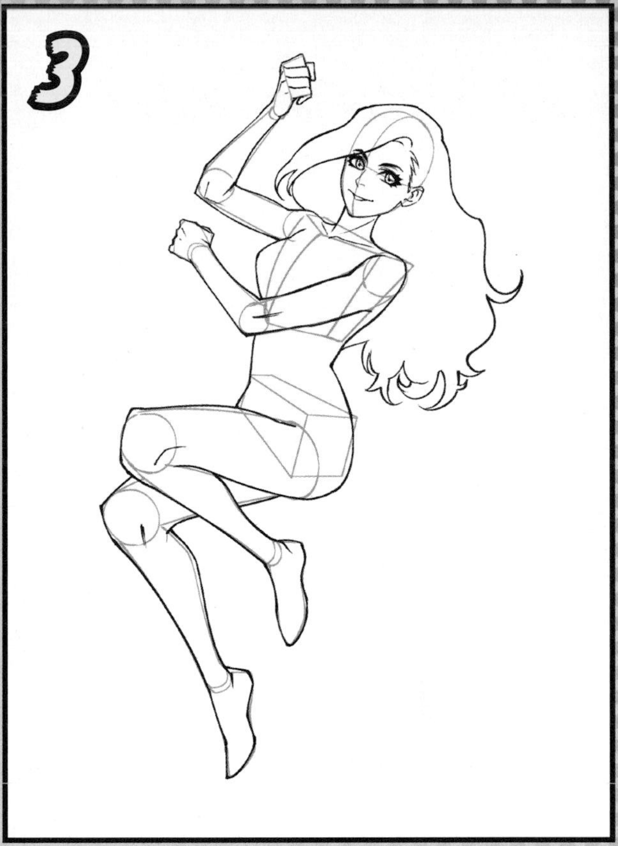
3
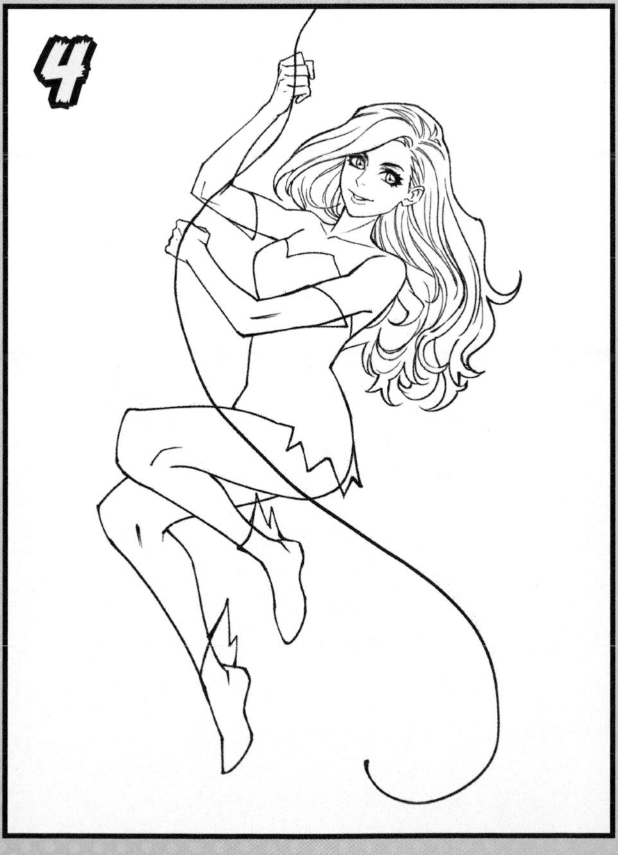
4
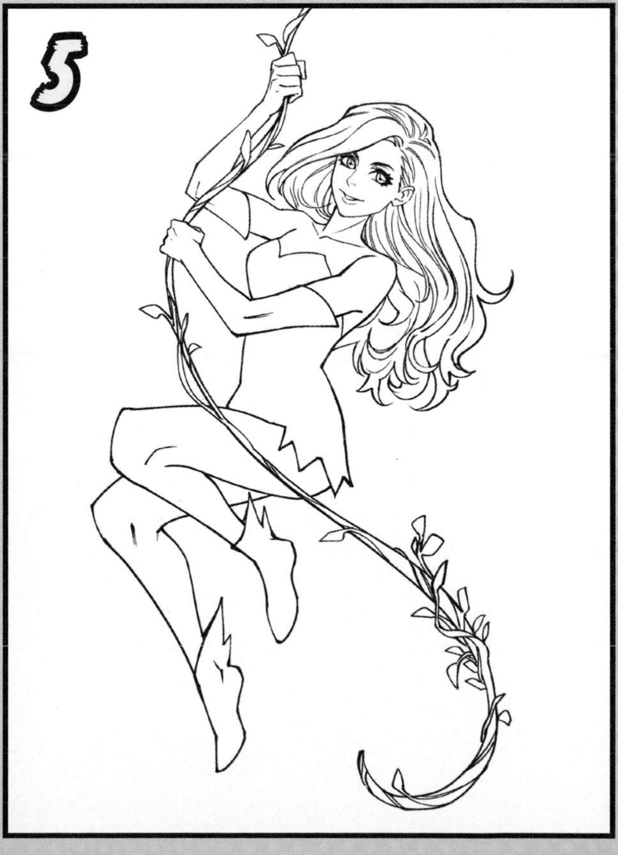
5

THE PENGUIN

The Penguin is a criminal kingpin who's as proud as a peacock. He's always dressed for success when pulling off his plots. With his trademark top hat, monocle, and tuxedo, the self-proclaimed "Gentleman of Crime" certainly looks the part. But beware this bad bird's tricky umbrella—or your goose is cooked!

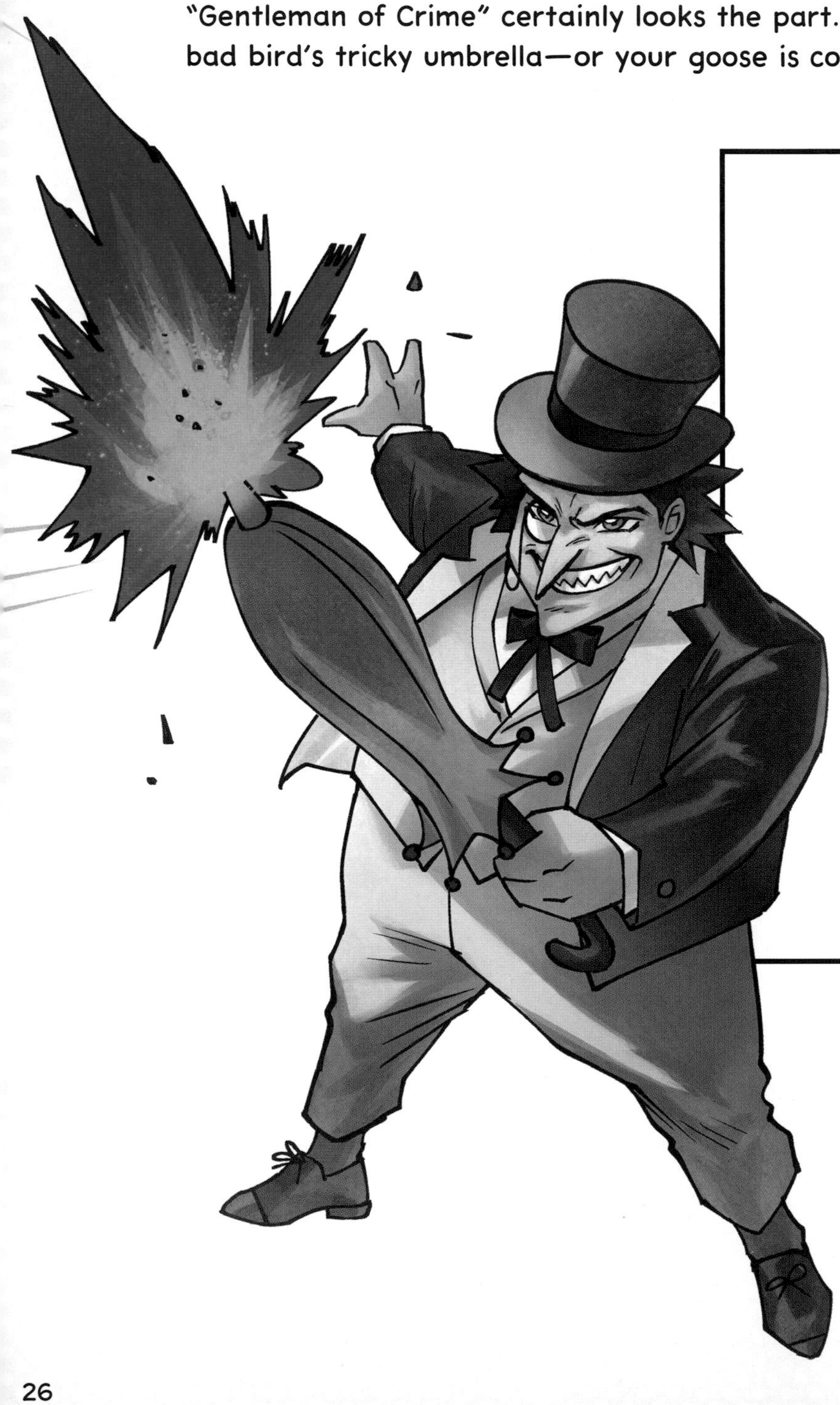

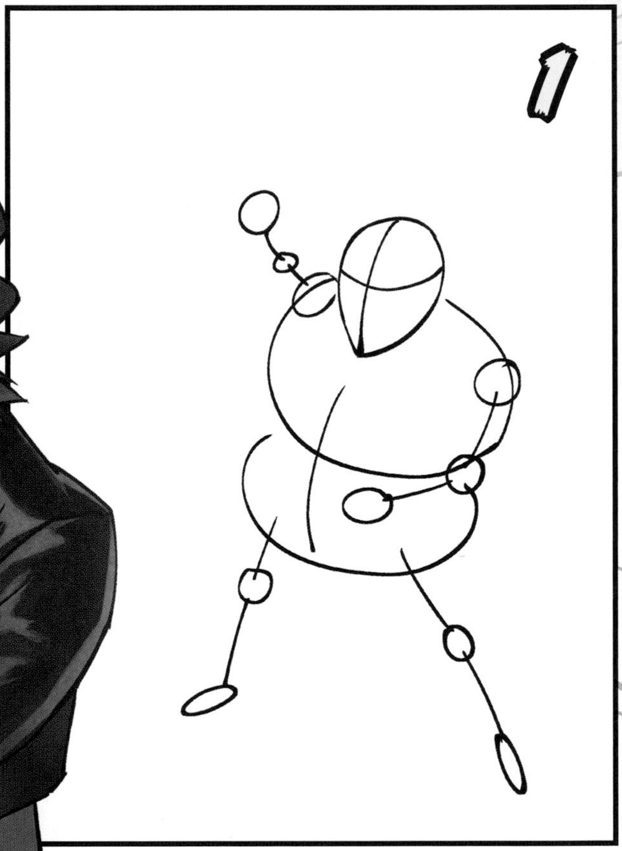
1

MANGA FACT

Manga series feature more than just super heroes and action adventures. From history and sports to fantasy and comedy, manga has many types of stories for everyone to enjoy.

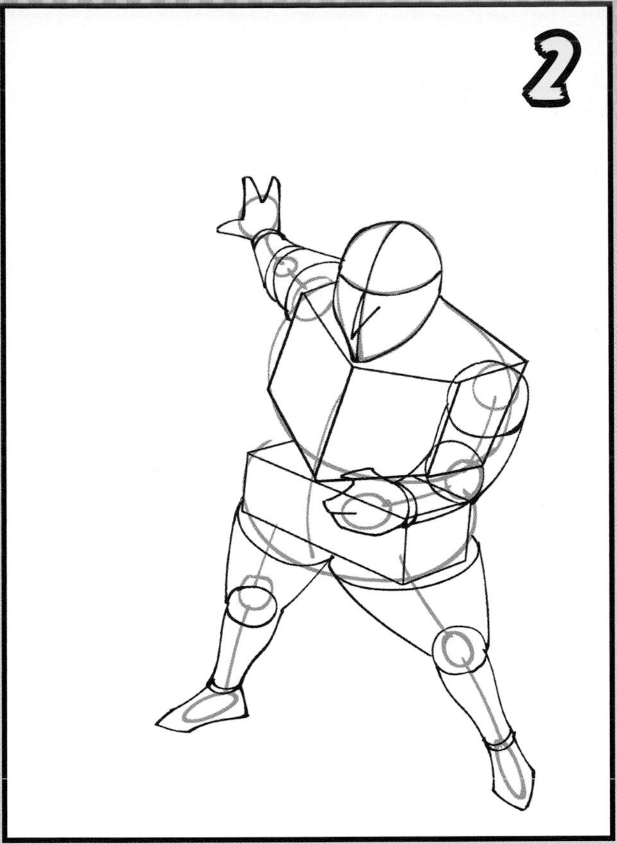
2
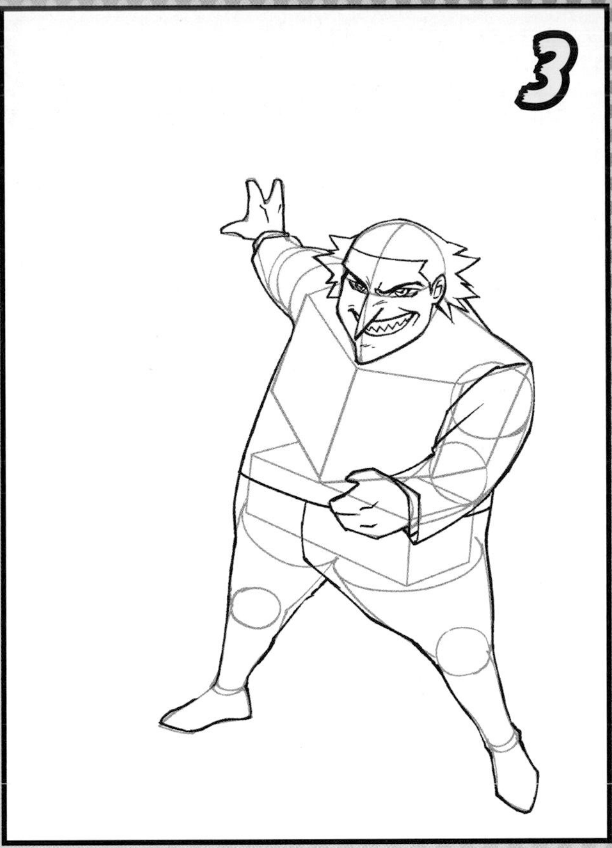
3
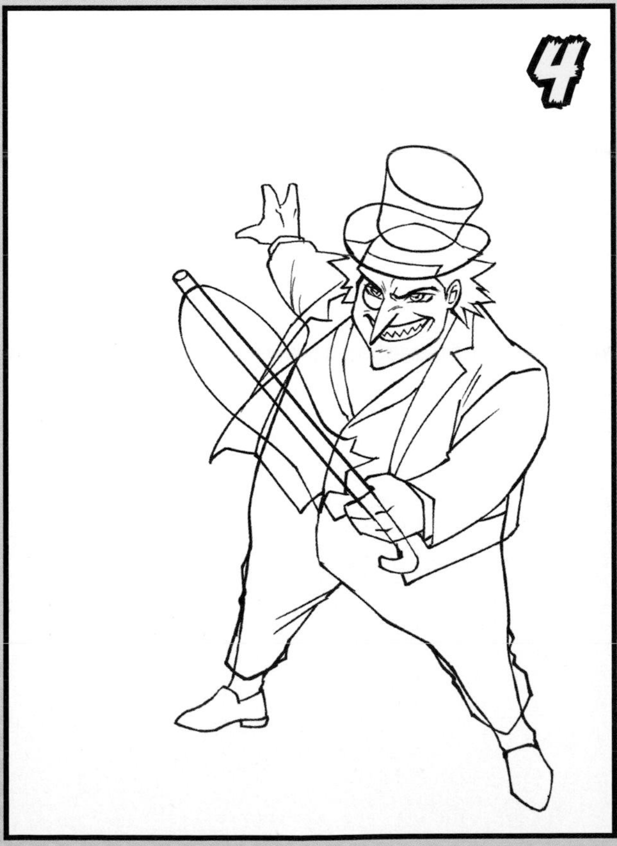
4
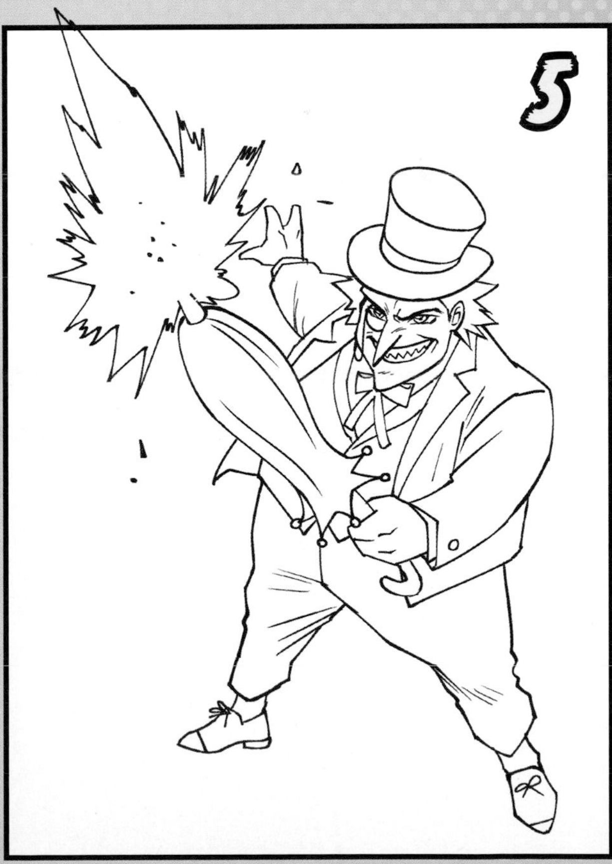
5

BATMAN VS. CLAYFACE

As Clayface rampages through the streets, Batman springs into action. Will the shape-shifting villain's twisted tentacle send the Dark Knight flying? Or can the Caped Crusader bring this muddy menace to justice? AS THE MANGAKA, THE FATE OF GOTHAM CITY IS IN YOUR HANDS!

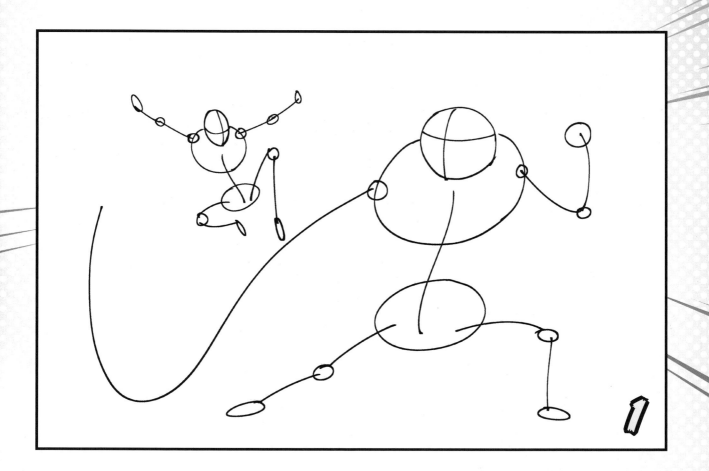

MANGA FACT
Osamu Tezuka is often called the "Godfather of Manga." During his career, he created more than 170,000 pages of manga! *Astro Boy* and *Princess Knight* were among his most popular.

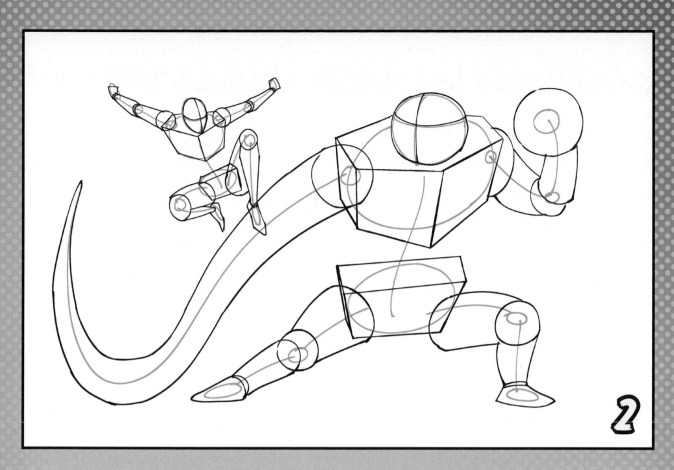

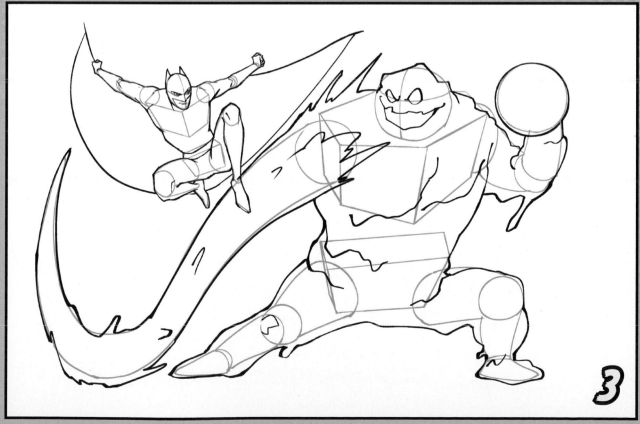

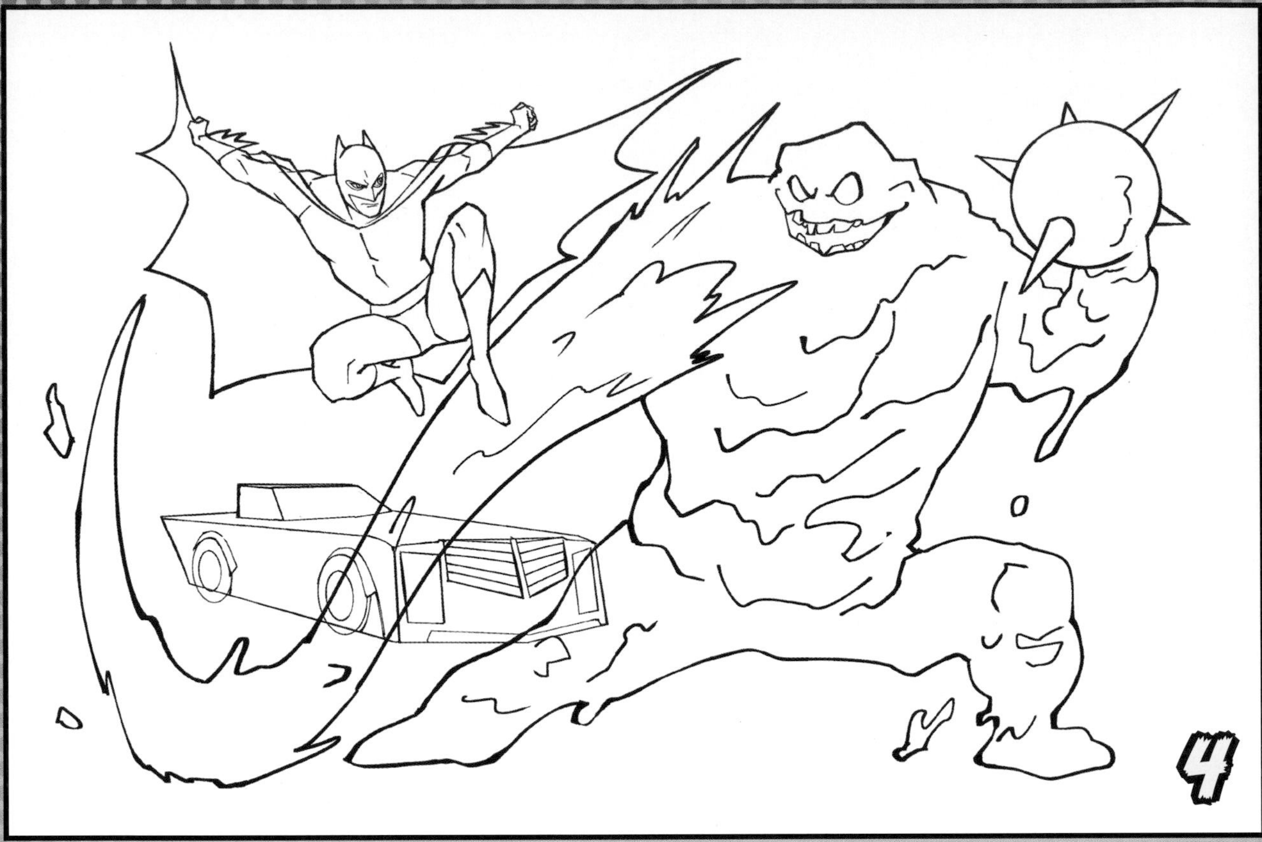
4

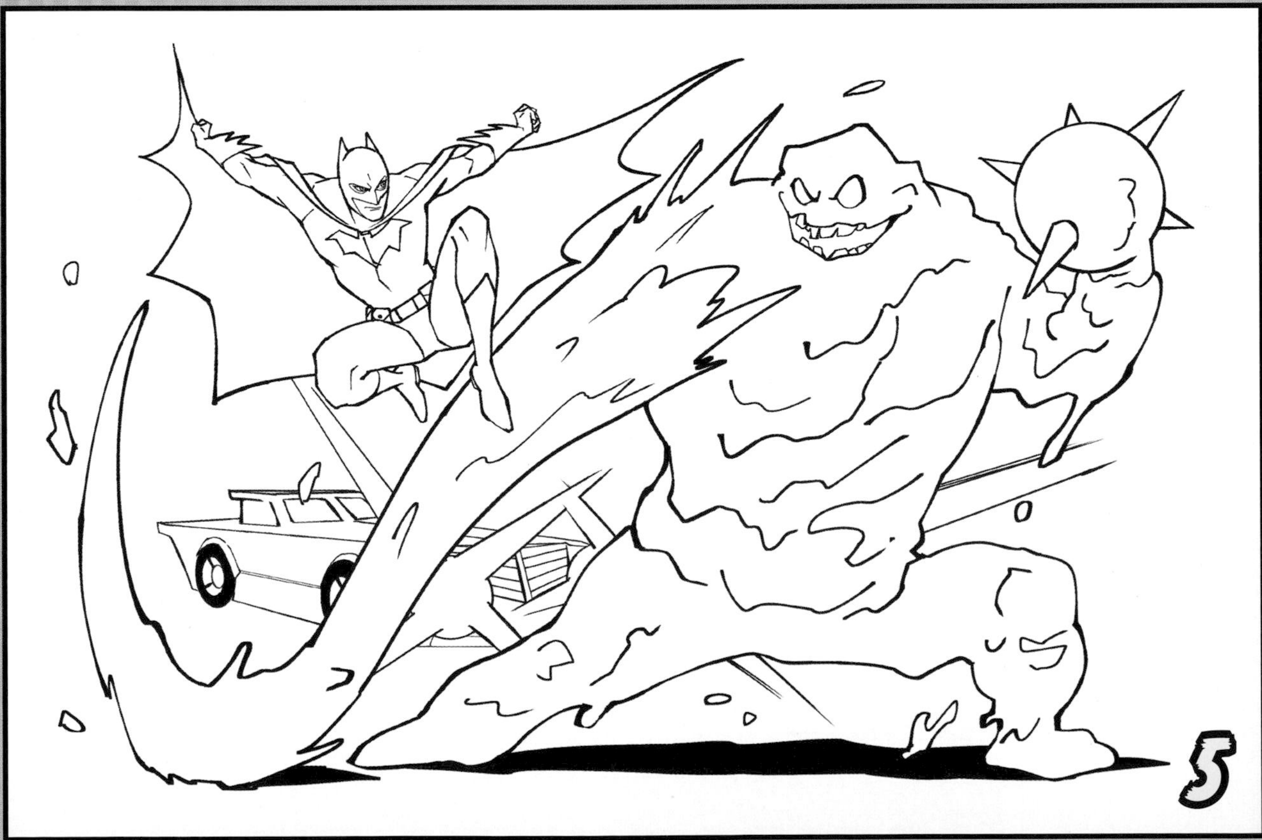
5

SUPERMAN

Supercharged by Earth's yellow sun, Superman is packed with powers. Super-strength? Check. Super-breath and super-hearing? Double check. Heat vision, X-ray vision, and flight? Triple check! But what is the Man of Steel's greatest strength? His solemn promise to use his might for all that is good and right!

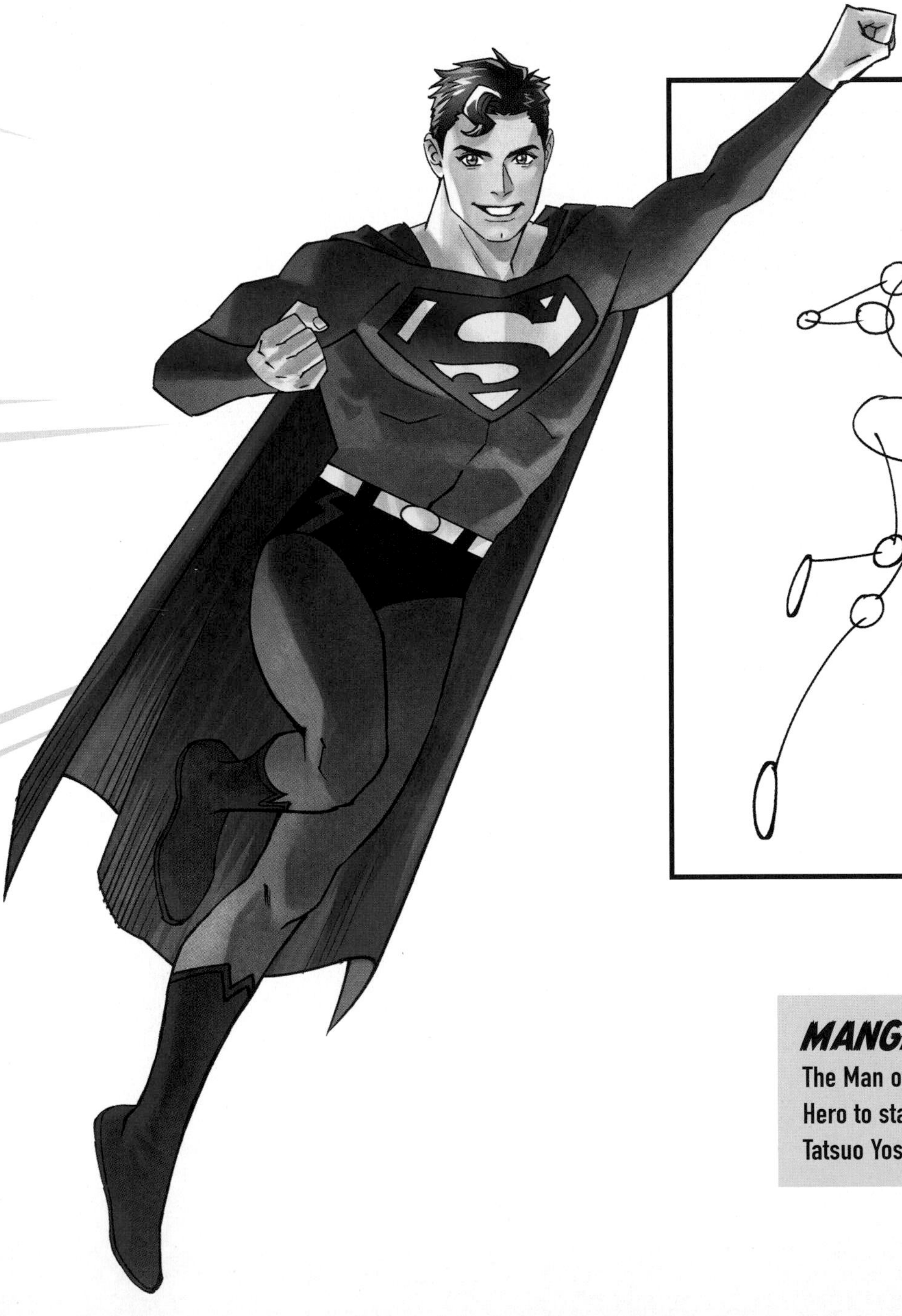

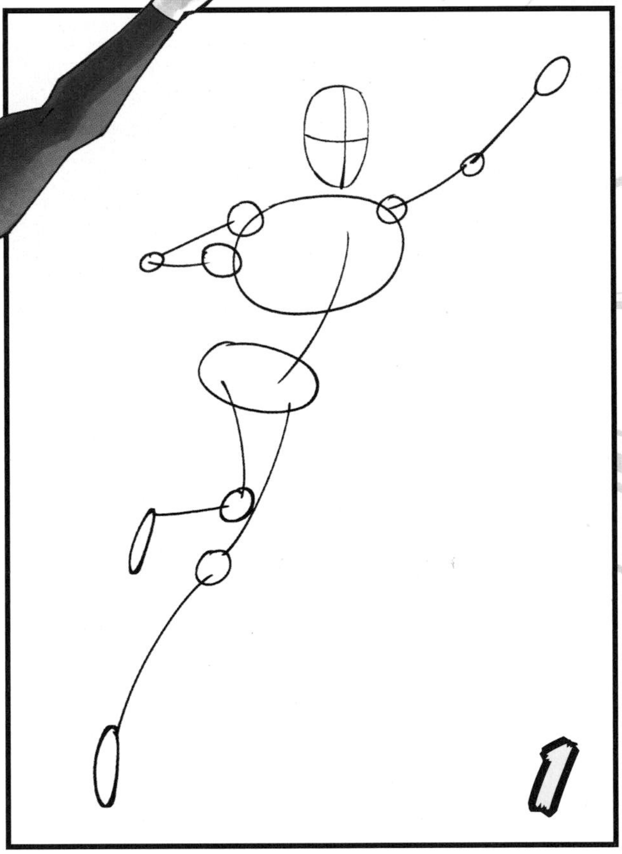
1

MANGA FACT

The Man of Steel was the first DC Super Hero to star in manga with *Superman* by Tatsuo Yoshida in 1959.

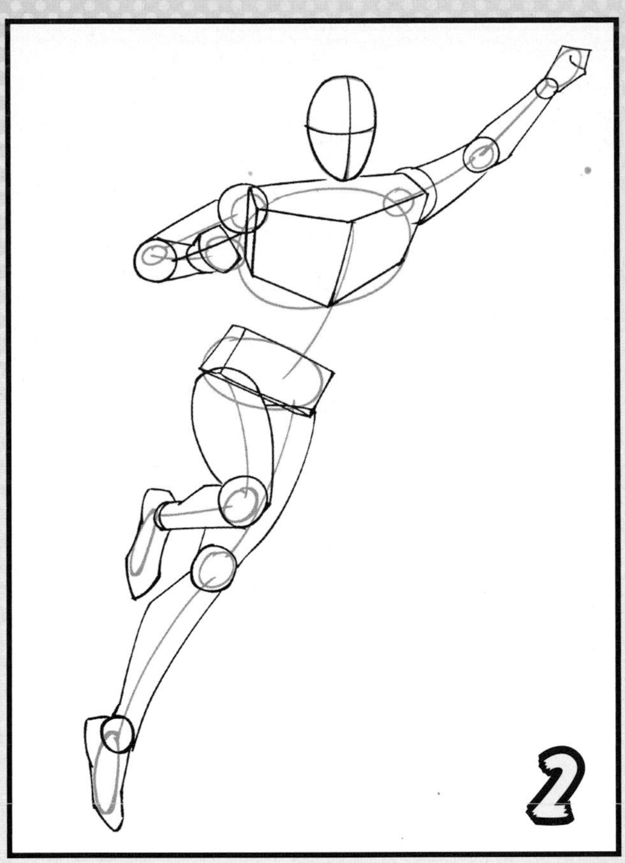
2
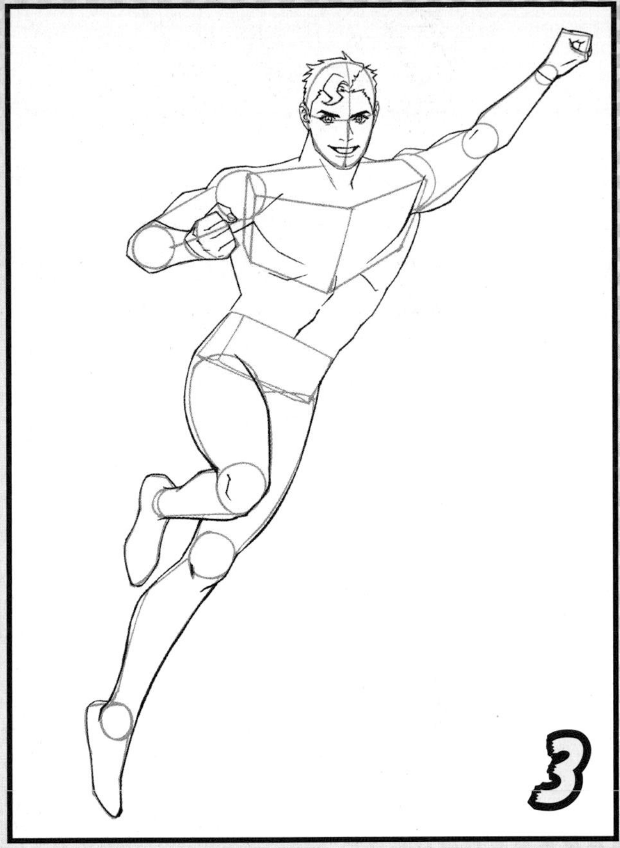
3
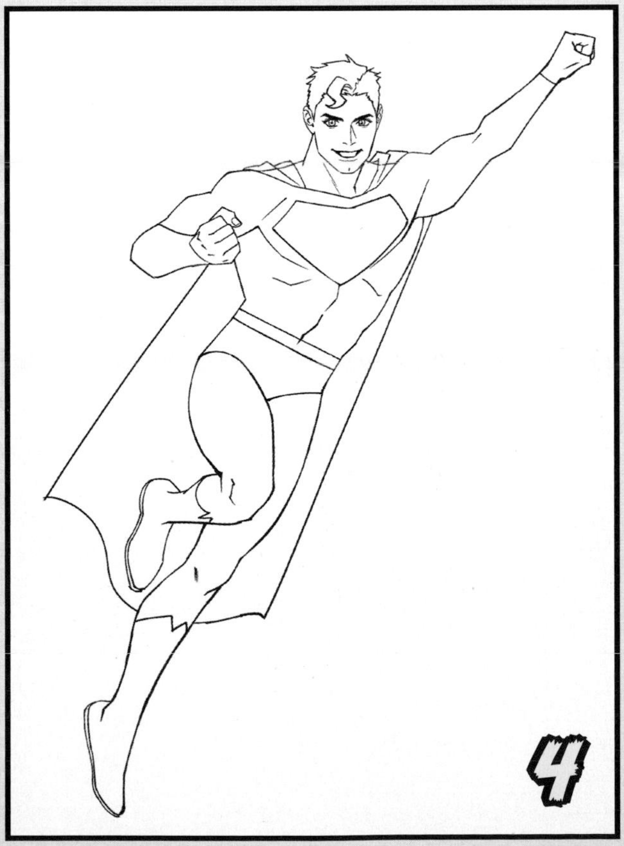
4
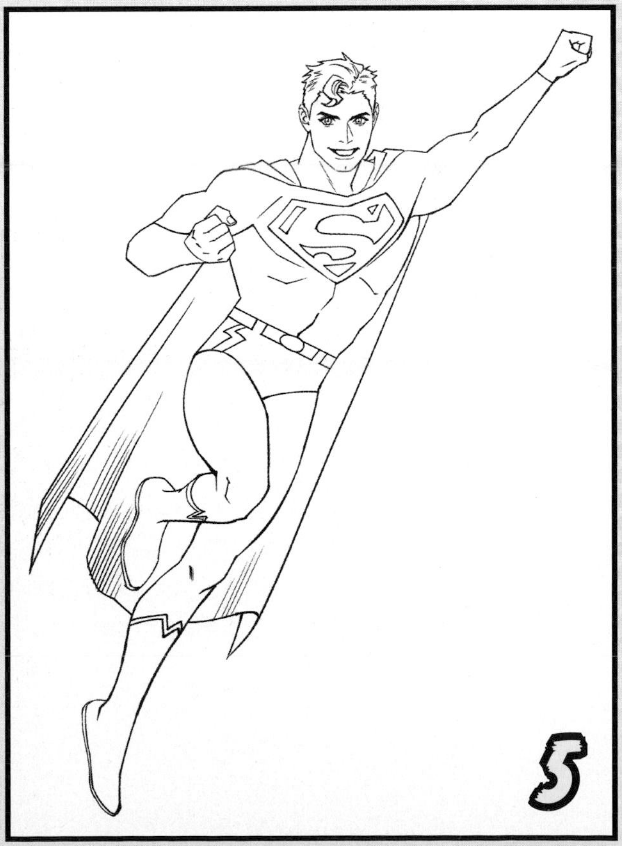
5

SUPERGIRL

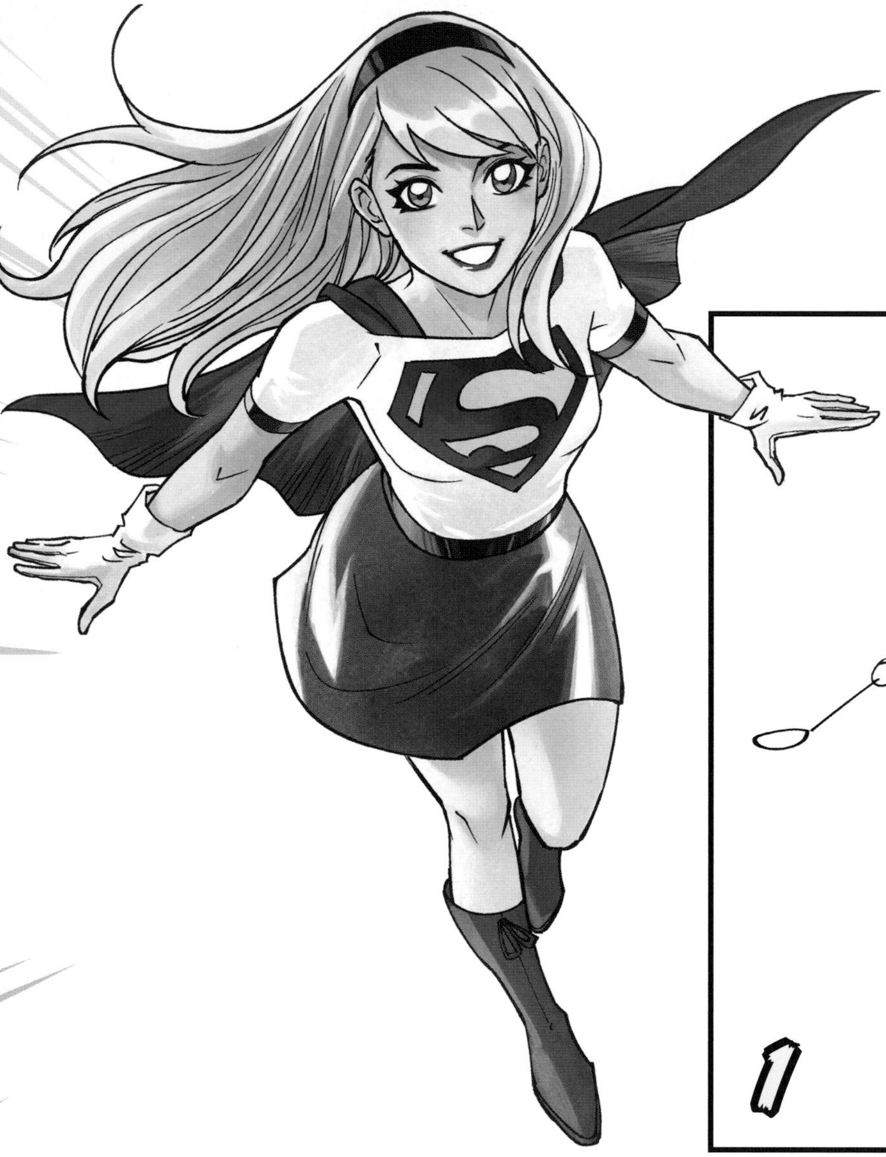

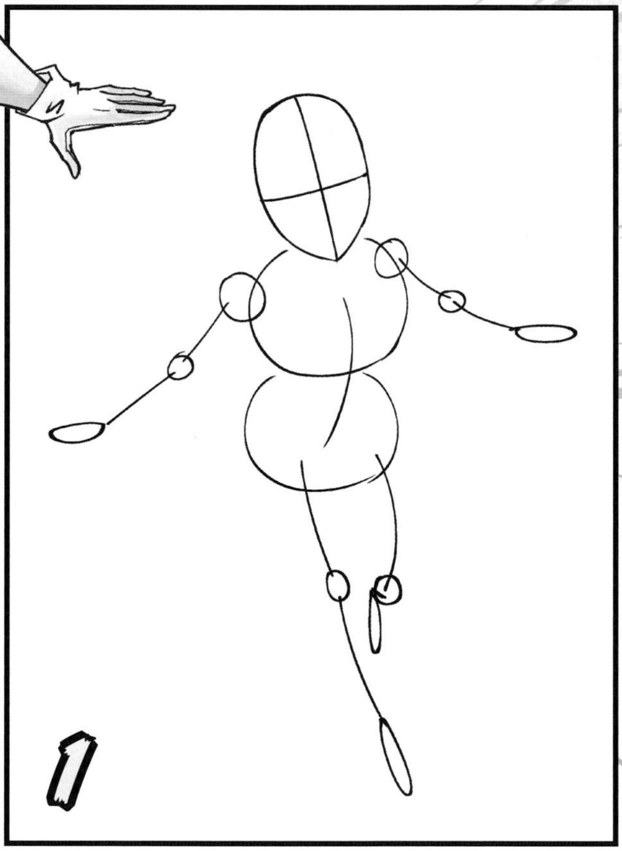
1

Supergirl is a hero with a heart of gold. Like her cousin, Superman, she can bend steel beams with her bare hands and blow out blazes with freeze-breath blasts. Most importantly, the teen shares her cousin's pledge to act with kindness and courage. The Girl of Steel will zoom to the ends of the Earth to protect people in peril!

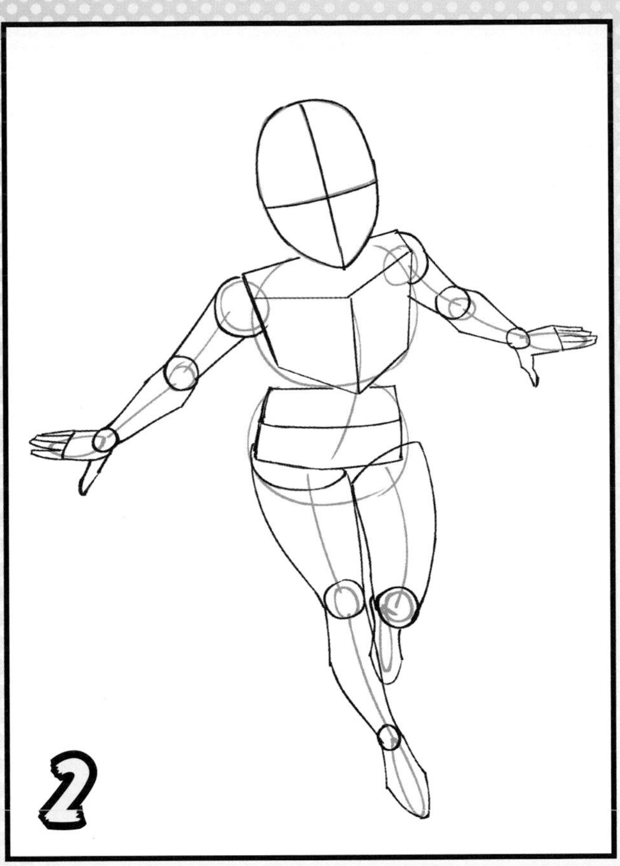
2
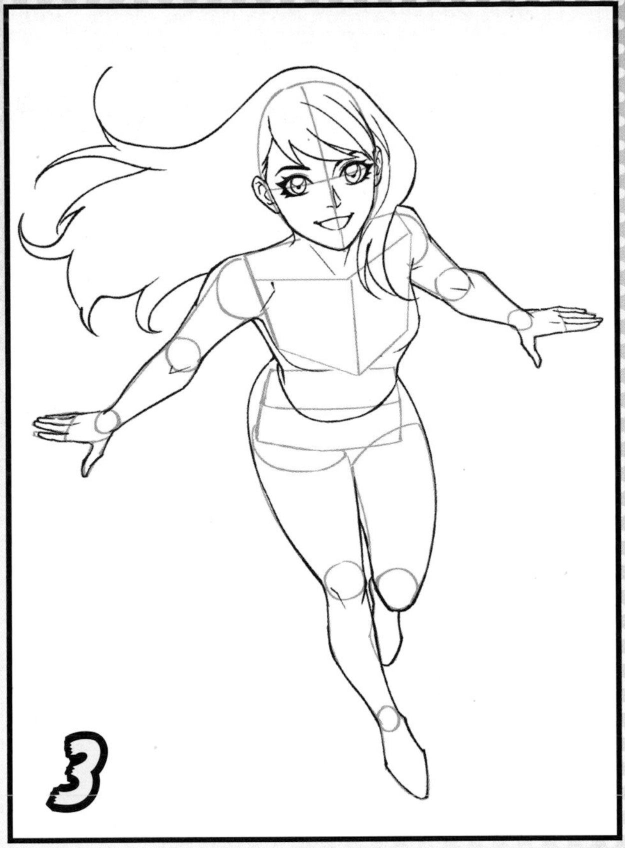
3
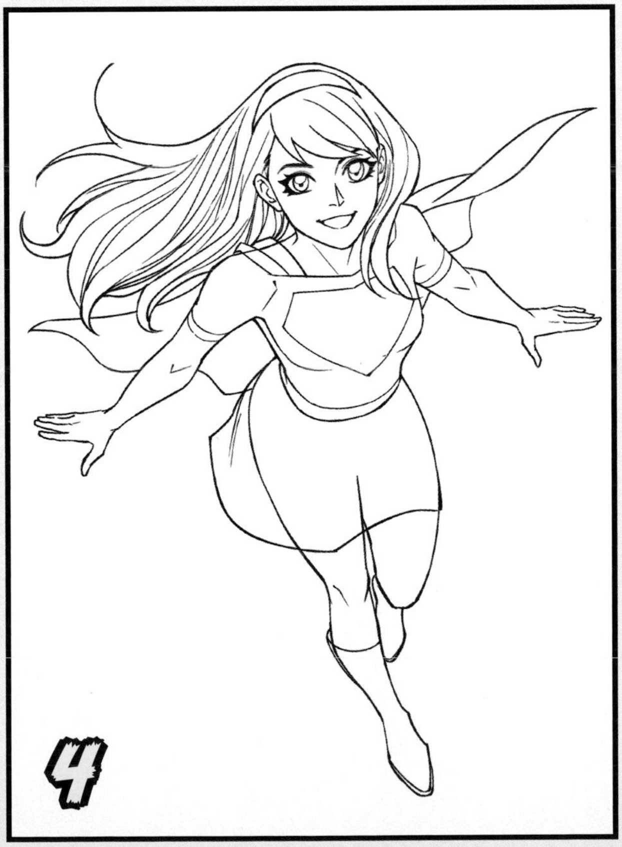
4
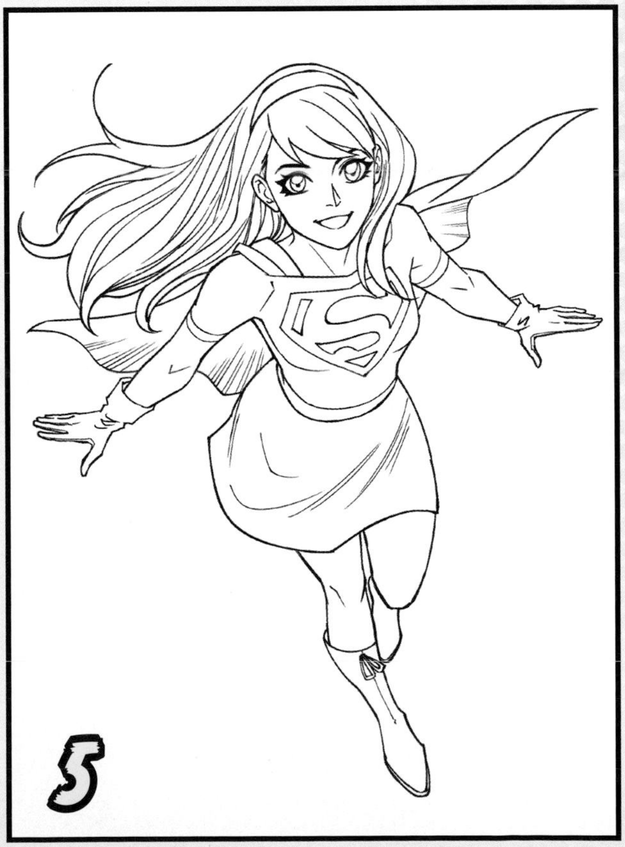
5

LOIS LANE

Lois Lane is always on the hunt for a headline. The star reporter for the *Daily Planet* has a knack for rooting out rogues with her unique brand of journalistic justice. But if Superman happens to swoop overhead, hang on tight! Lois will dash into danger on a dime to nab her next big scoop!

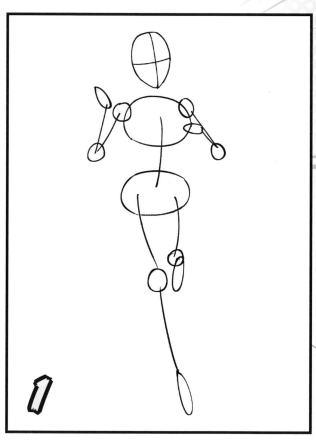

MANGA FACT
While *manga* refers to comics and graphic novels from Japan, the word itself means "whimsical pictures" in Japanese.

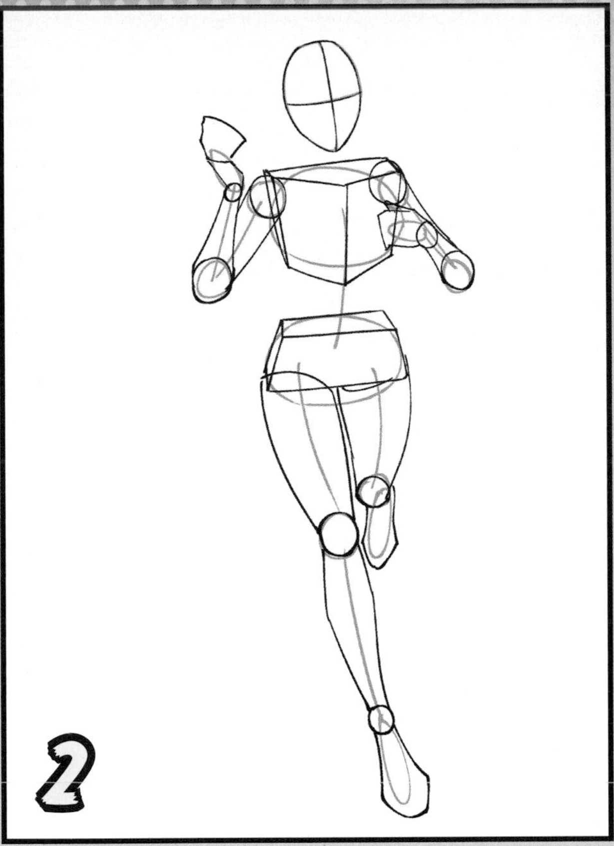
2

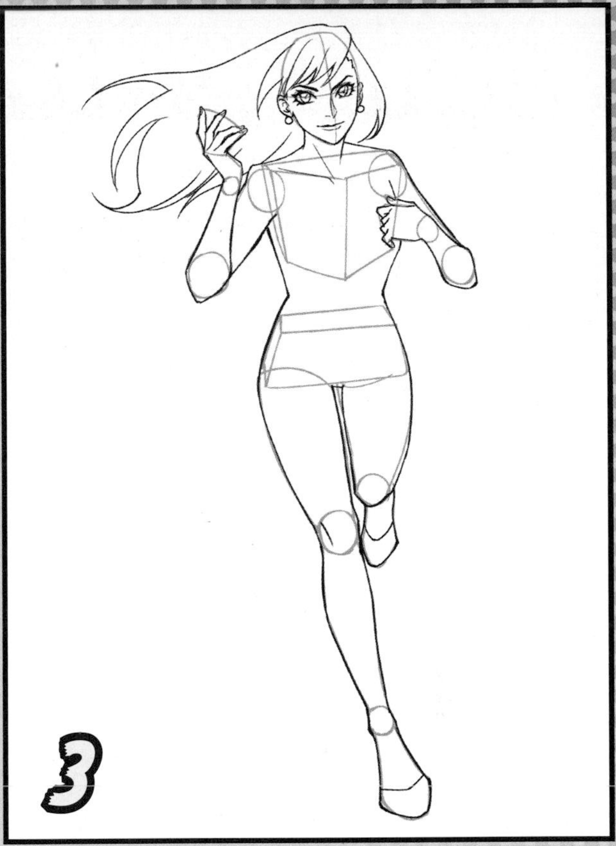
3

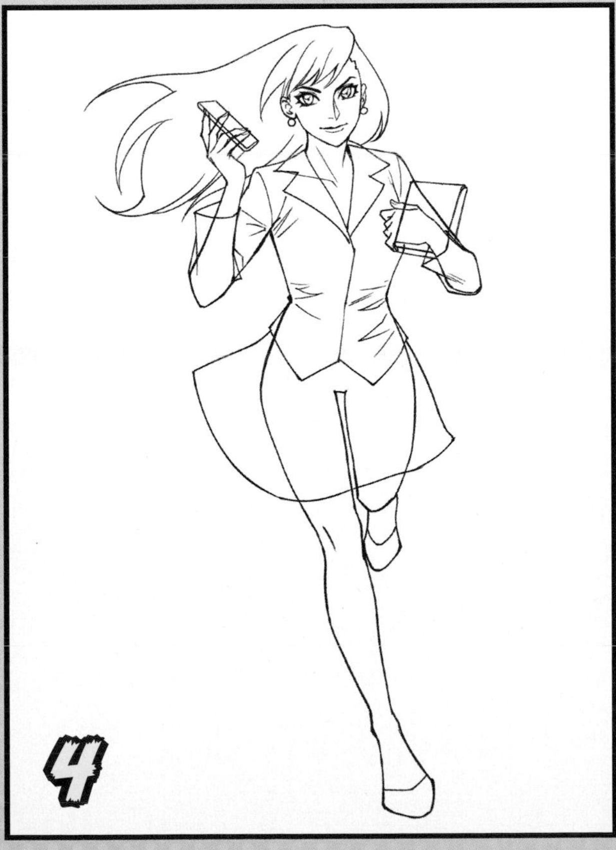
4

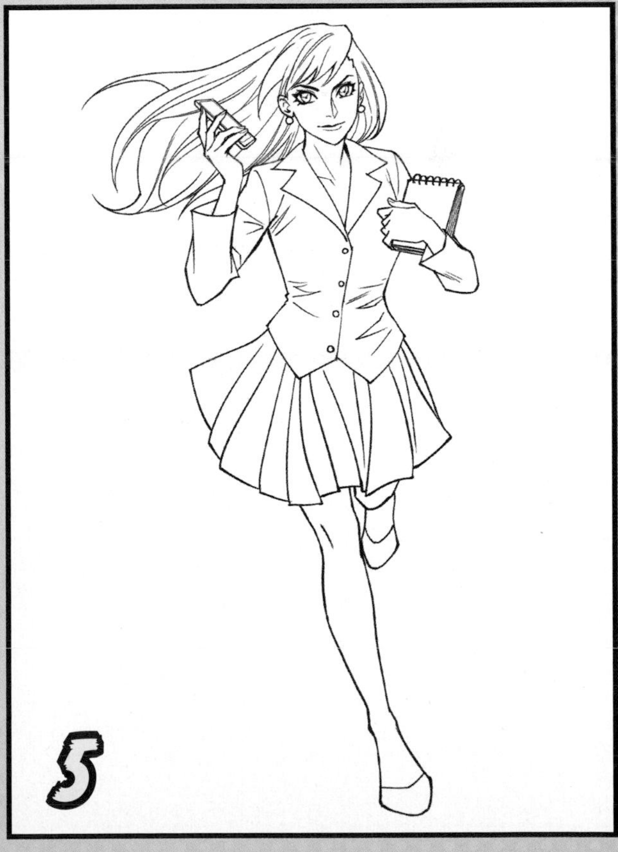
5

JIMMY OLSEN

If a picture is worth a thousand words, then Jimmy Olsen may be one of the world's greatest storytellers. The *Daily Planet* photographer has captured hundreds of amazing moments—including many of the Man of Steel's greatest feats. Whenever Lois needs snapshots for her news stories, Jimmy's pics do the trick!

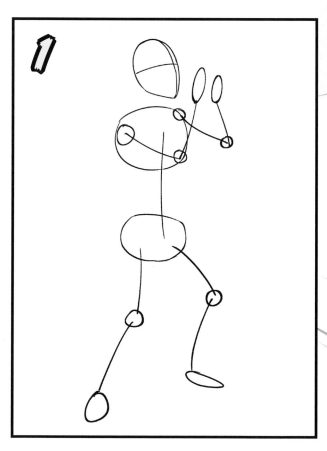

MANGA FACT
Manga characters may be stylized, but most are based on real human anatomy. Study pictures of people to help get your characters' proportions just right.

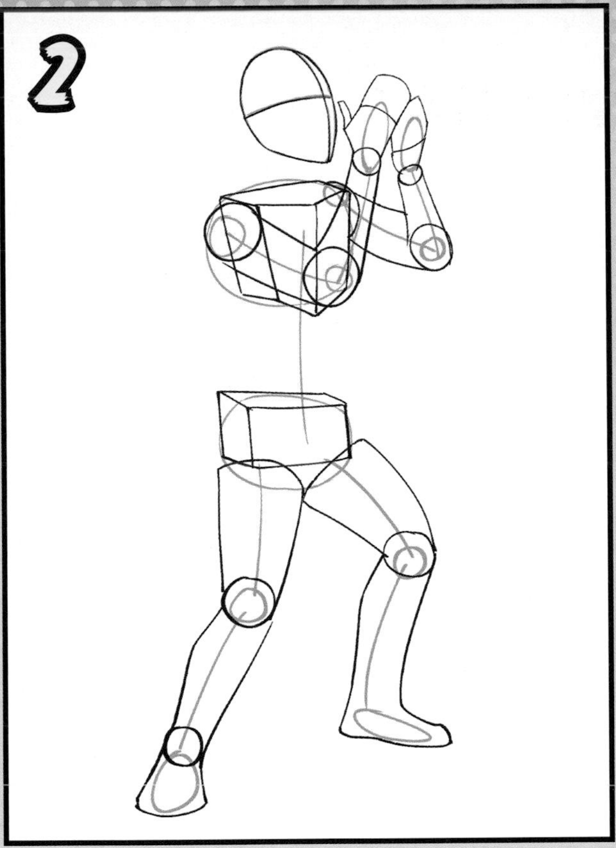
2

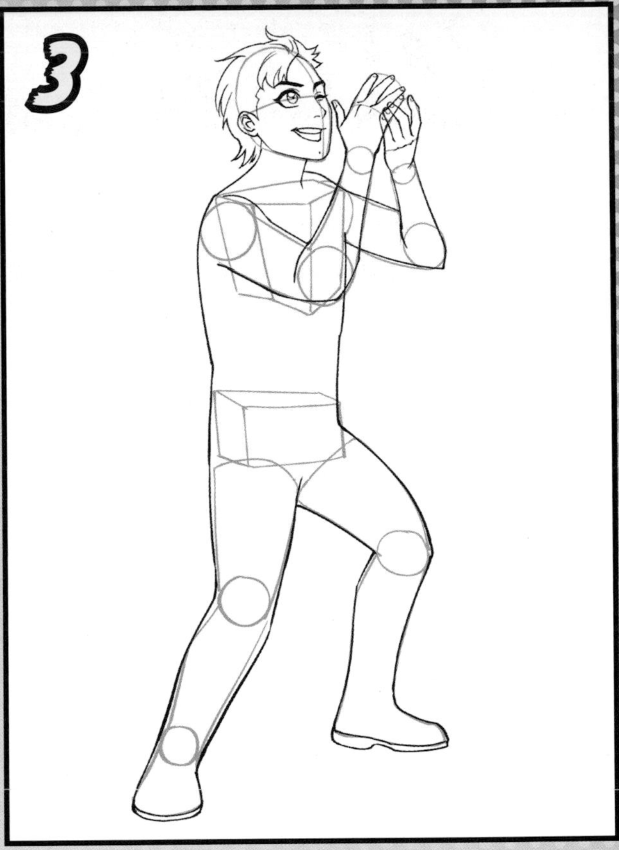
3

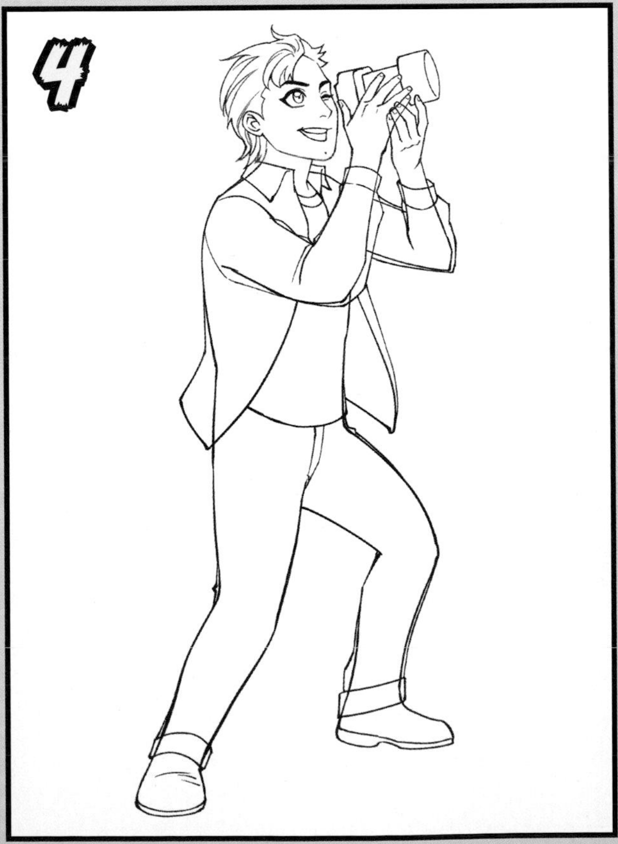
4

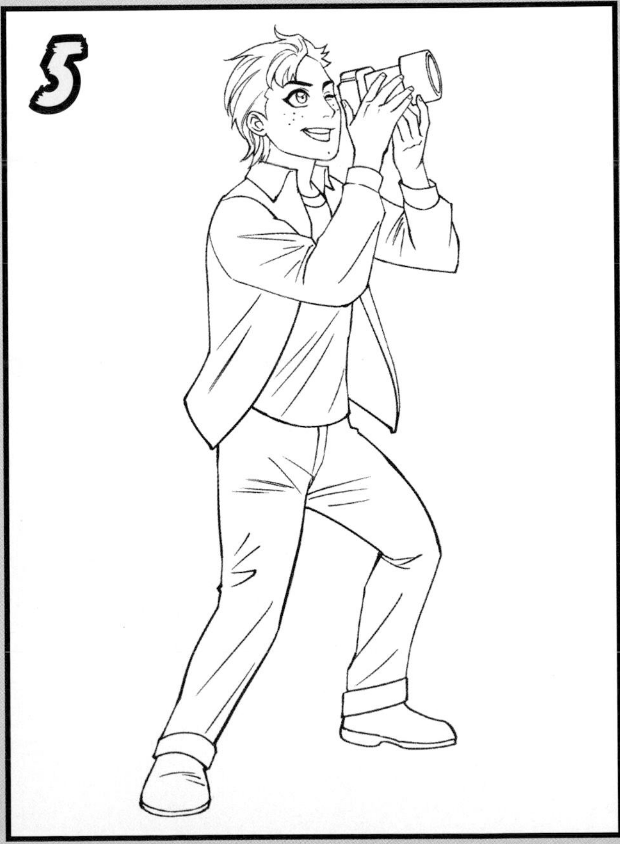
5

POWER GIRL

Behold Power Girl as she descends to defend the defenseless! She may be Supergirl's double from an alternate universe, but this Super Hero has a style that's all her own. With amazing Kryptonian abilities, expert boxing skills, and a whip-smart mind, Power Girl quickly takes any criminal to the cleaners!

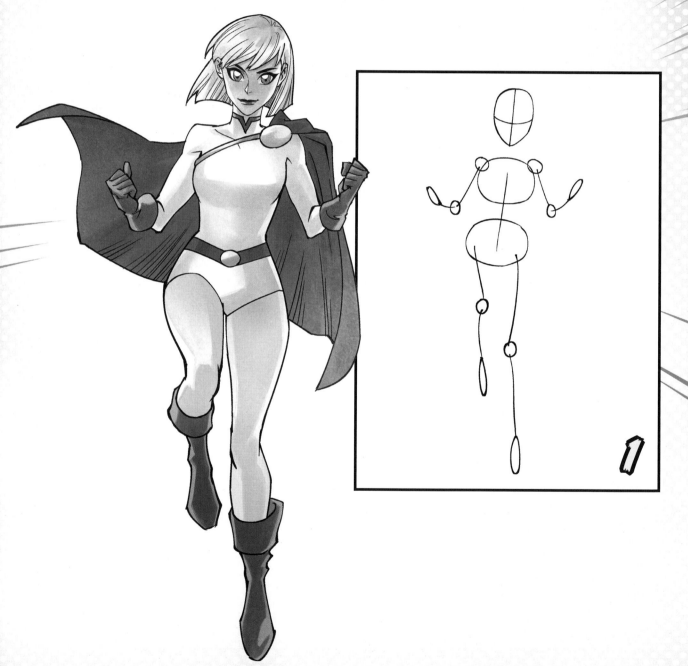

1

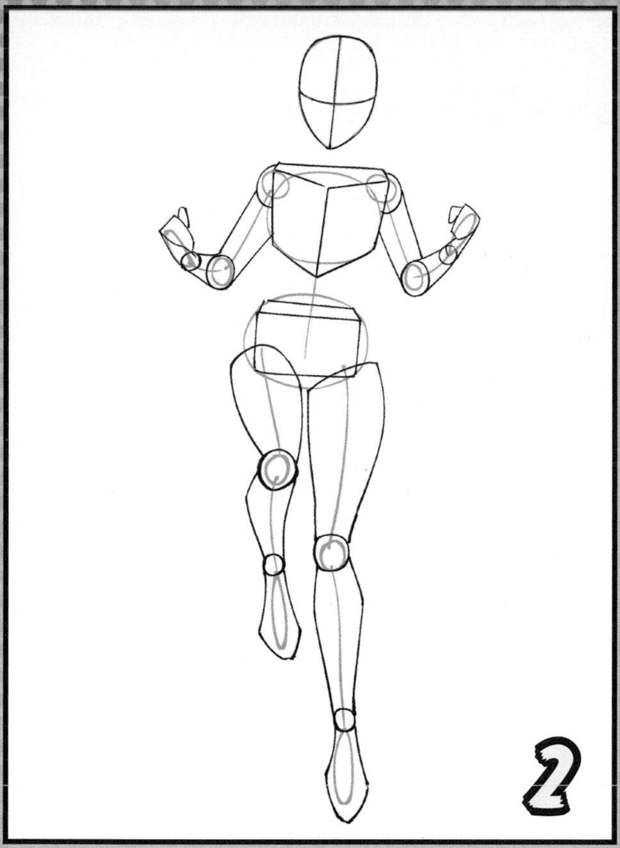
2
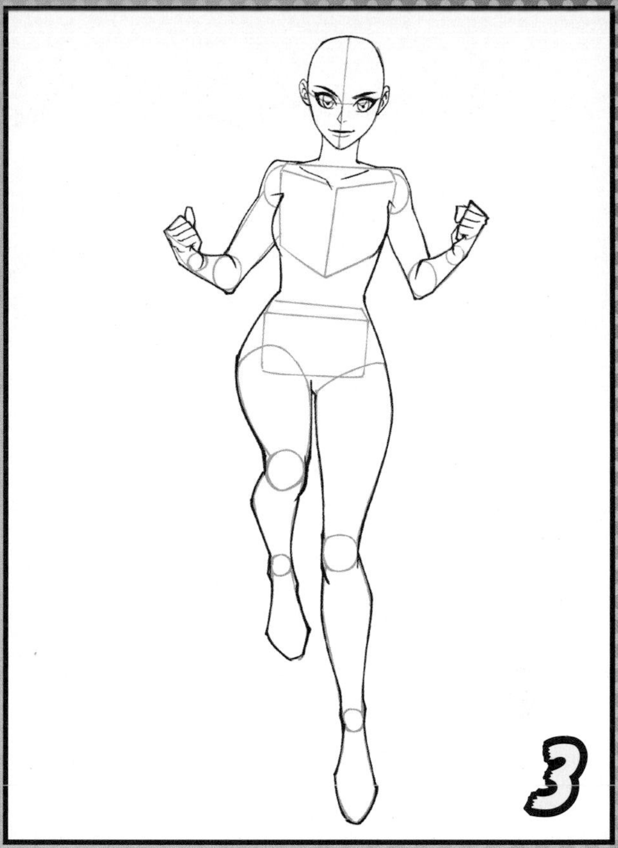
3
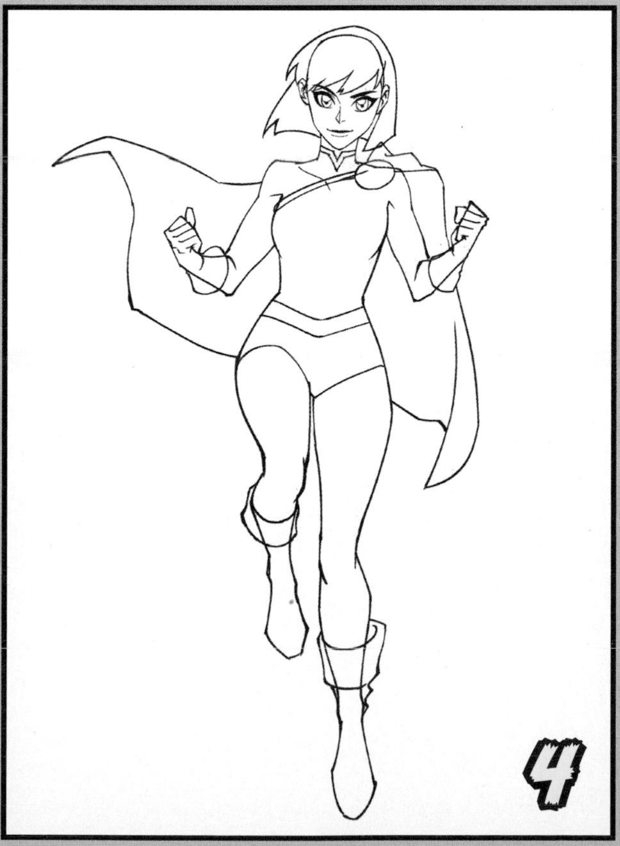
4
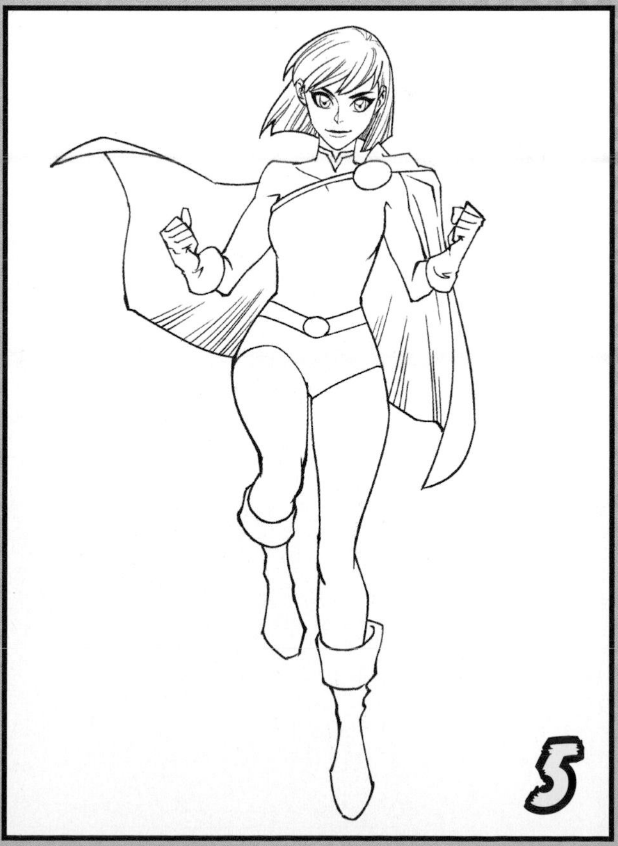
5

LEX LUTHOR

Lex Luthor's envy is as green as Kryptonite—and just as dangerous. Jealous of Superman's power and popularity, the CEO of LexCorp will stop at nothing to crush the Super Hero. That's why the criminal mastermind often dons his warsuit. Wearing the alien-tech armor, Luthor can pack a wallop to challenge even the Man of Steel!

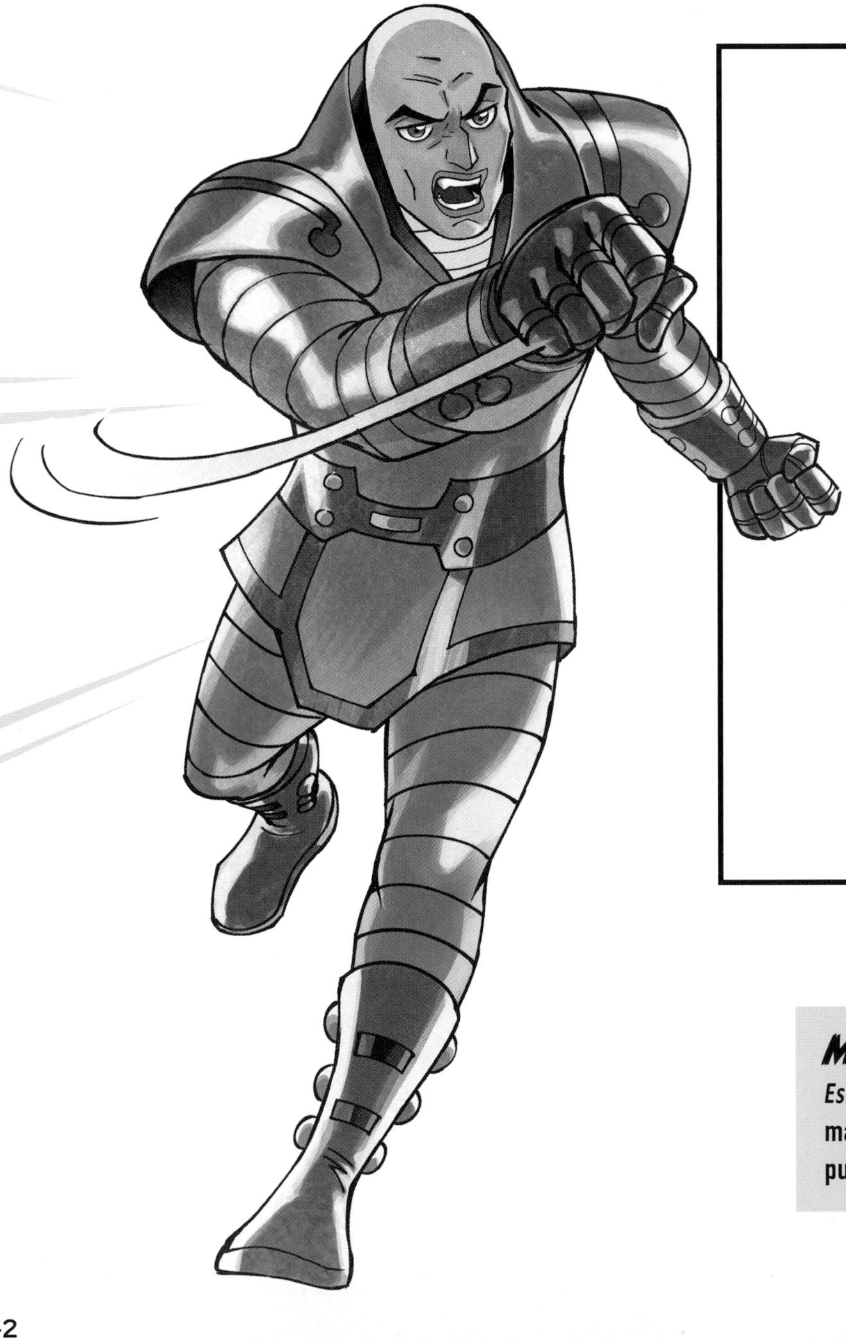

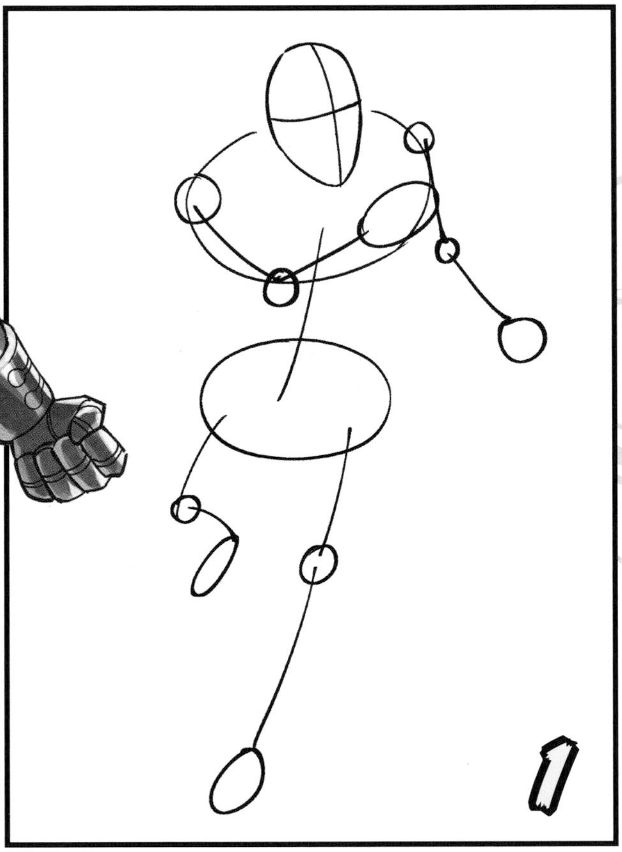
1

MANGA FACT

Eshinbun Nipponchi is considered the first manga magazine ever created. It was published in 1874 and ran for three issues.

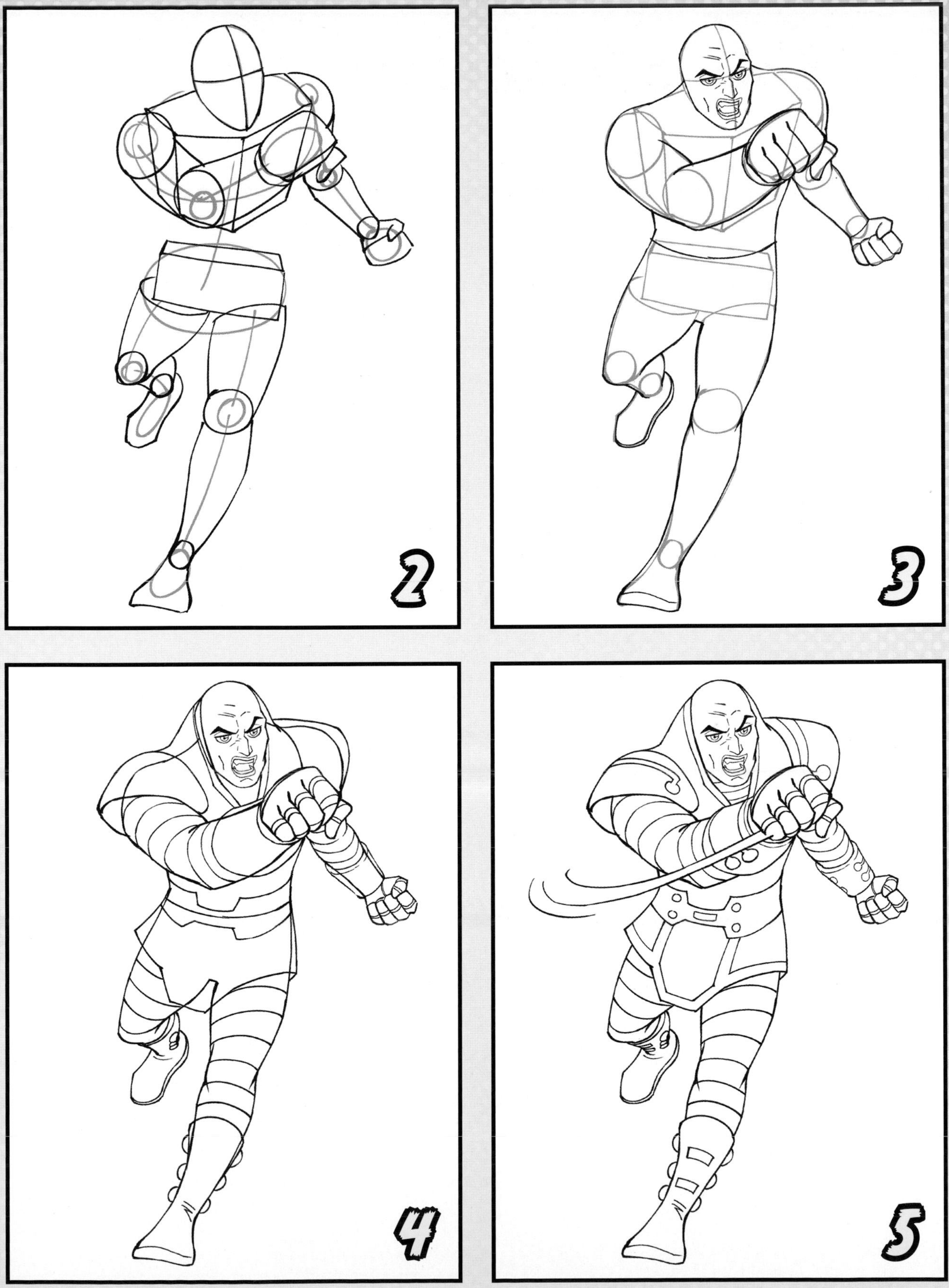
2
3
4
5

BIZARRO

Is Bizarro a duplicate of doom or an adorable goofball? The jury is still out. This clone of Superman has all the Super Hero's powers, but in reverse. Instead of heat vision and freeze-breath, he unleashes freeze vision and flame-breath. Bizarro's backward heroics often harm more than help. But as he'll tell you, "Bizarro am perfectly imperfect!"

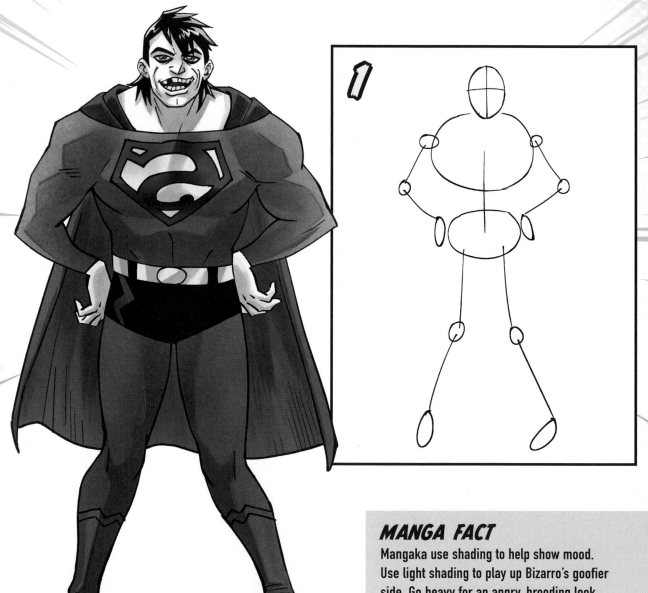

MANGA FACT
Mangaka use shading to help show mood. Use light shading to play up Bizarro's goofier side. Go heavy for an angry, brooding look.

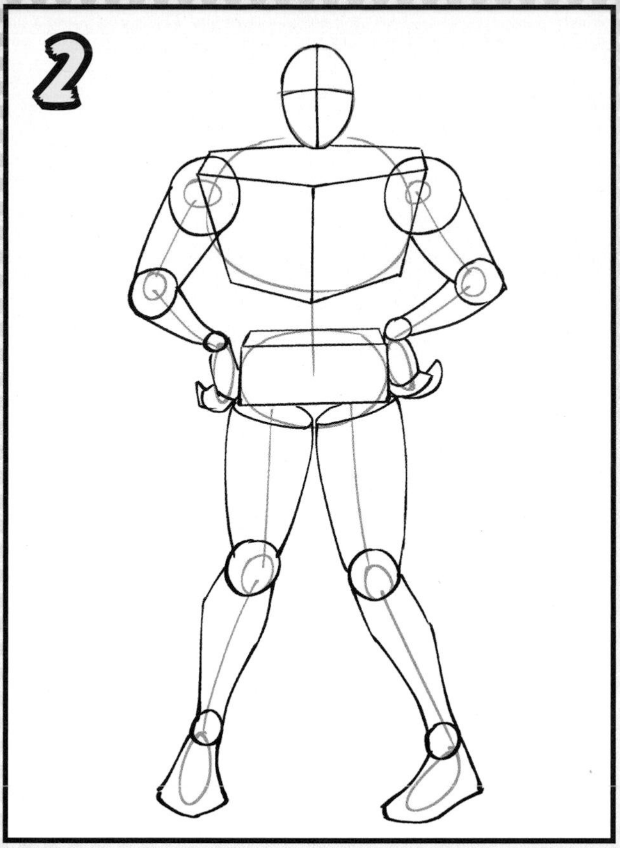
2
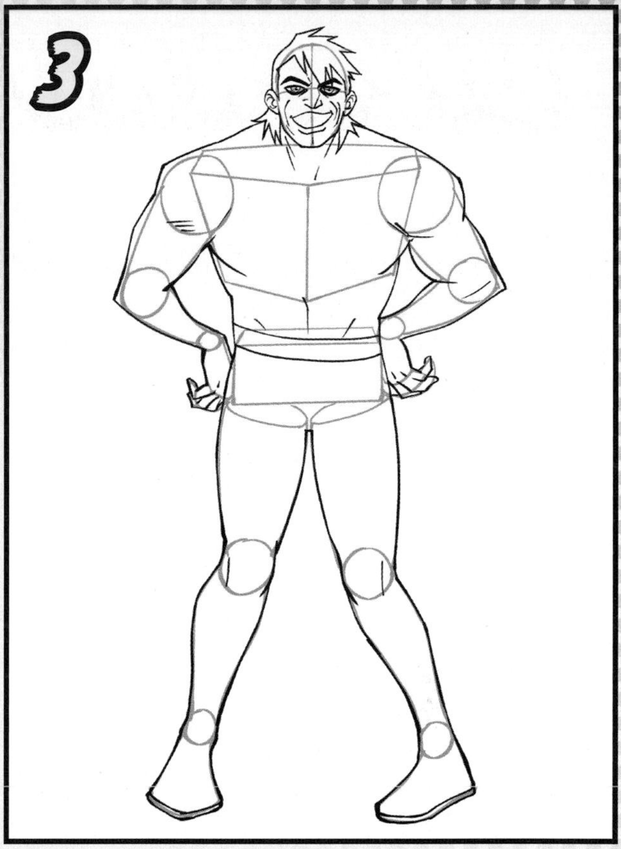
3
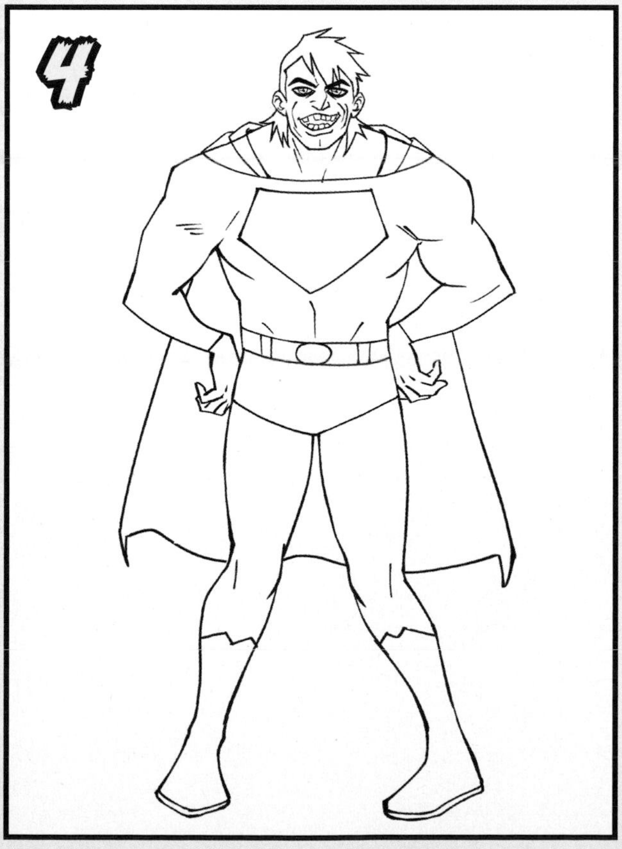
4
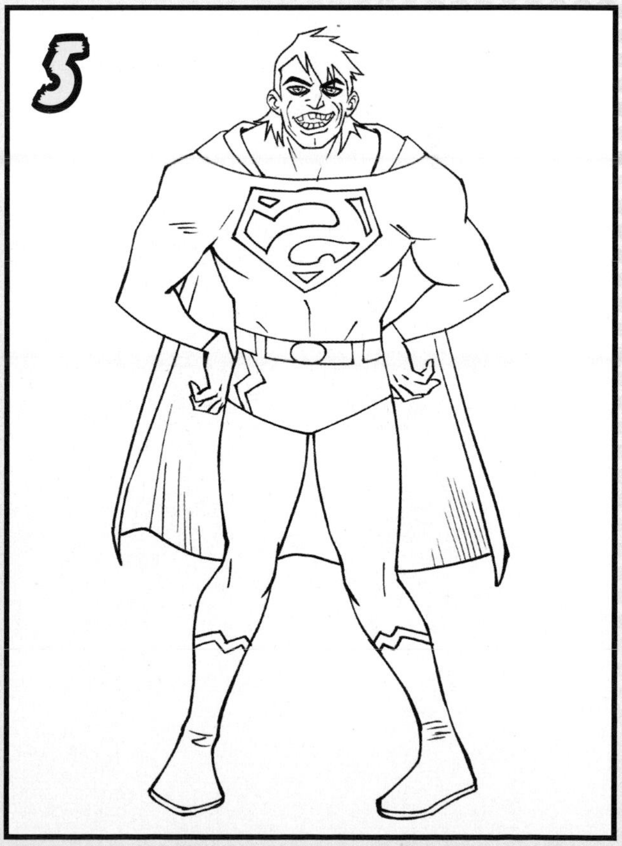
5

DARKSEID

A word to the wise—don't mess with Darkseid. The ruthless ruler of planet Apokolips is called the God of Tyranny for a reason. His sights are set on conquering the universe! Anyone who dares to defy Darkseid must beware the tyrant's mighty Omega Beams, which can bring even Superman to his knees.

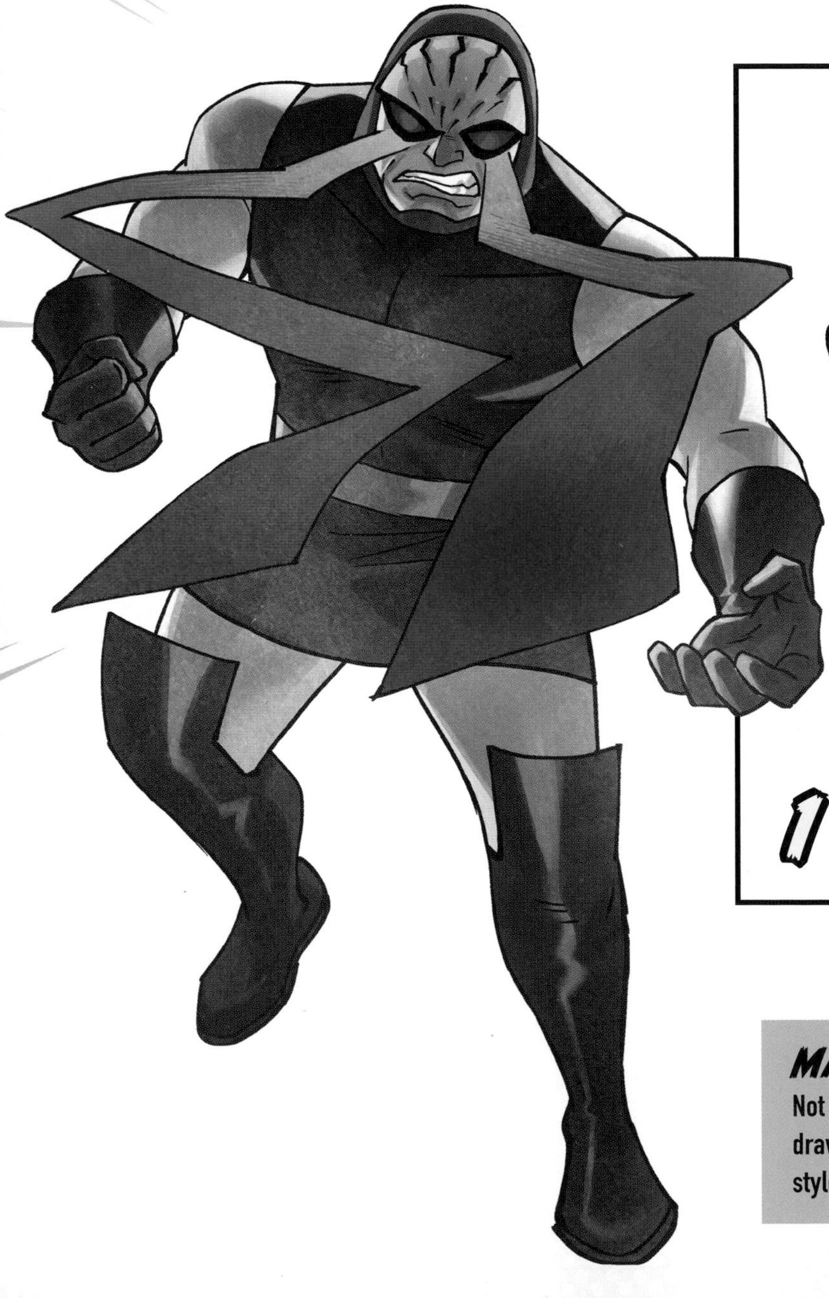

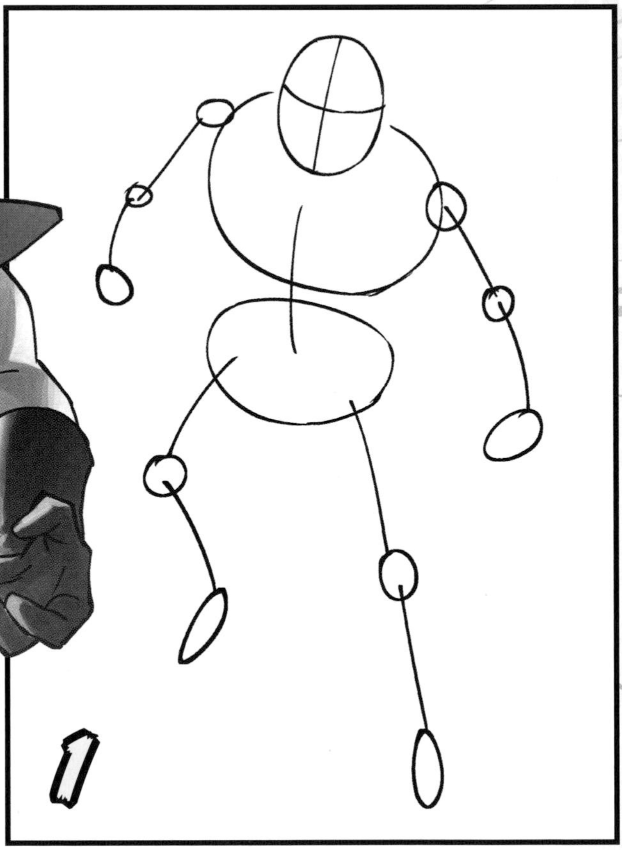
1

MANGA FACT

Not feeling serious? Manga characters are sometimes drawn as chibis to add humor. Try using the super-cute style to make the menacing Darkseid look hilarious!

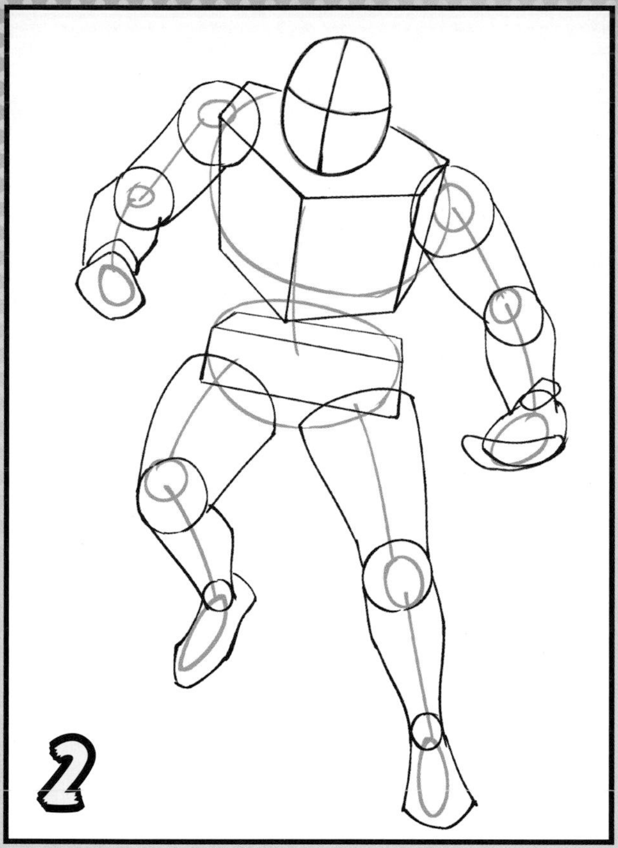
2
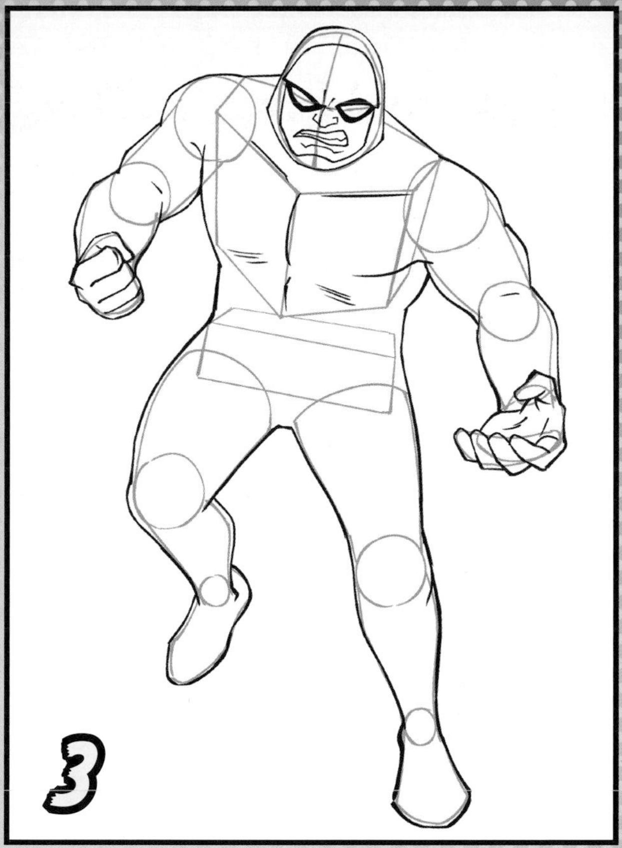
3
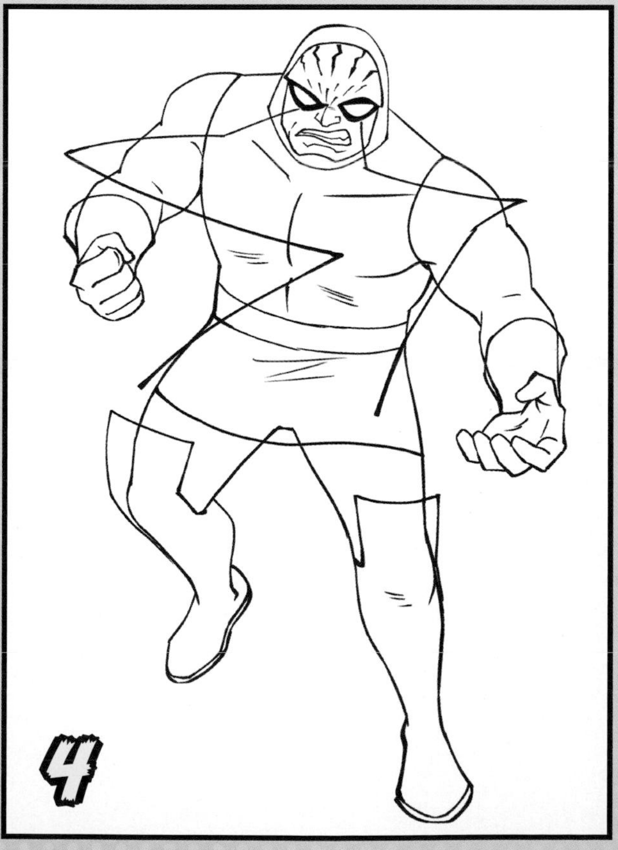
4
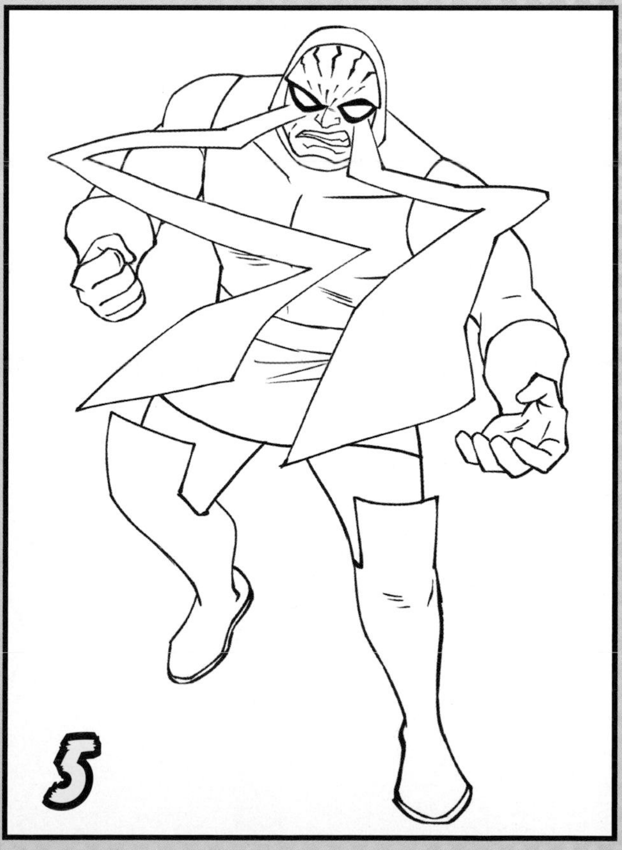
5

LIVEWIRE

Look out for Livewire! She is positively supercharged with negative energy. The high-voltage Super-Villain can unleash huge amounts of electricity with shocking results. From melting metal to flinging electric energy balls, Livewire has *watt* it takes to conduct mayhem in Metropolis!

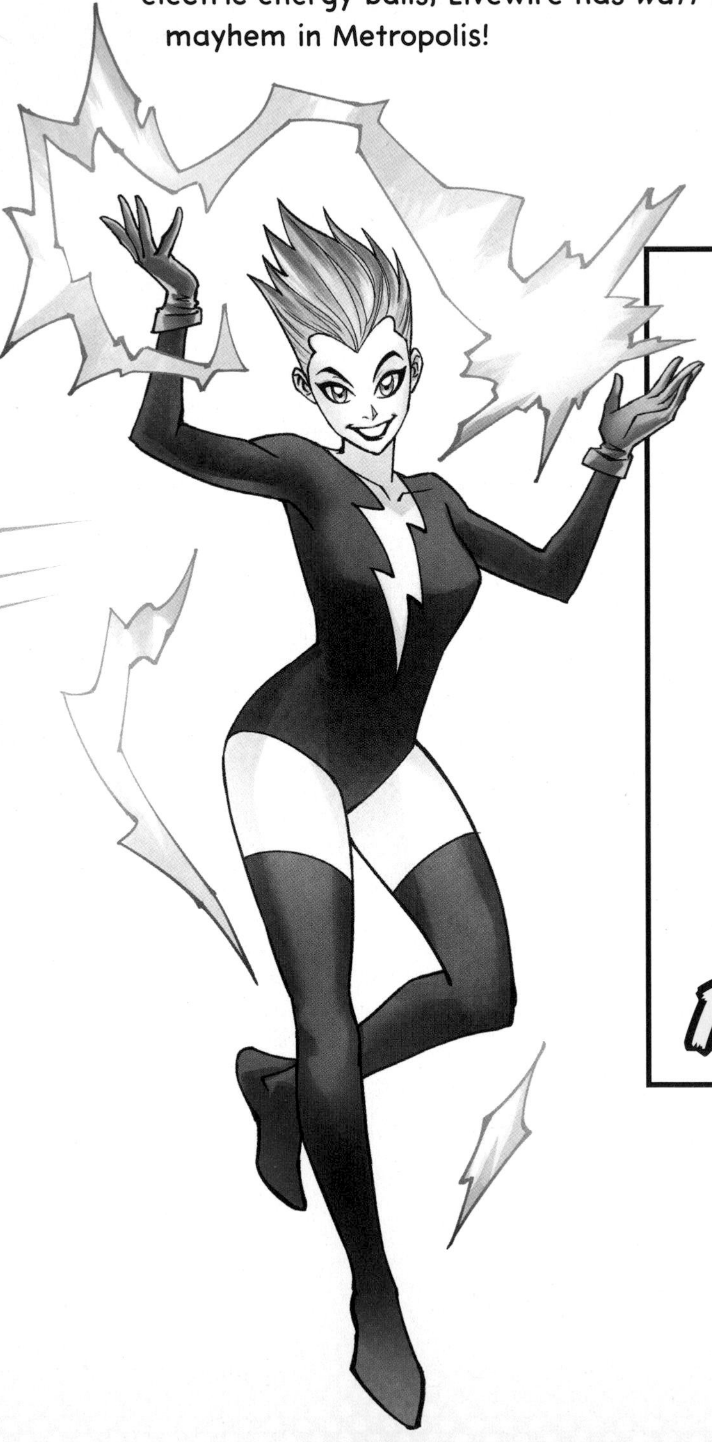

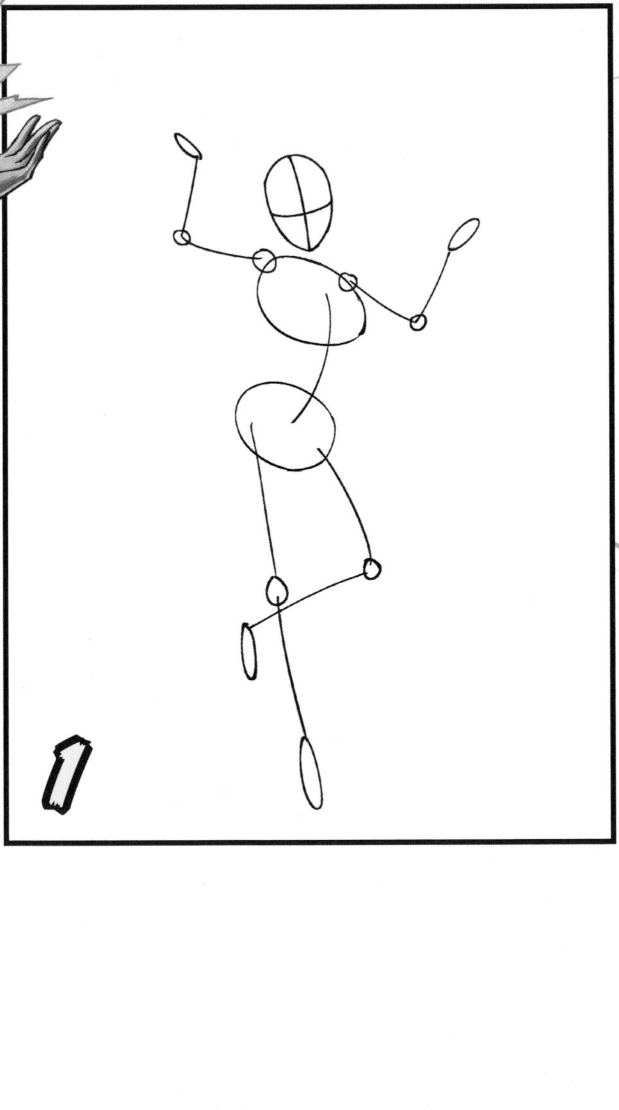
1

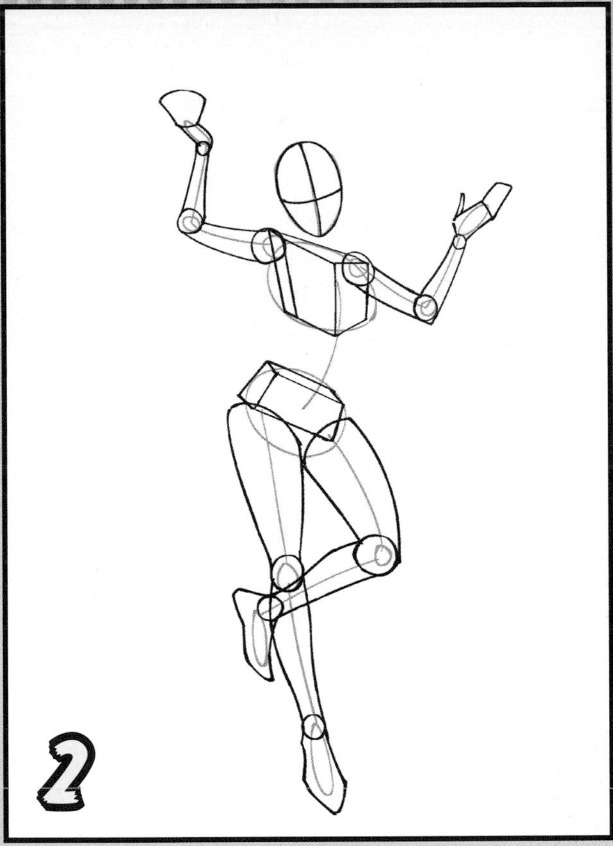
2
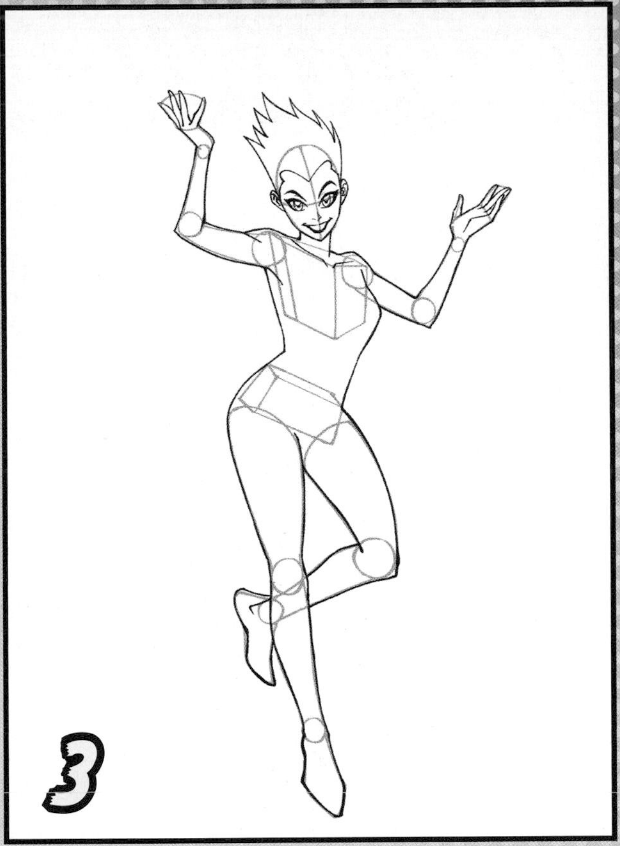
3
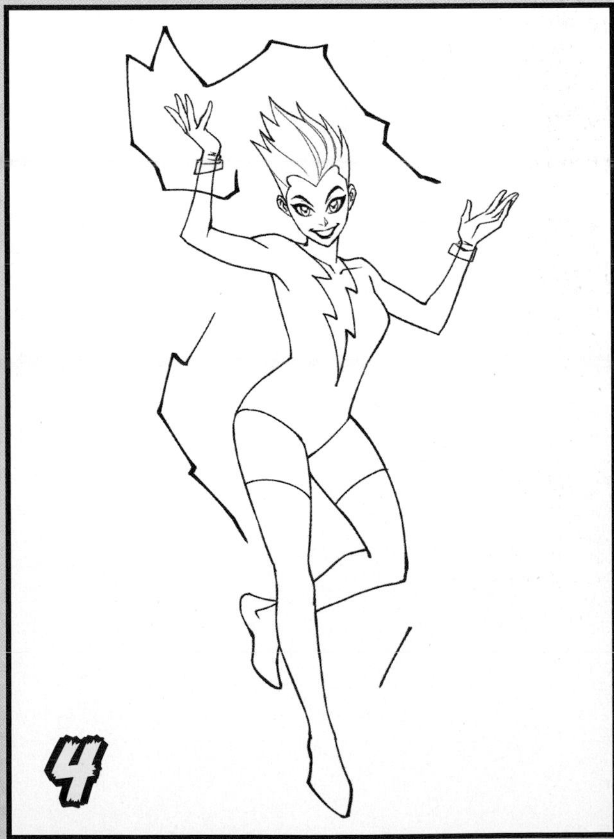
4
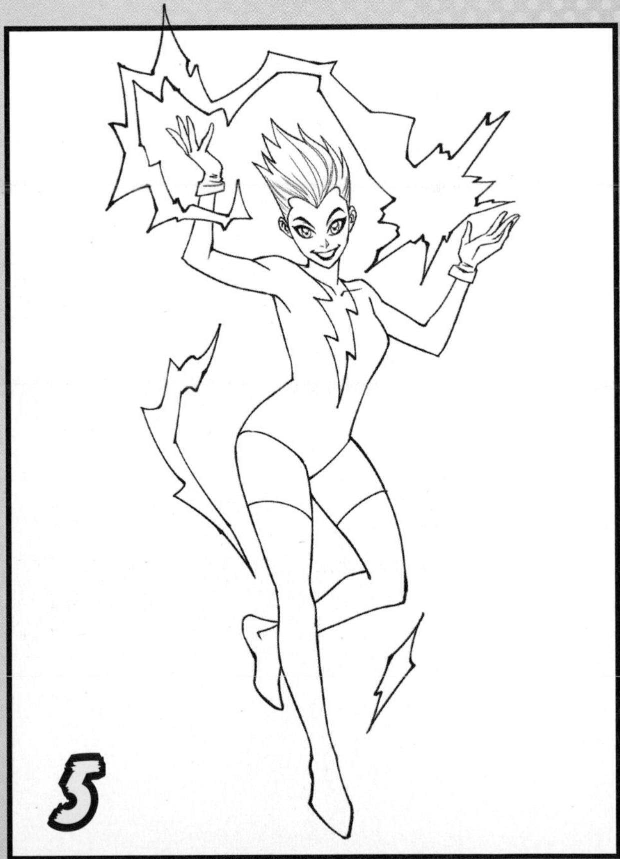
5

BRAINIAC

For Brainiac, knowledge is power. And this superintelligent supercomputer has a goal that's sinister in its simplicity: Seek out planets, download their raw data, and then destroy them. Naturally, Superman isn't too keen on the evil AI hacking into Earth's databanks with twisting tendrils!

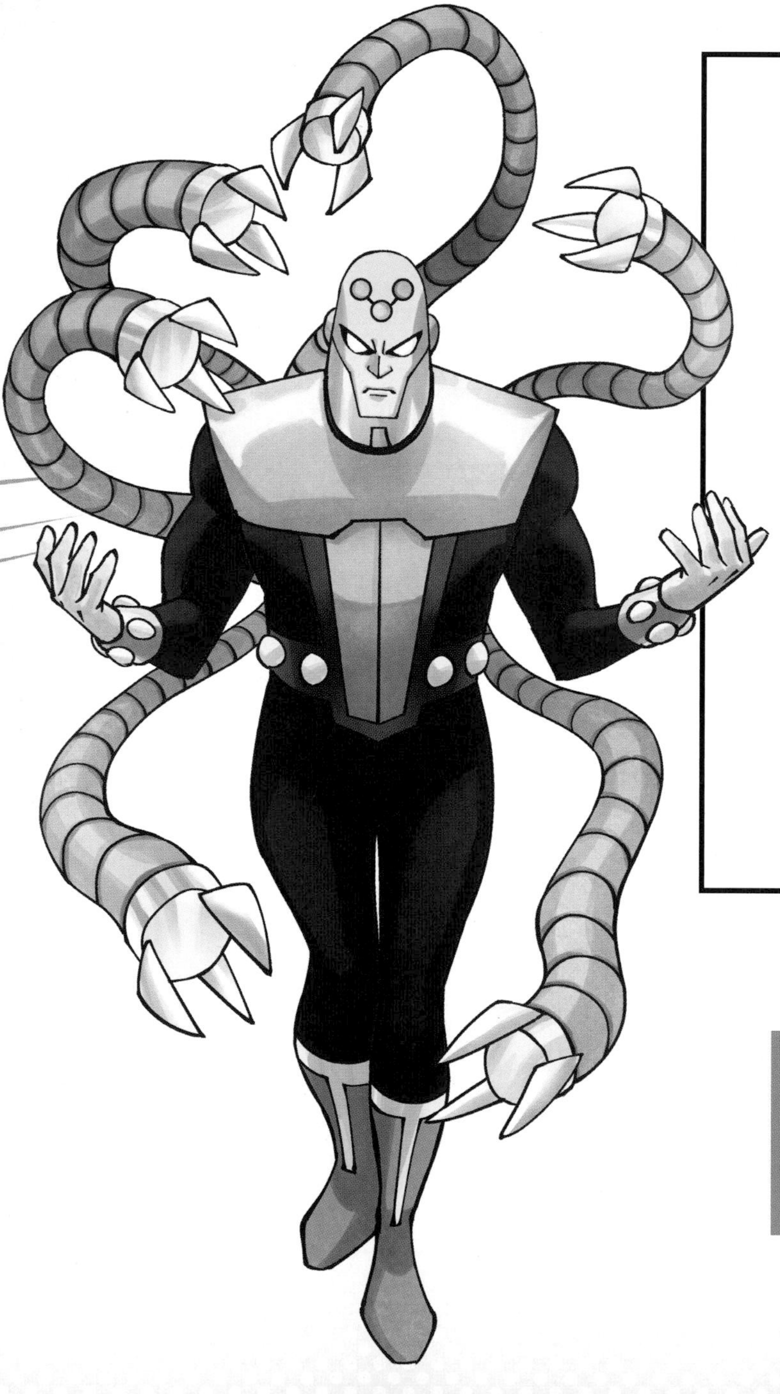

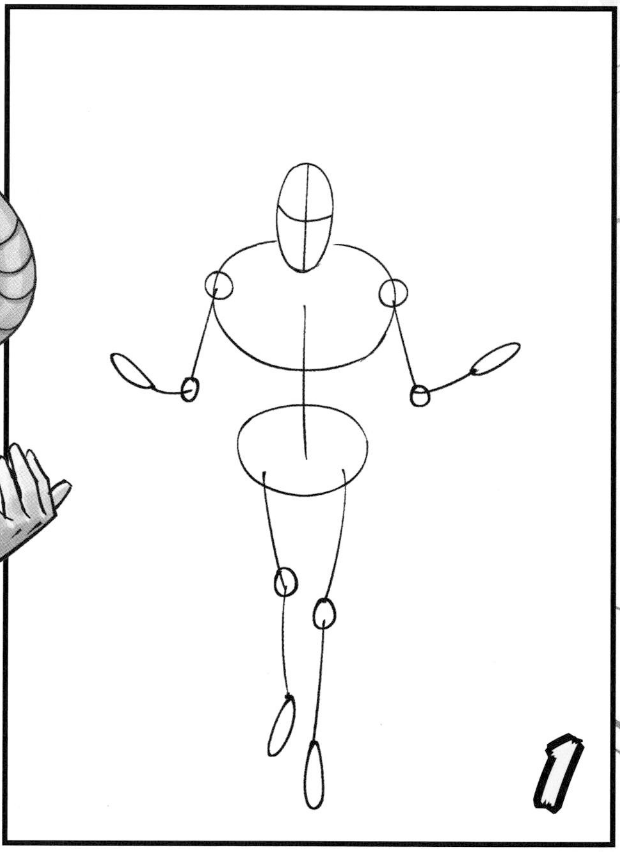
1

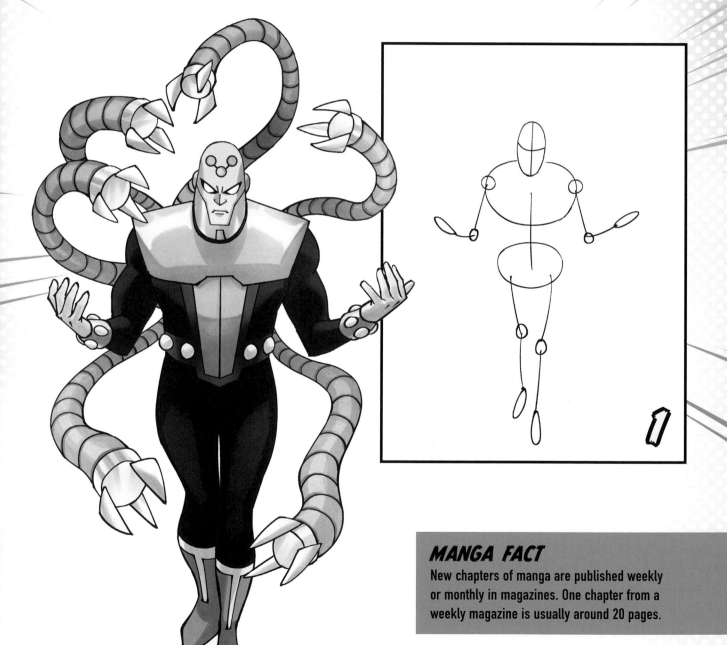

MANGA FACT

New chapters of manga are published weekly or monthly in magazines. One chapter from a weekly magazine is usually around 20 pages.

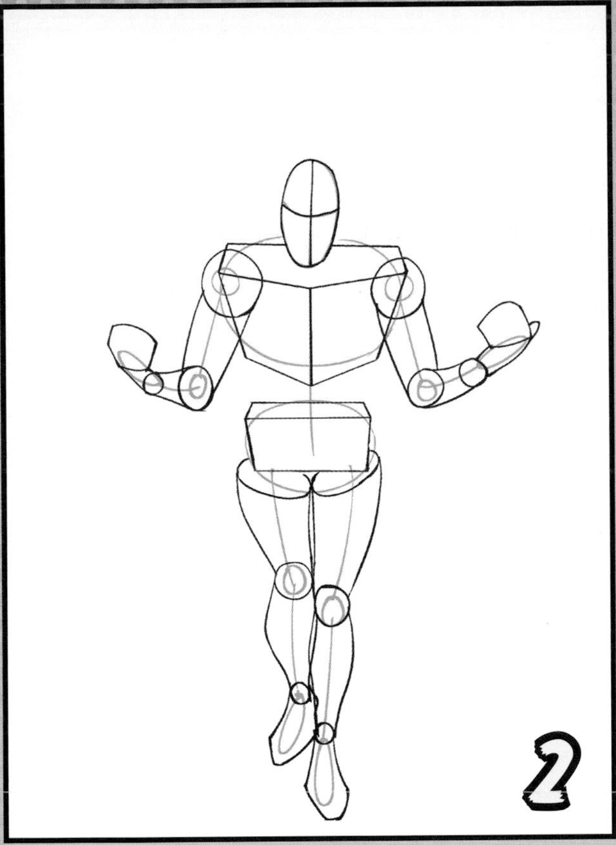
2

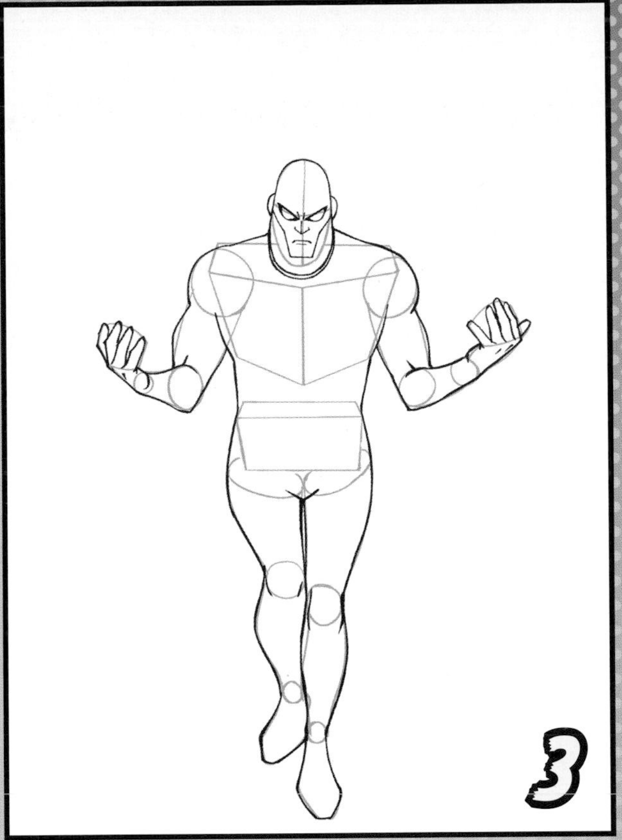
3

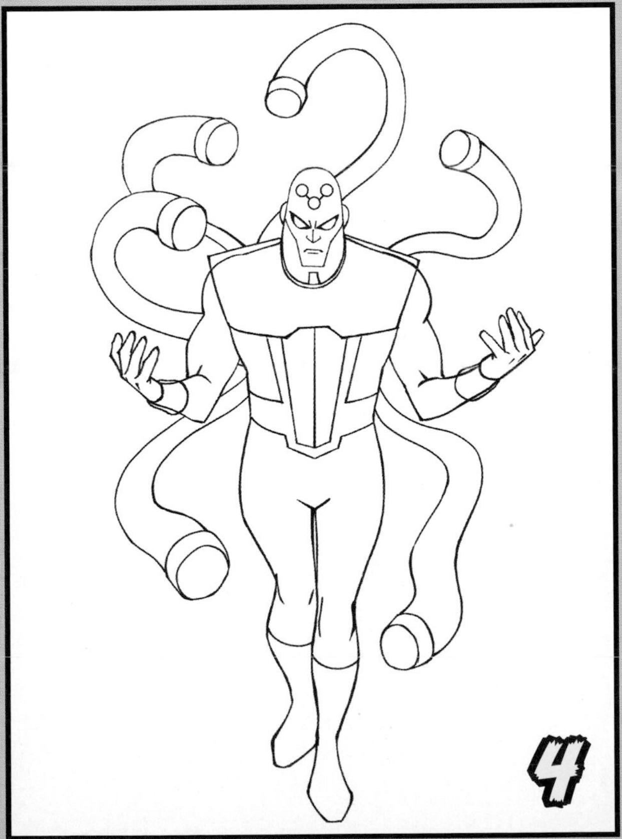
4

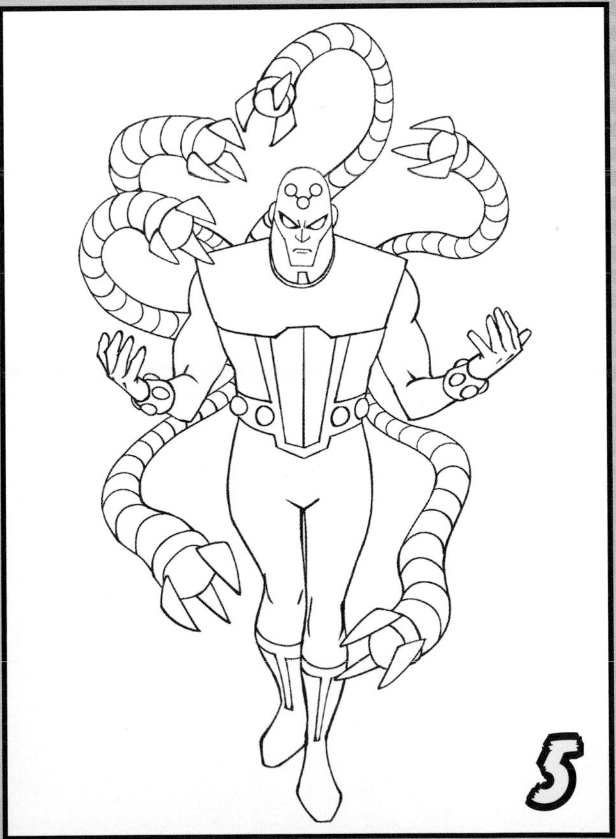
5

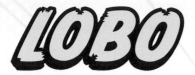

LOBO

Lobo's word is his bond. When this intergalactic bounty hunter takes a contract, nothing stands in his way. The Main Man—as he's dubbed himself—crisscrosses the galaxy on a souped-up space-bike in pursuit of prey. And when he corners a quarry, he restrains his game with a hook and chain!

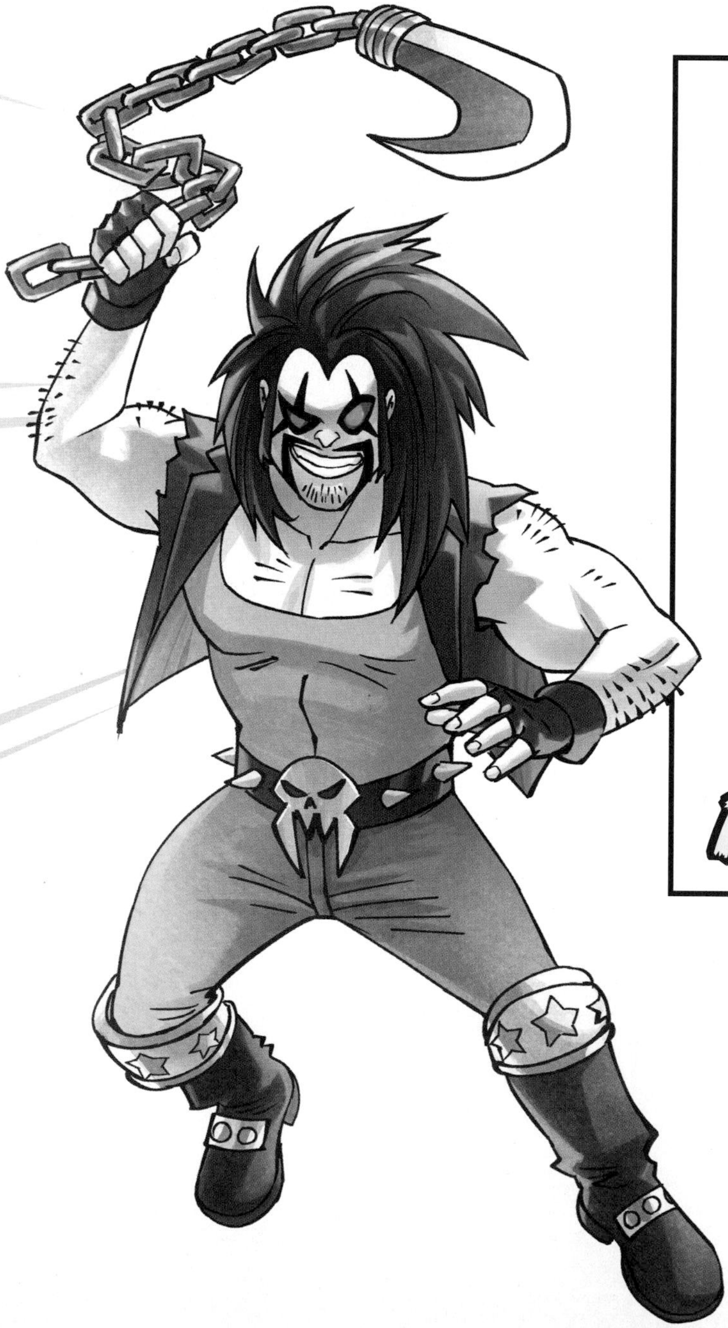

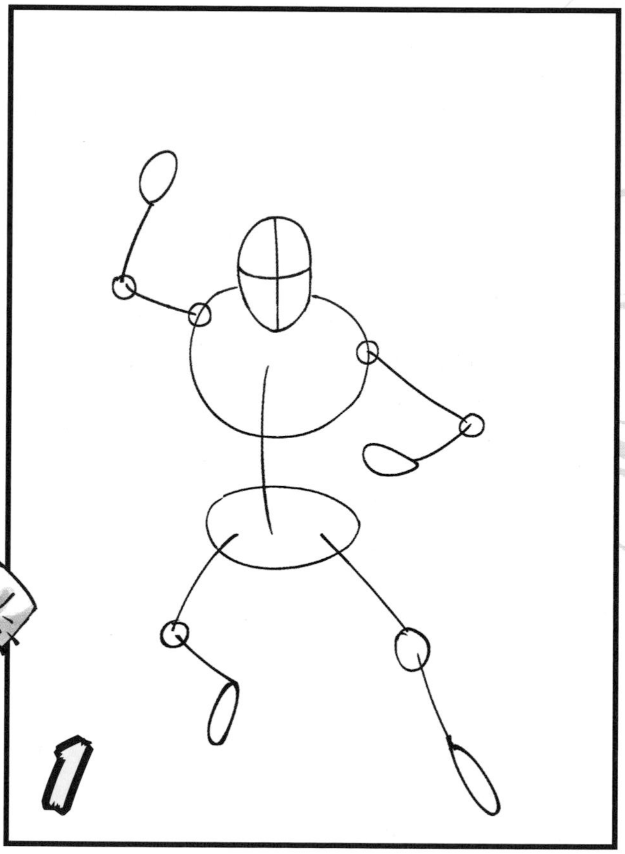
1

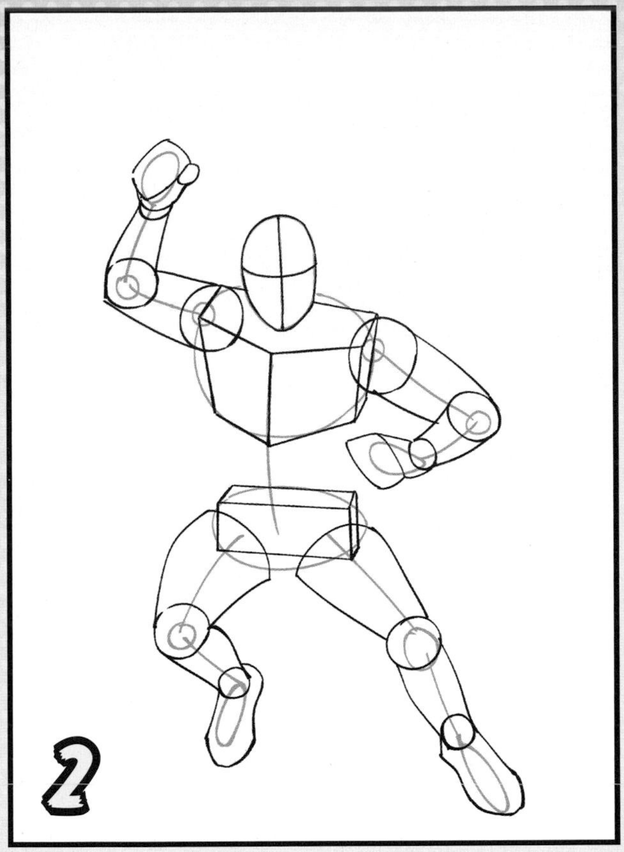
2
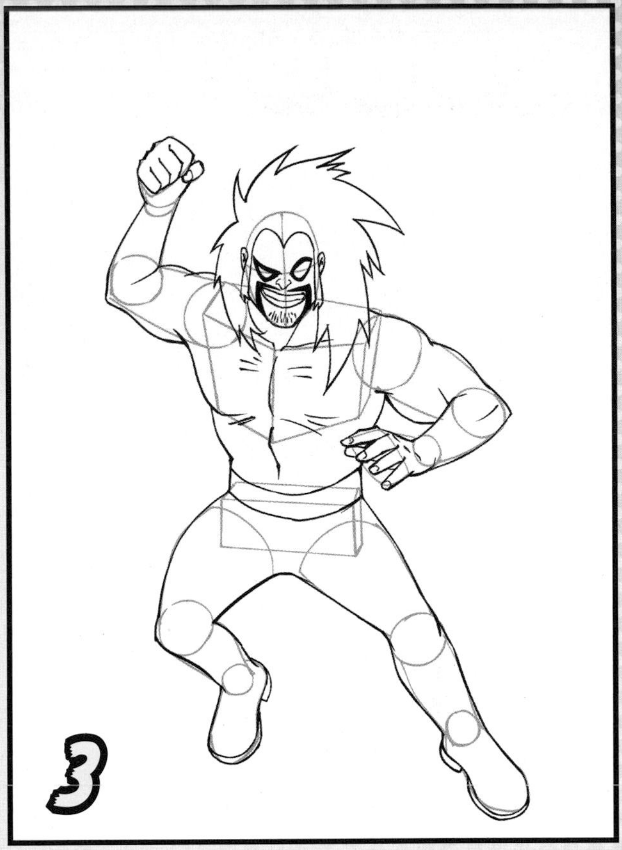
3
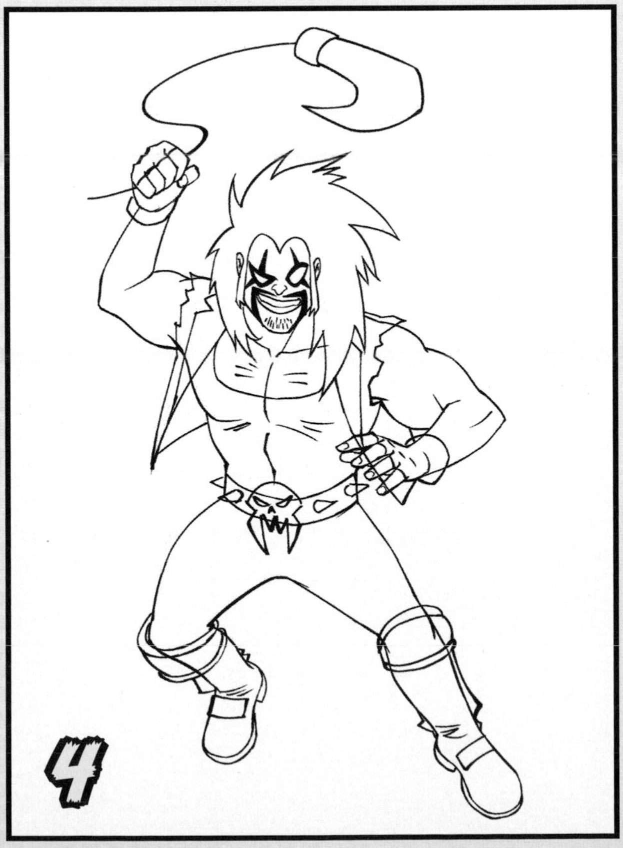
4
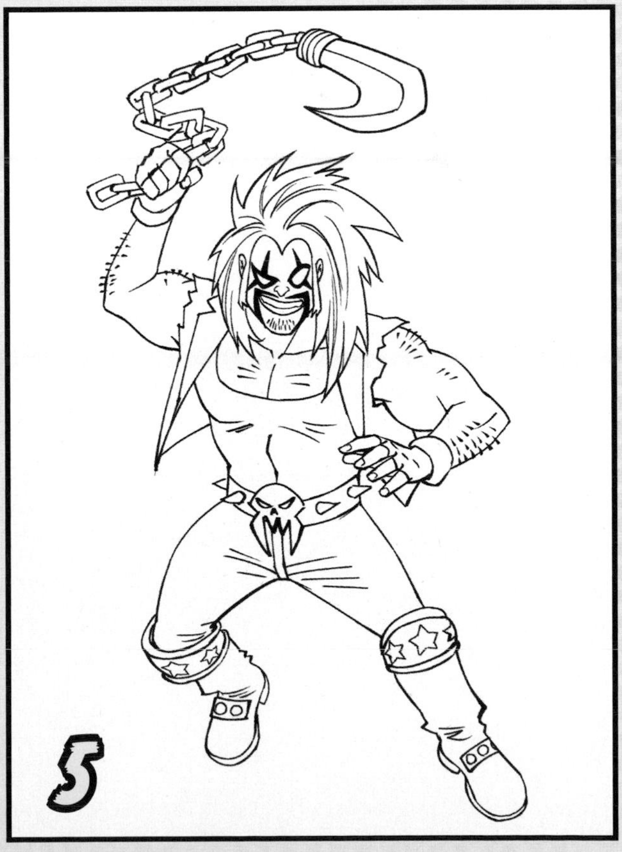
5

SUPERMAN VS. DOOMSDAY

An epic battle erupts when the World's Greatest Super Hero faces his fiercest foe! Will the dreaded Doomsday release his rage on all of Metropolis? Or can Superman take down the creature of chaos and catastrophe? YOU'RE THE MANGAKA. THE FATE OF THE CITY IS IN YOUR HANDS!

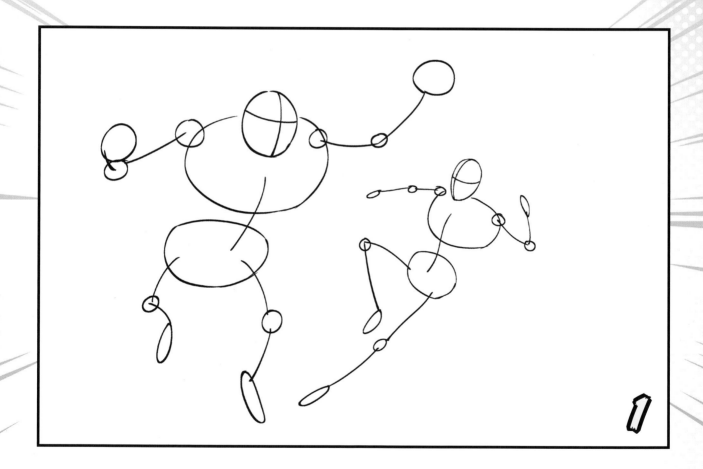

MANGA FACT
Eiichiro Oda is one of the most successful mangaka of all time. Since 1997, his blockbuster series, *One Piece*, has sold more than 500 million volumes worldwide!

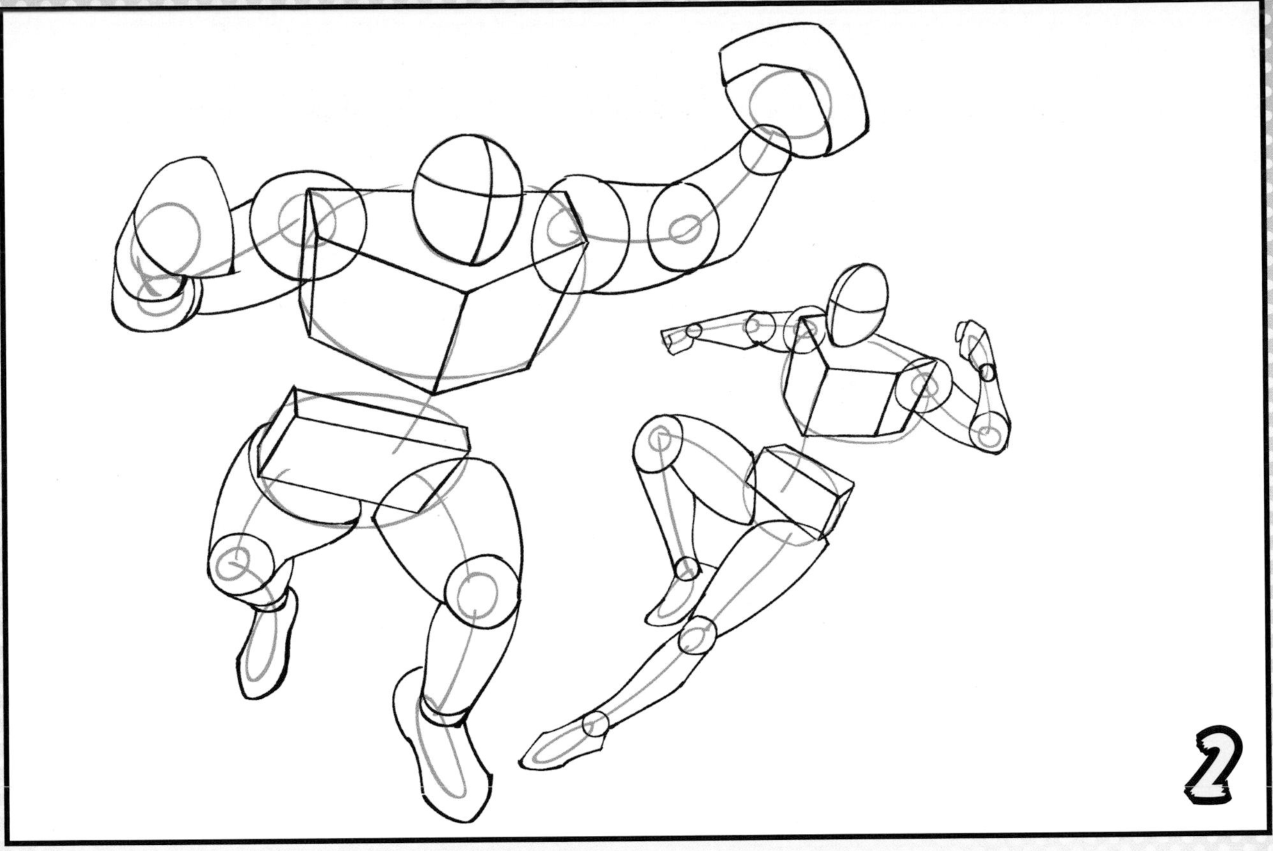
2

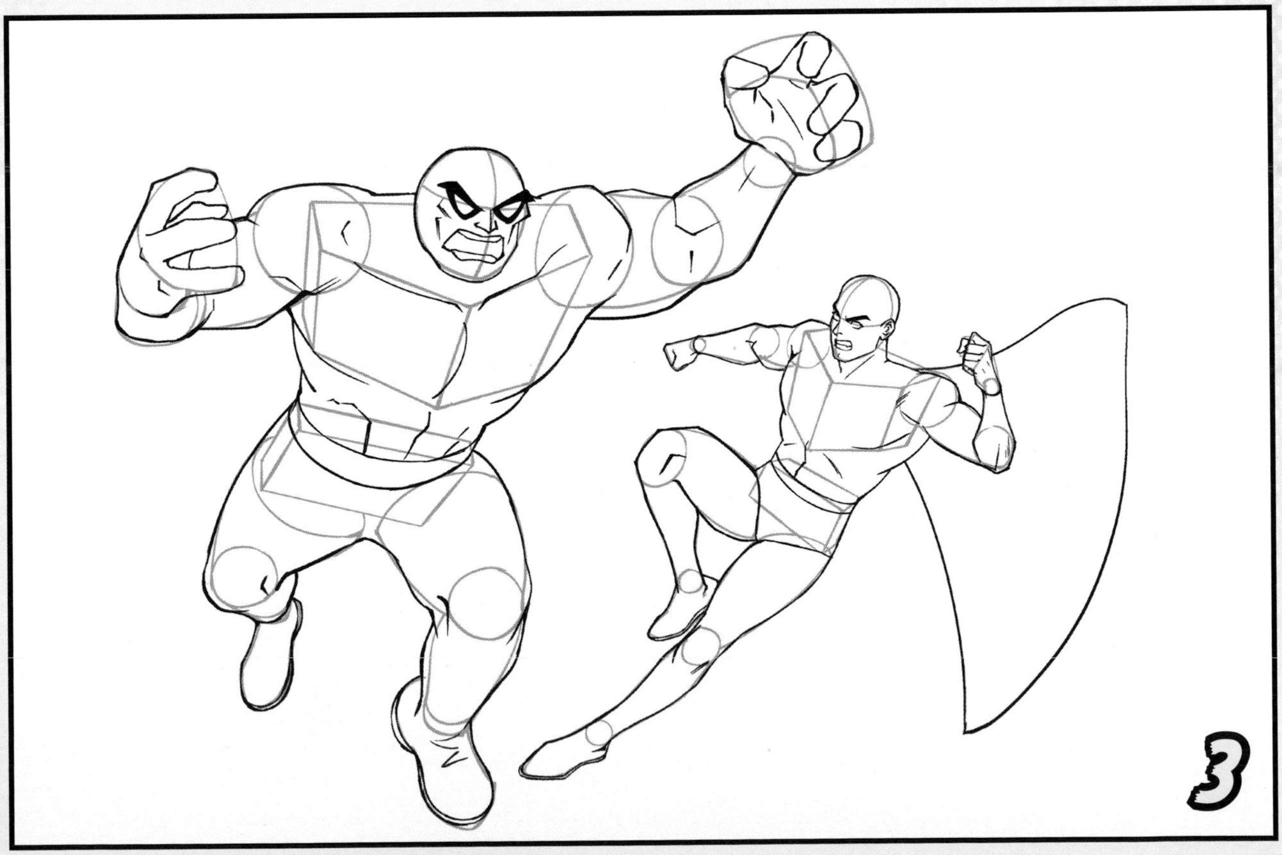
3

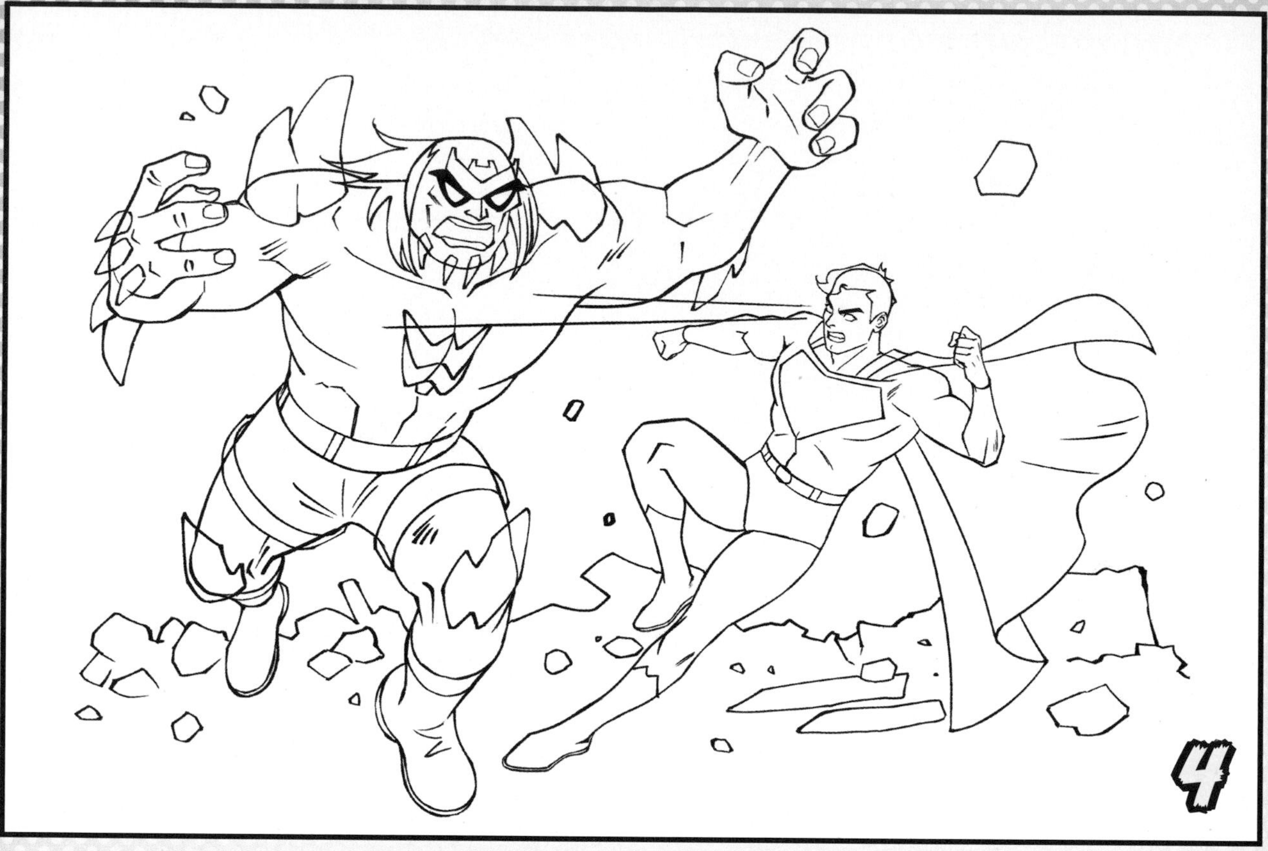

4

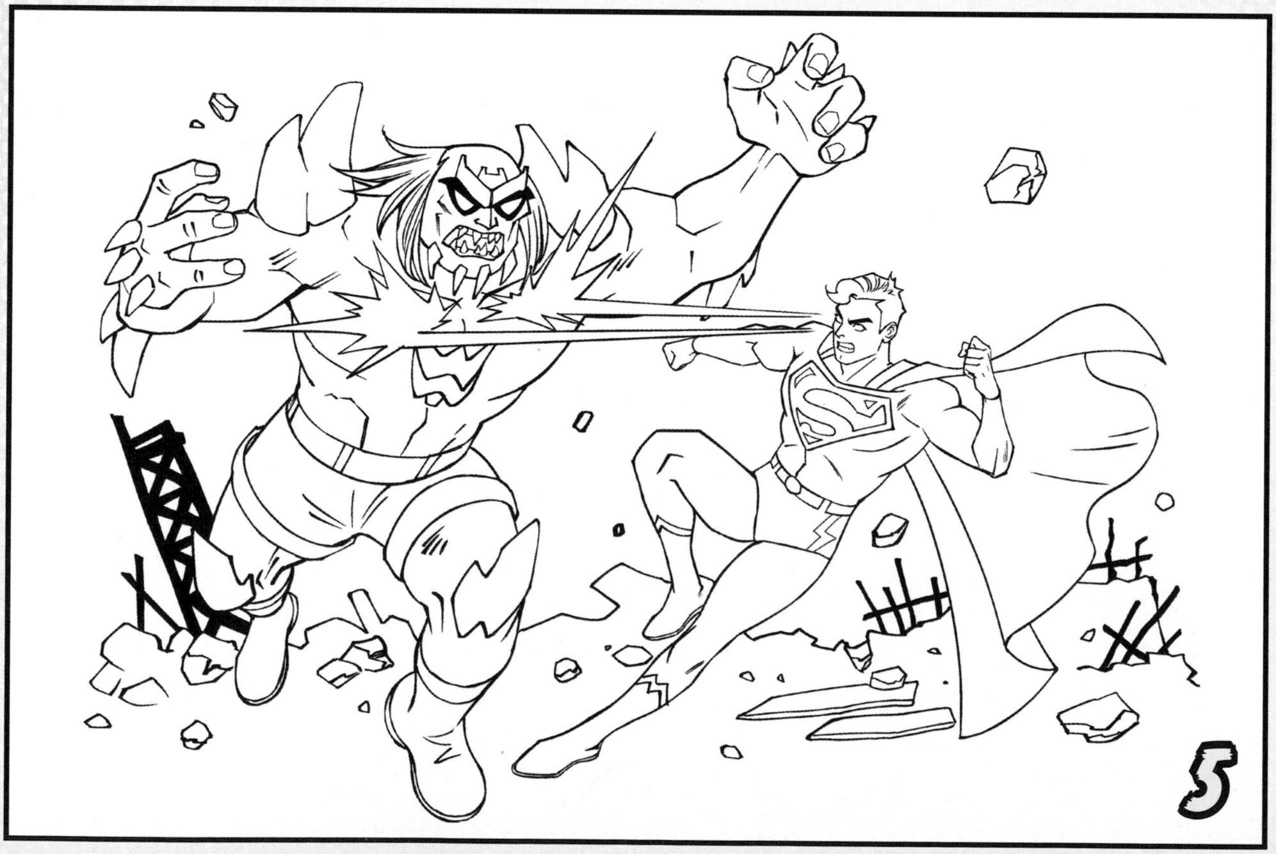

5

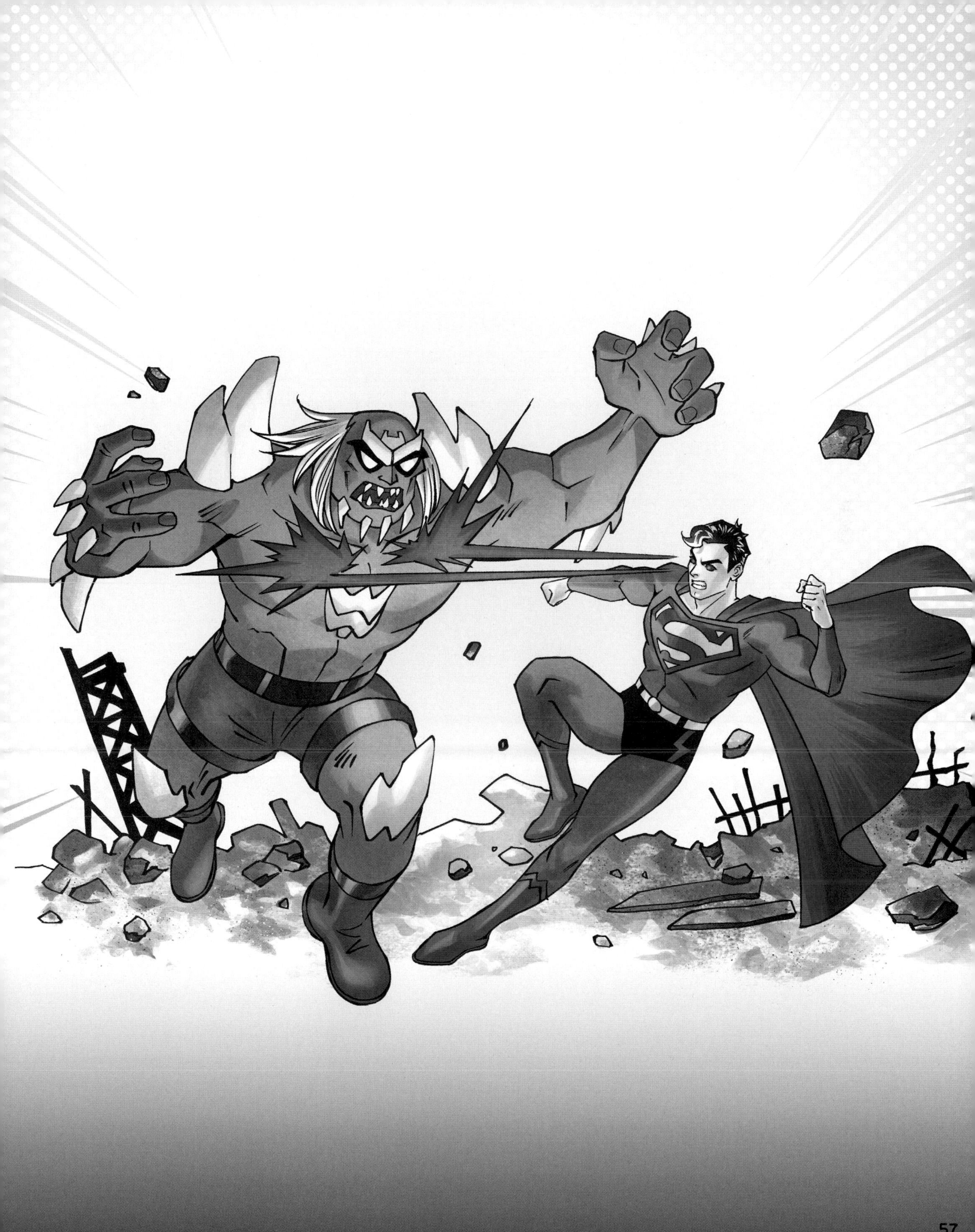

WONDER WOMAN

When the world gets walloped by the wicked, Wonder Woman is a warrior who never wavers. Blessed by the Greek gods, Princess Diana boasts super-strength, lightning reflexes, and the power of flight. But her greatest tool for foiling felons may be her magnificent magic lasso. With its golden coils, the Amazing Amazon can compel even the most tight-lipped troublemaker to tell the truth!

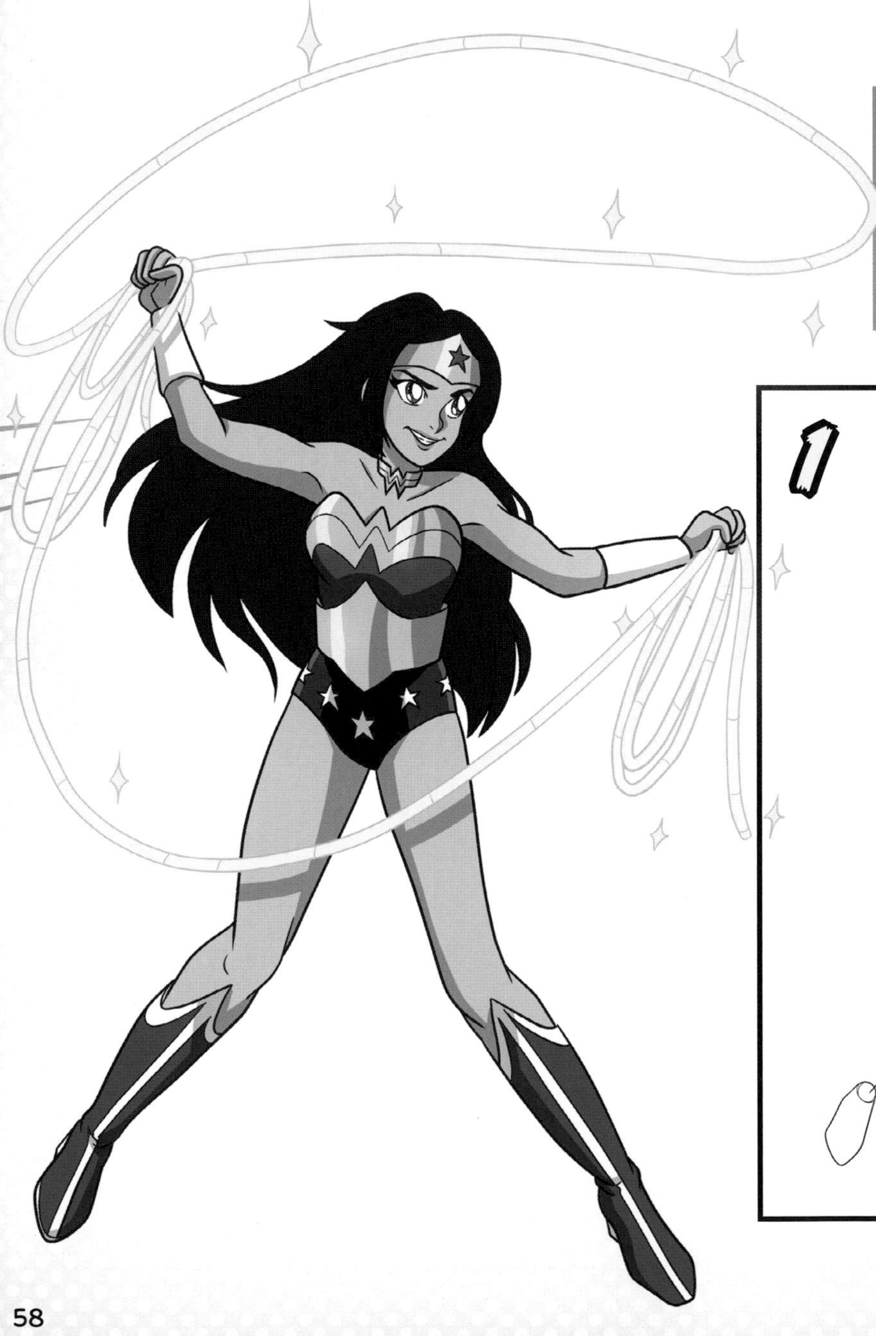

MANGA FACT

Mangaka first started drawing big and shiny eyes because they were inspired by early Disney films, such as *Bambi*. Leave white spots in your characters' eyes to add sparkle.

1

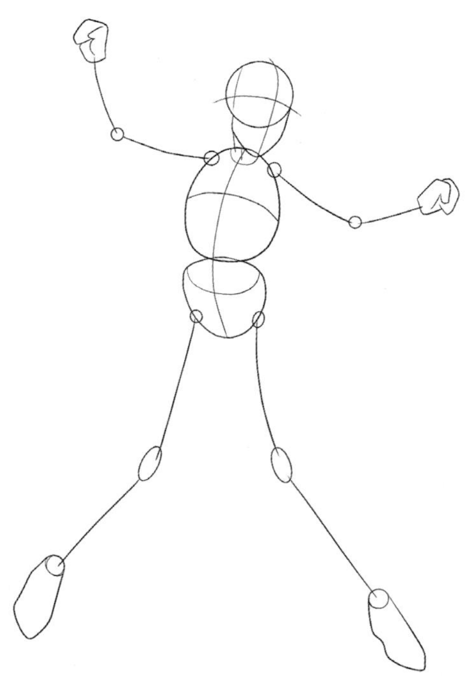

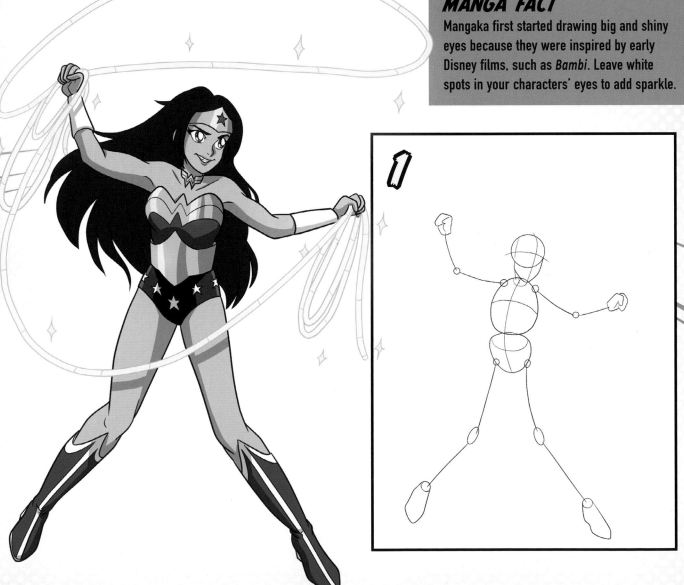

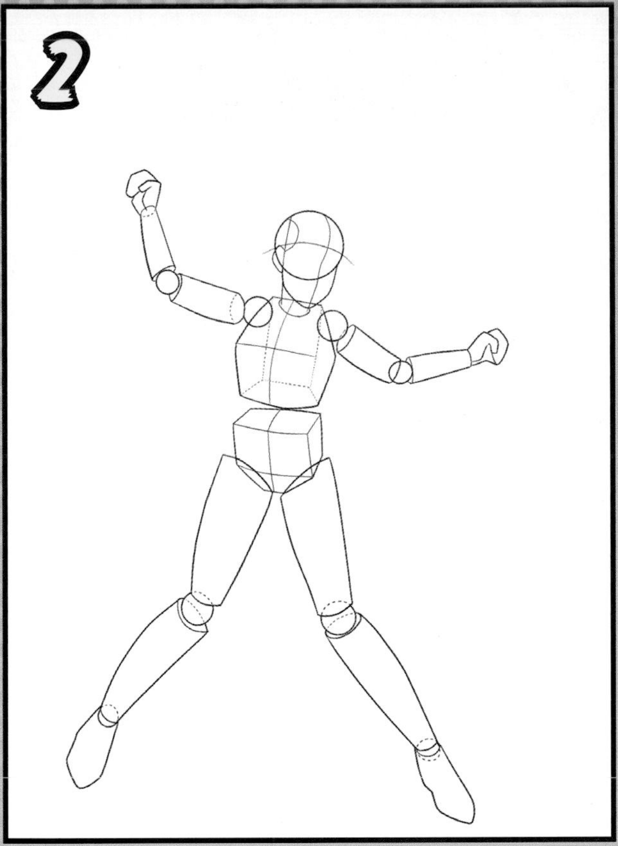
2

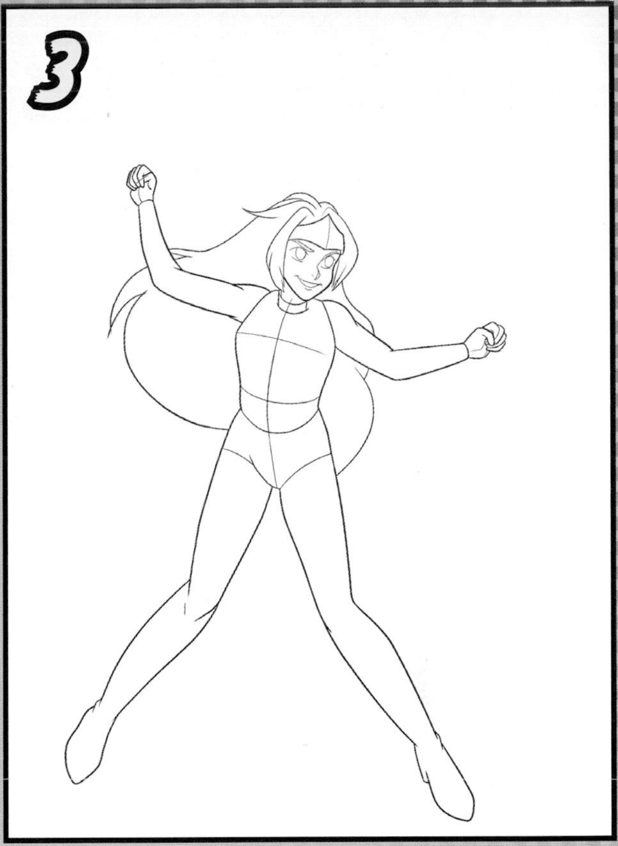
3

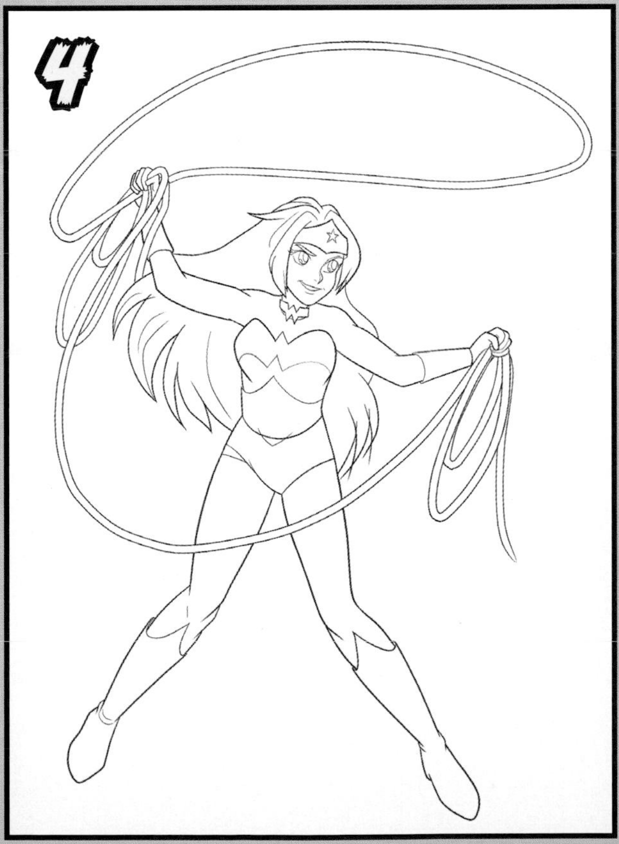
4

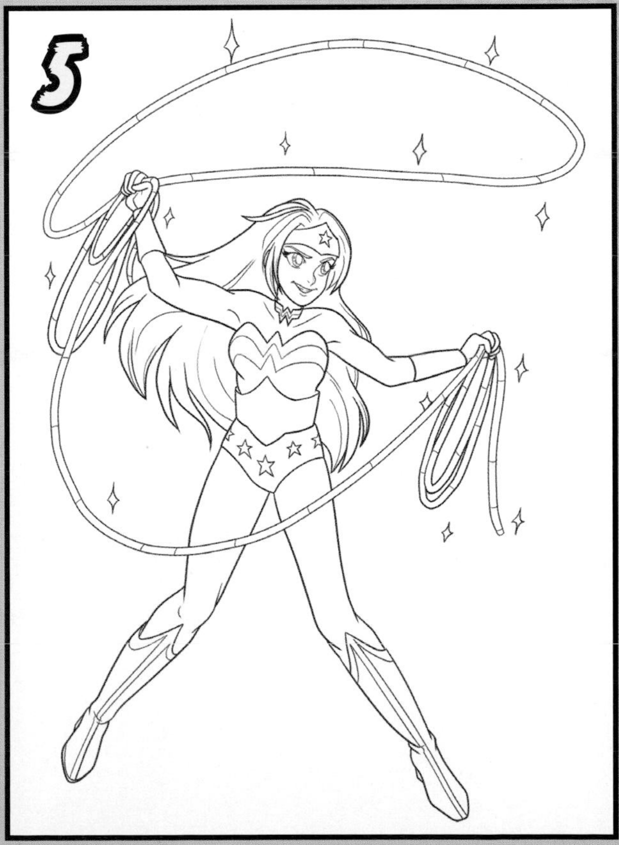
5

STEVE TREVOR

Every Super Hero benefits from a little backup. Luckily, Wonder Woman has Steve Trevor on her side. Not only is Trevor one of the Amazon warrior's most trusted friends, but he's also an agent of A.R.G.U.S. (Advanced Research Group Uniting Super-Humans). As a man with a plan and an appetite for action, Trevor is always ready to take a swing at crime.

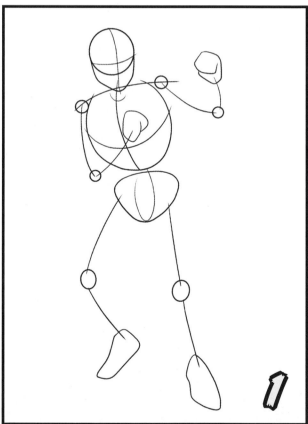

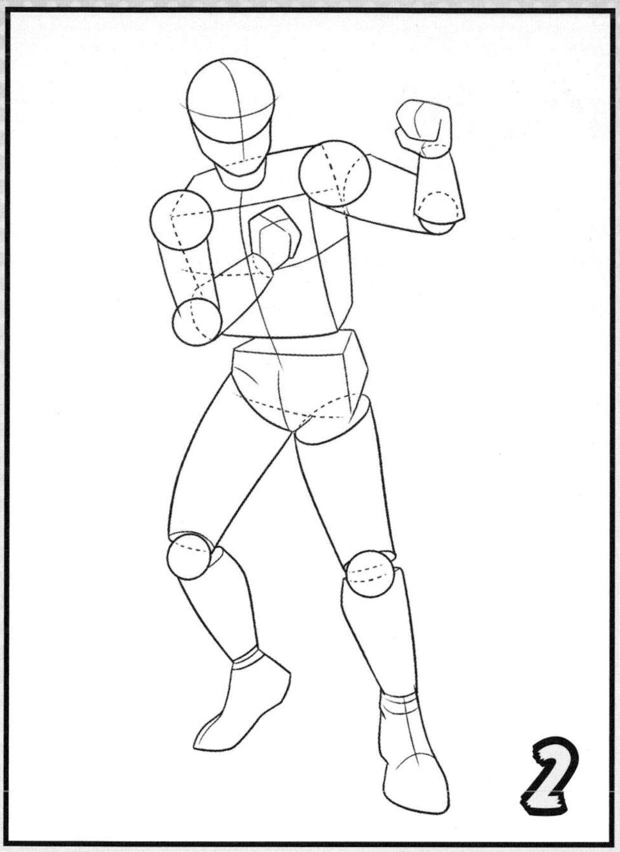
2
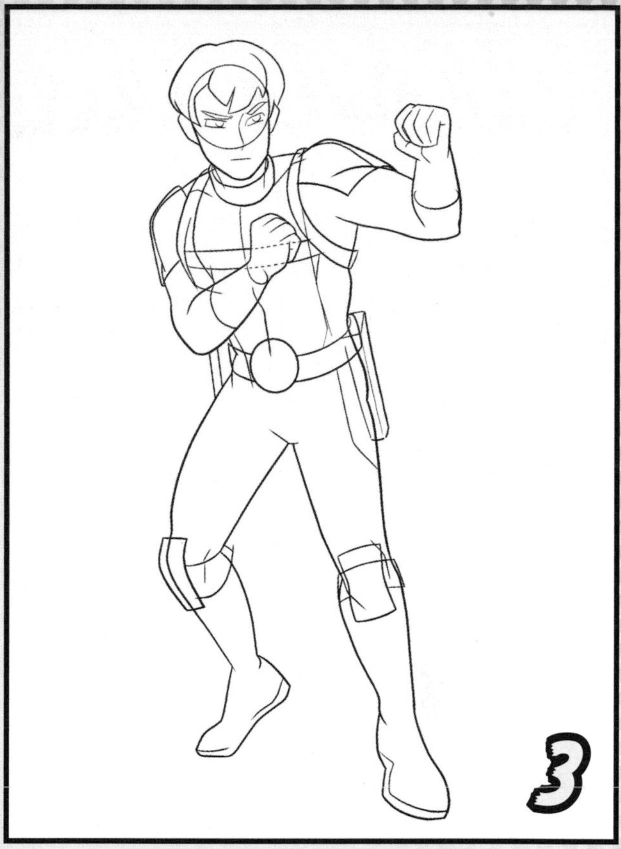
3
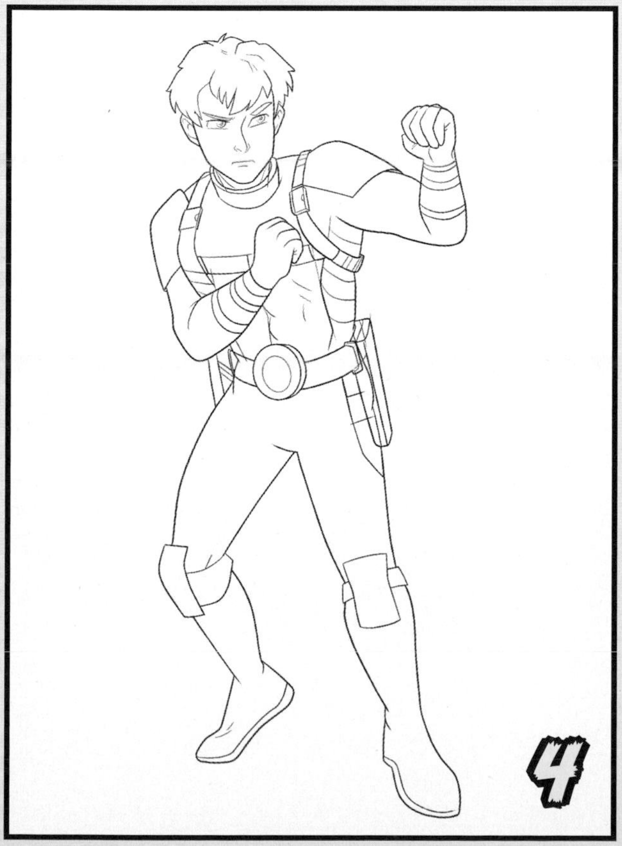
4
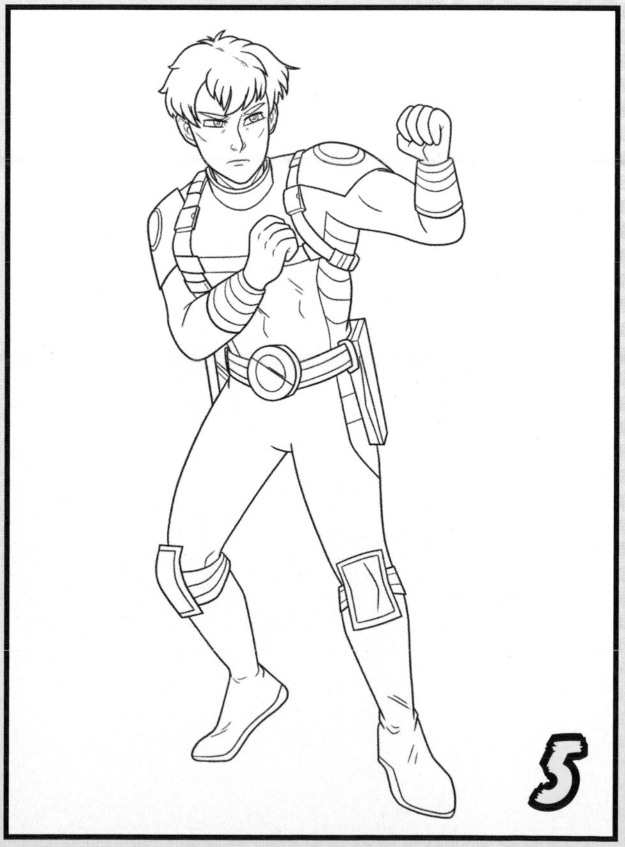
5

ETTA CANDY

A.R.G.U.S. agent Etta Candy's sweet spot is saving the day alongside Wonder Woman. The bold and bubbly intelligence officer is just as happy decoding data as she is bounding into battle. Whenever Princess Diana gets in a bind, Etta comes in to kick things up a notch!

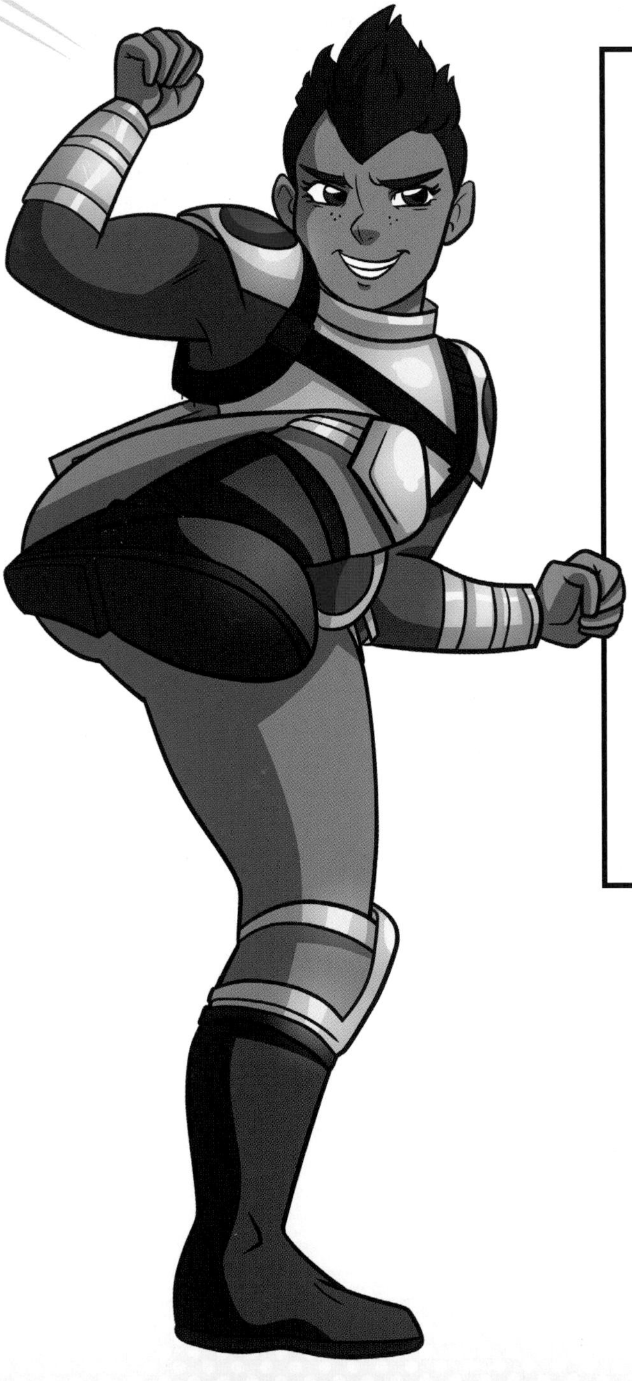

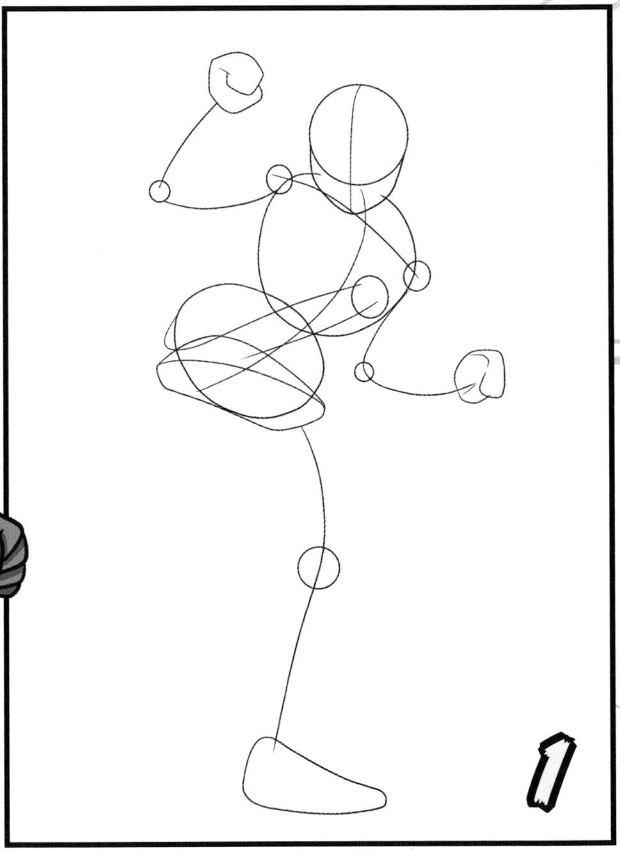
1

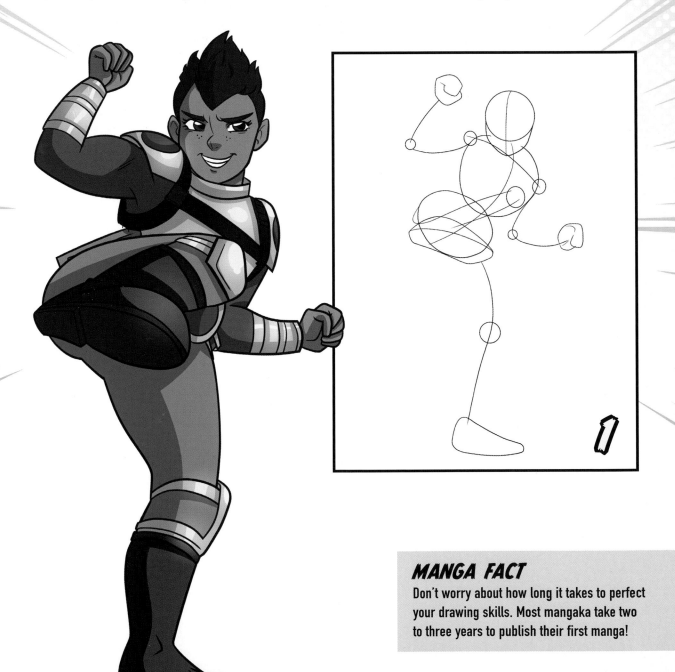

MANGA FACT

Don't worry about how long it takes to perfect your drawing skills. Most mangaka take two to three years to publish their first manga!

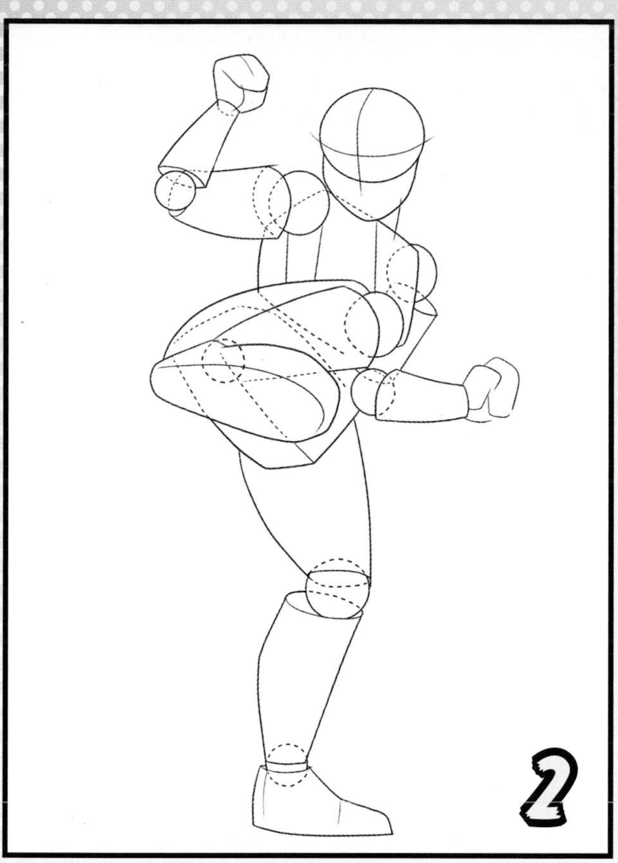
2
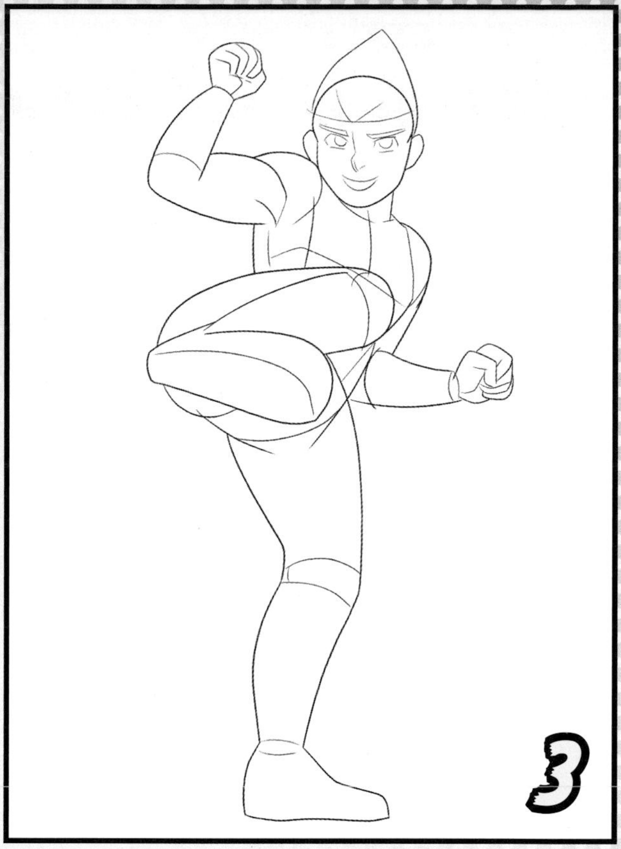
3
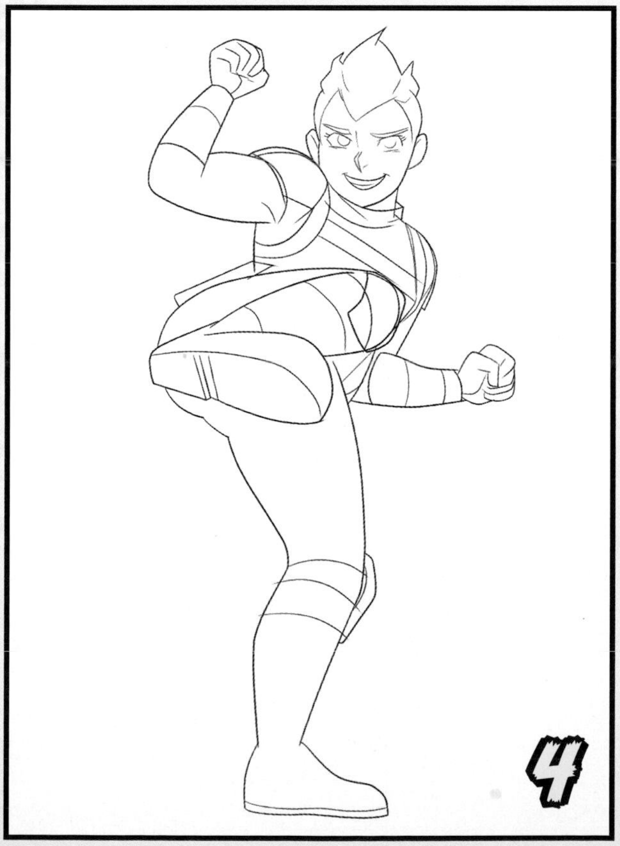
4
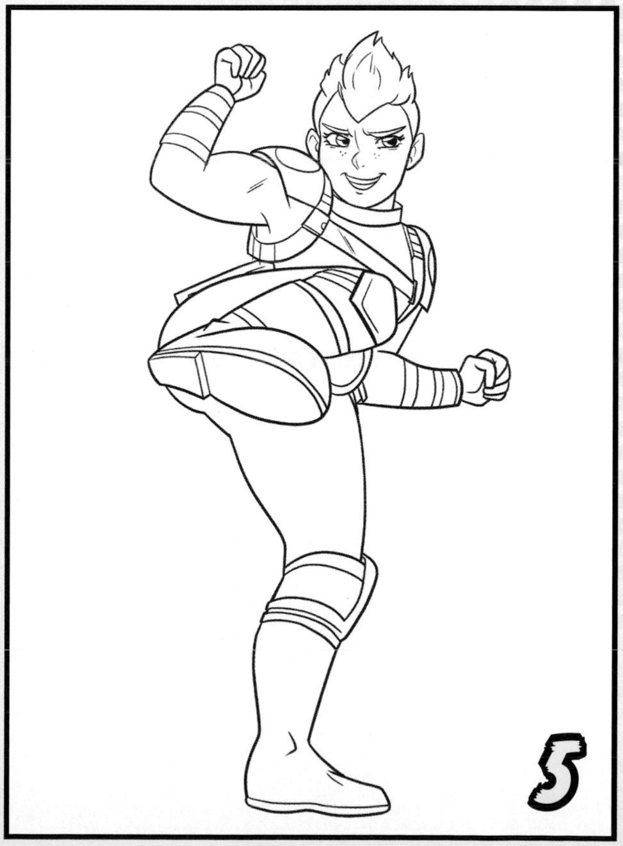
5

QUEEN HIPPOLYTA

All hail Queen Hippolyta! She is the wise ruler of the island of Themyscira, the fierce leader of the Amazons . . . and a marvelous mother. Long ago Hippolyta was blessed by the gods with a daughter, Diana. With such a majestic mom, it's no wonder Princess Diana grew up to become Wonder Woman!

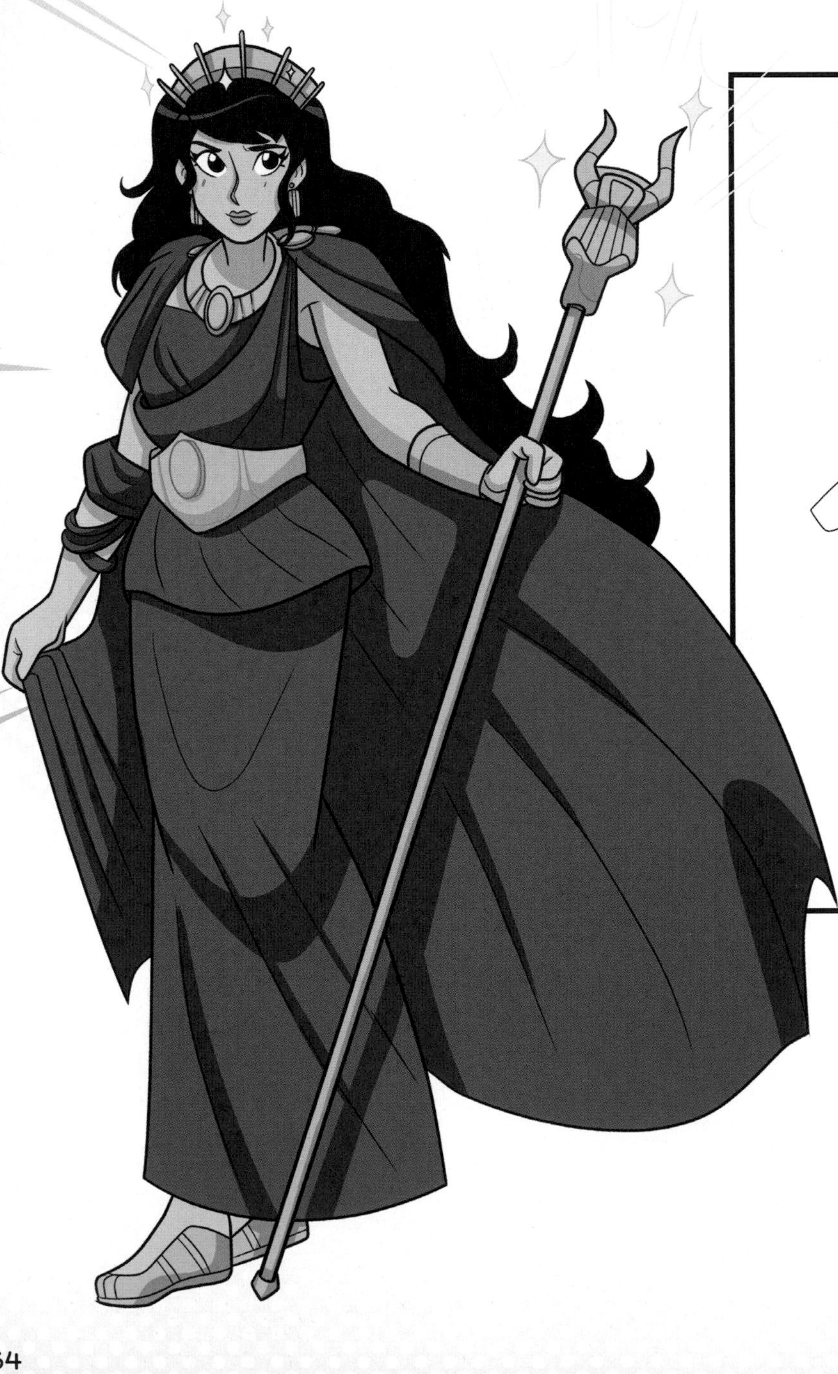

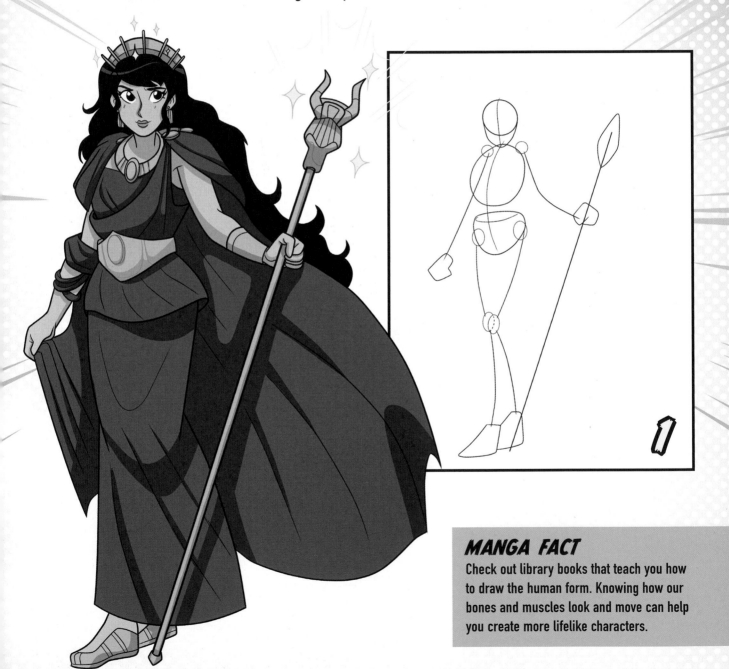

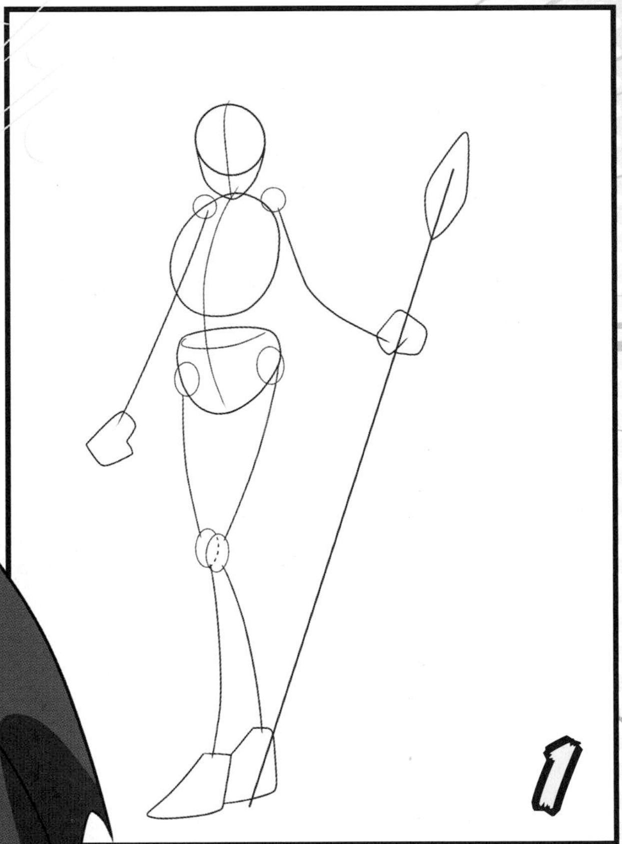
1

MANGA FACT

Check out library books that teach you how to draw the human form. Knowing how our bones and muscles look and move can help you create more lifelike characters.

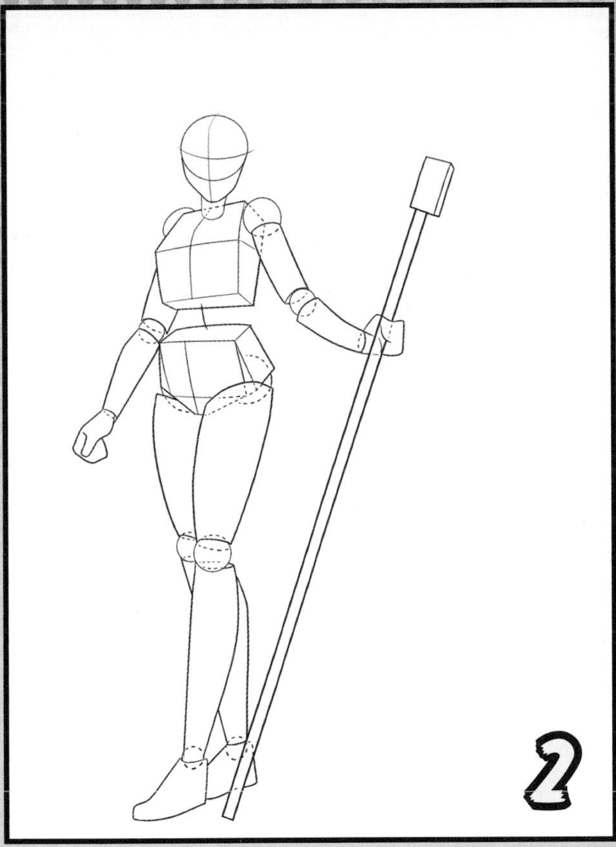
2
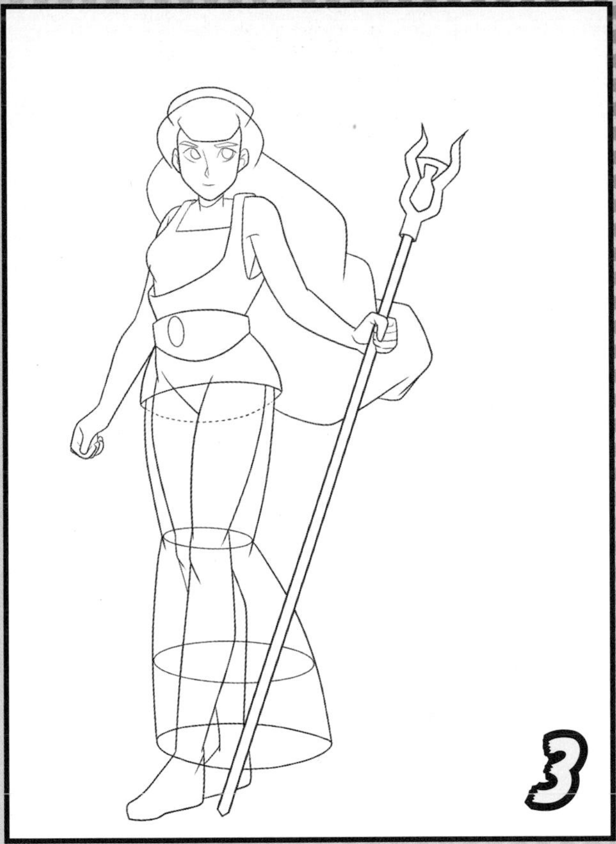
3
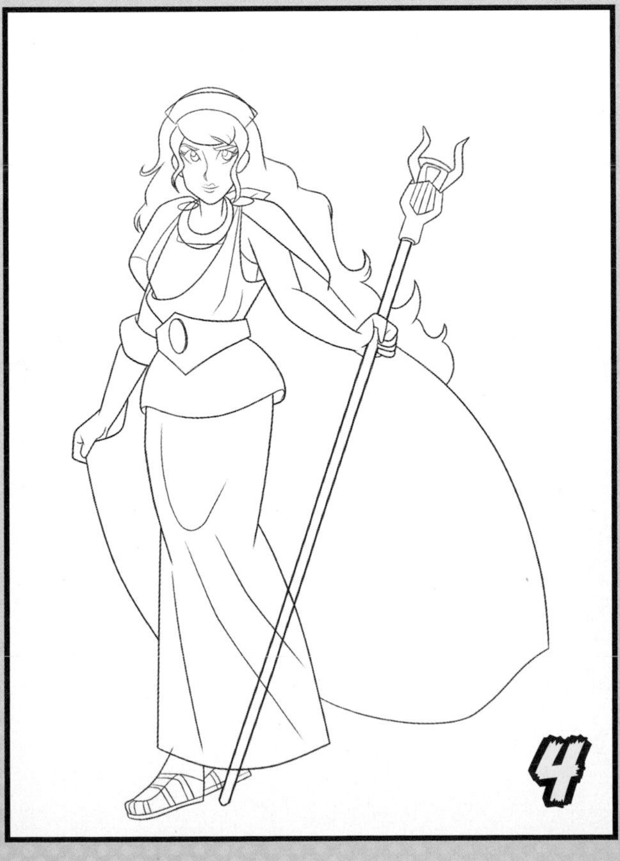
4
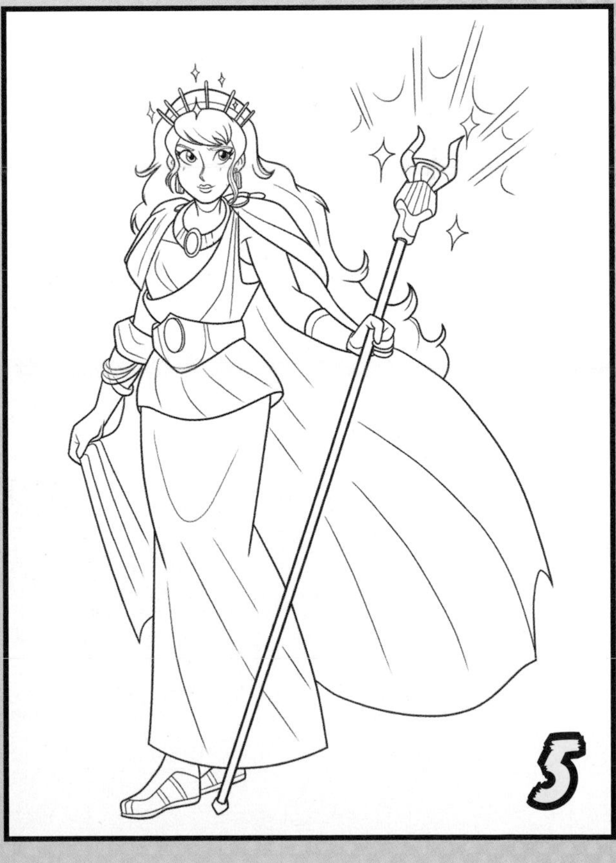
5

PHILIPPUS

When Wonder Woman wanted to learn the ways of the warrior, she turned to Philippus. It'd be hard to find a better teacher. The immortal Amazon general has more than 3,000 years of battle experience! She's not afraid to enter the fray. She skillfully fends off foes with a flurry of her fists or a slash of her sword!

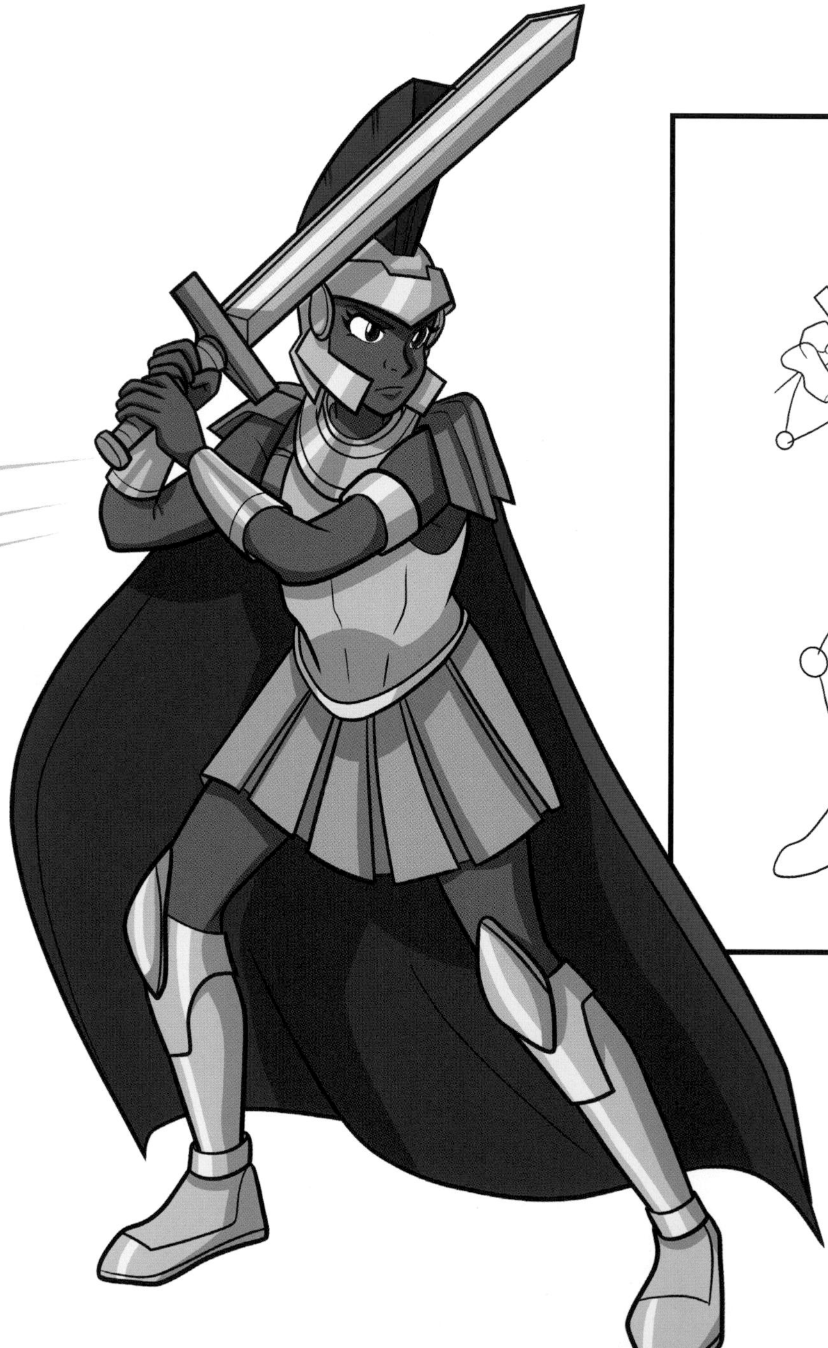

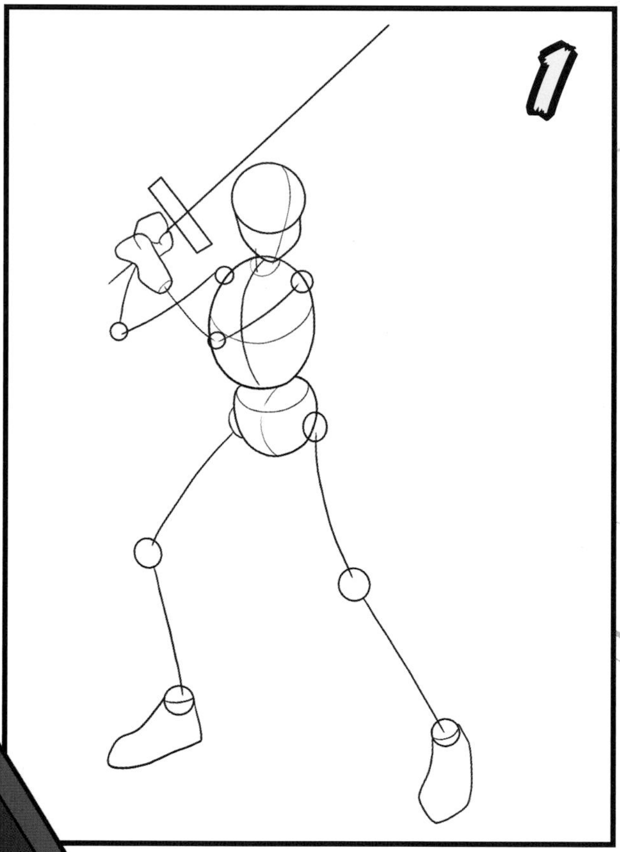
1

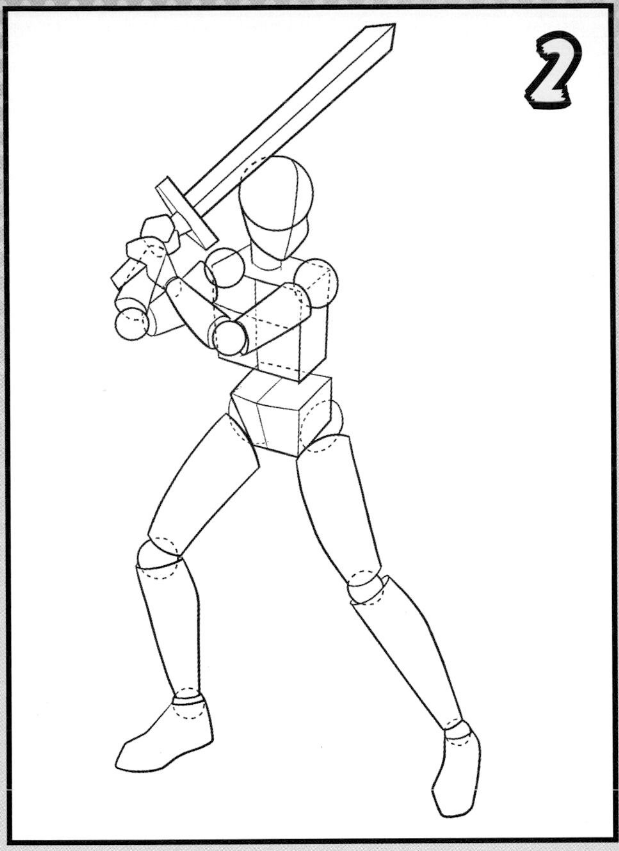
2
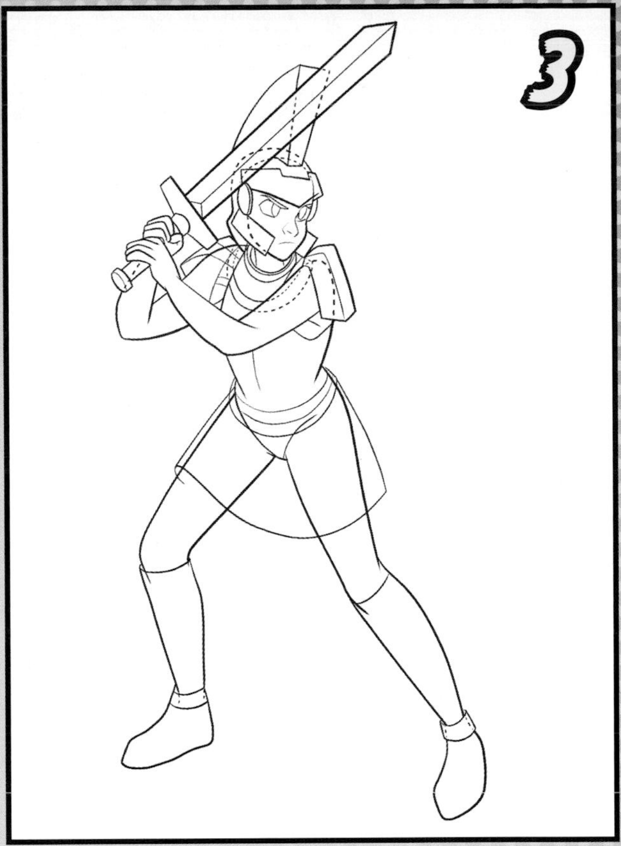
3
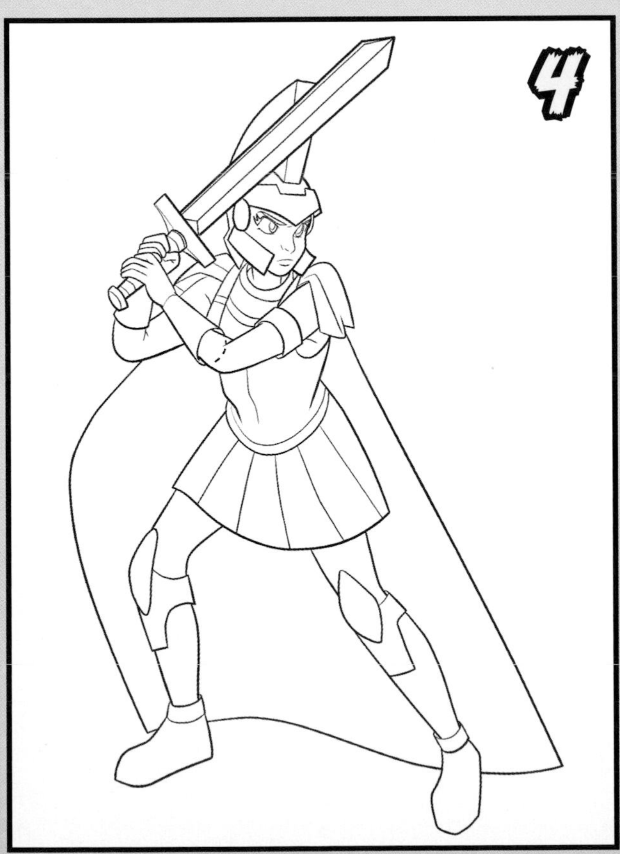
4
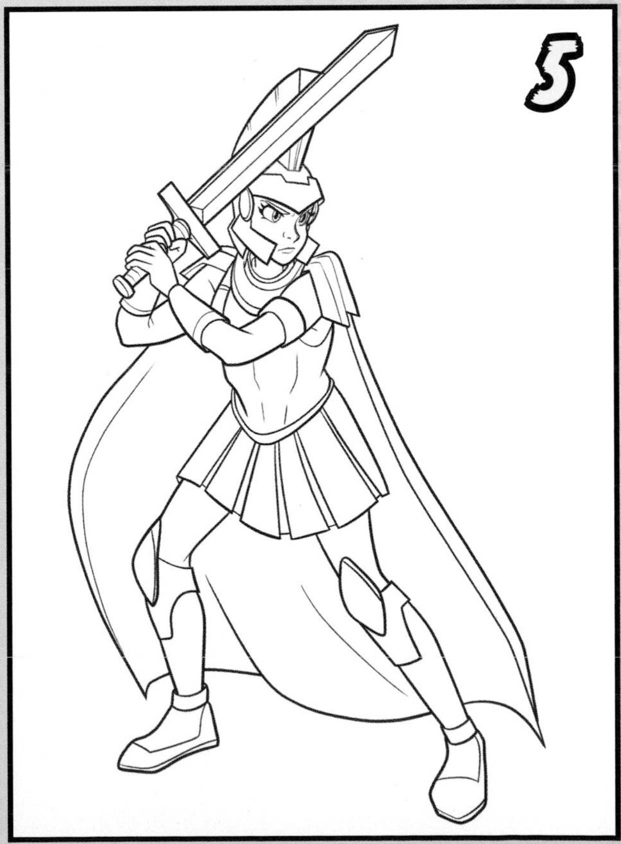
5

THE CHEETAH

Watch out! The Cheetah is on the prowl! This scientist-turned-Super-Villain is a *fur*-ocious fighter. She sports catlike agility, beastly strength, and razor-sharp claws that are capable of slashing straight through solid stone. The Cheetah will never *paws* while taking a swipe at Wonder Woman!

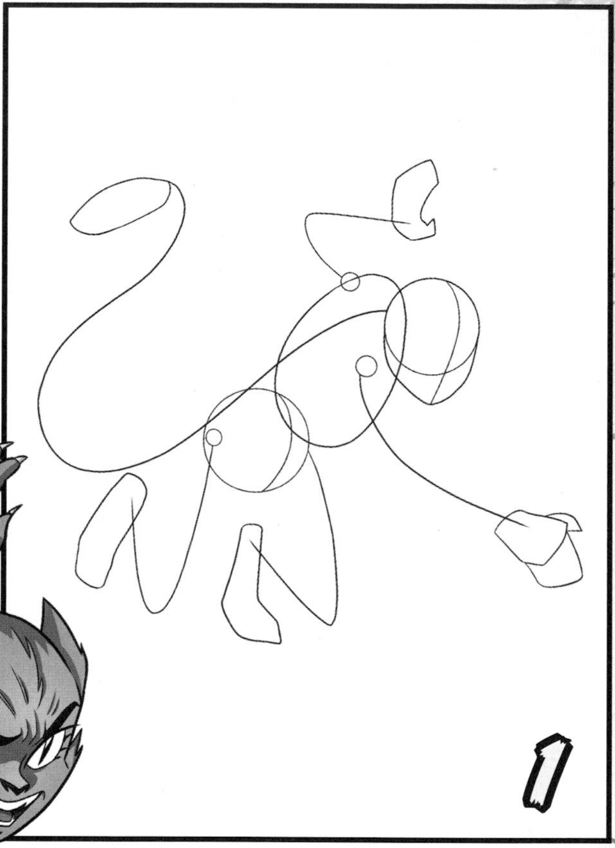
1

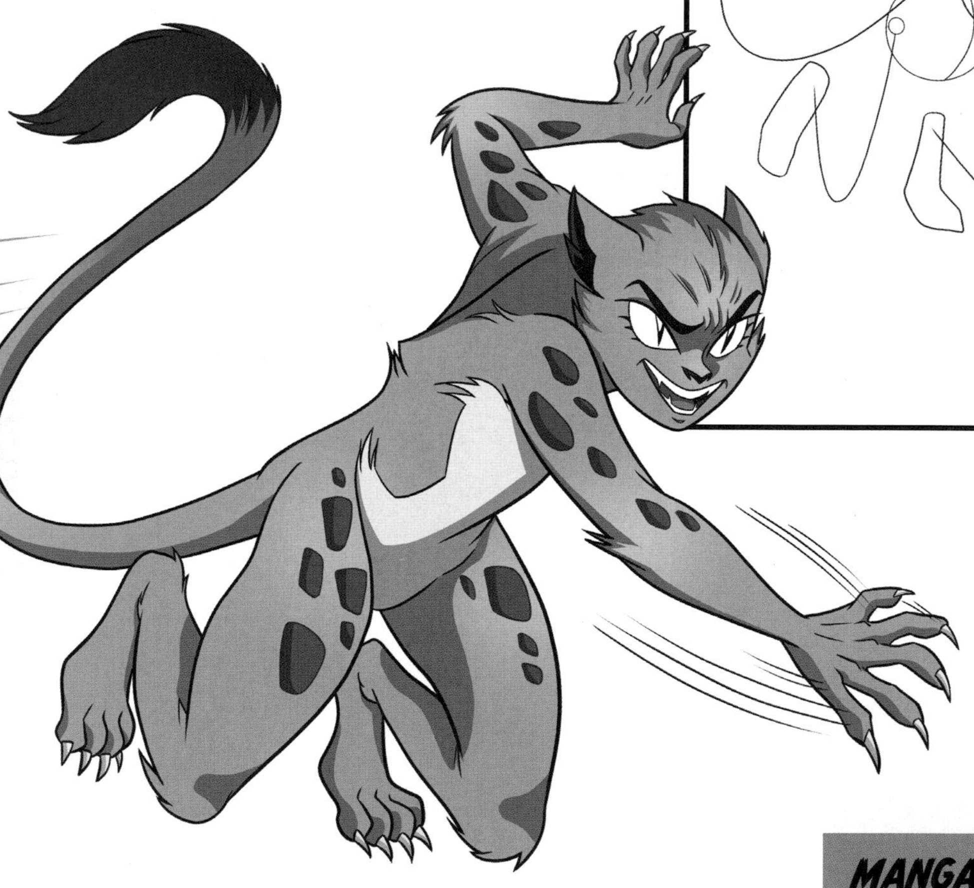

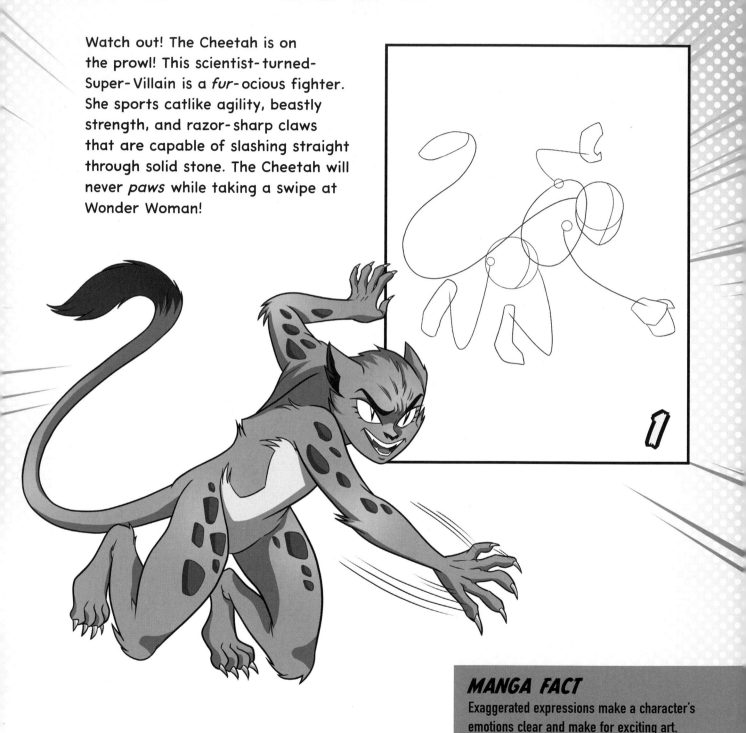

MANGA FACT

Exaggerated expressions make a character's emotions clear and make for exciting art. So don't be afraid to punch them up!

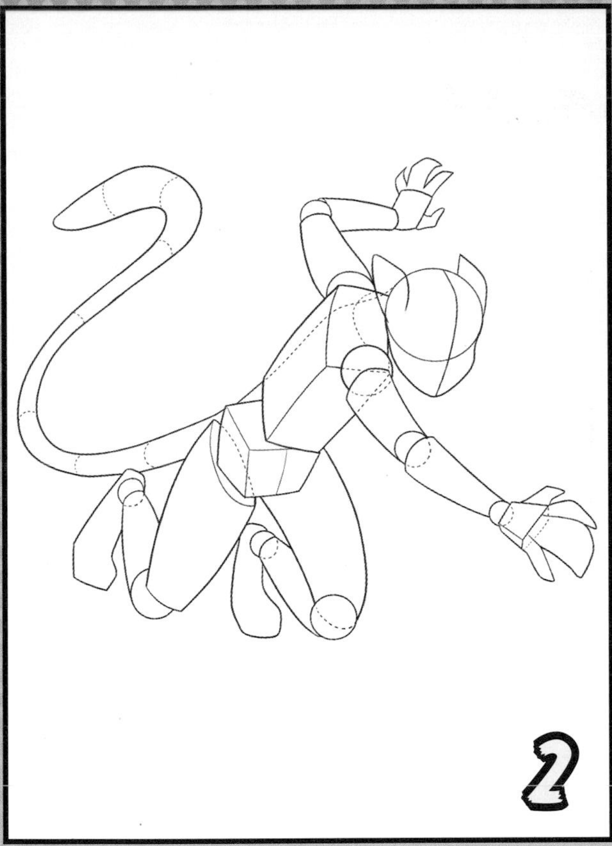
2
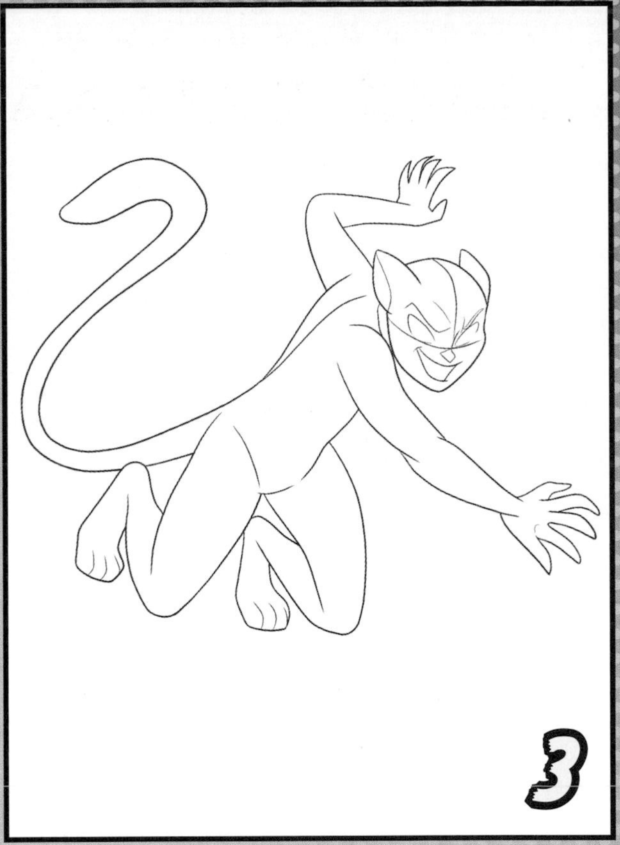
3
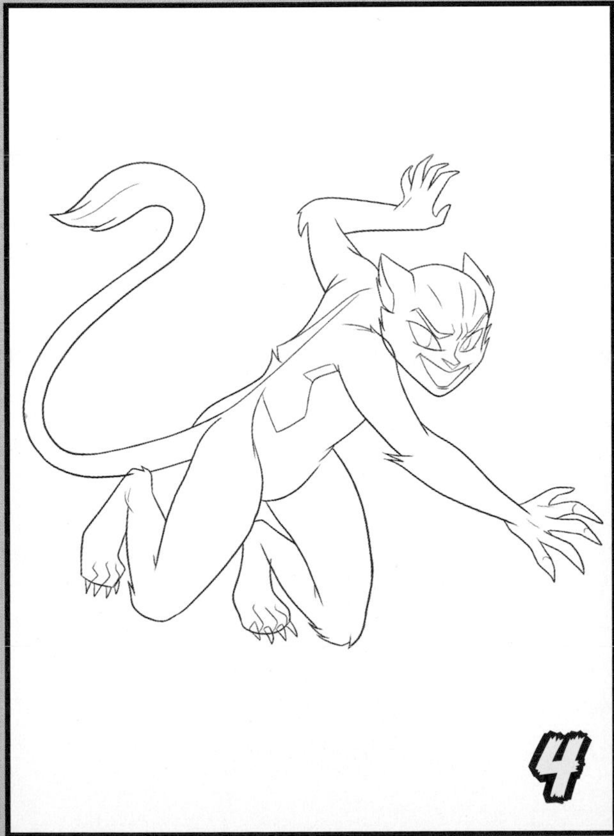
4
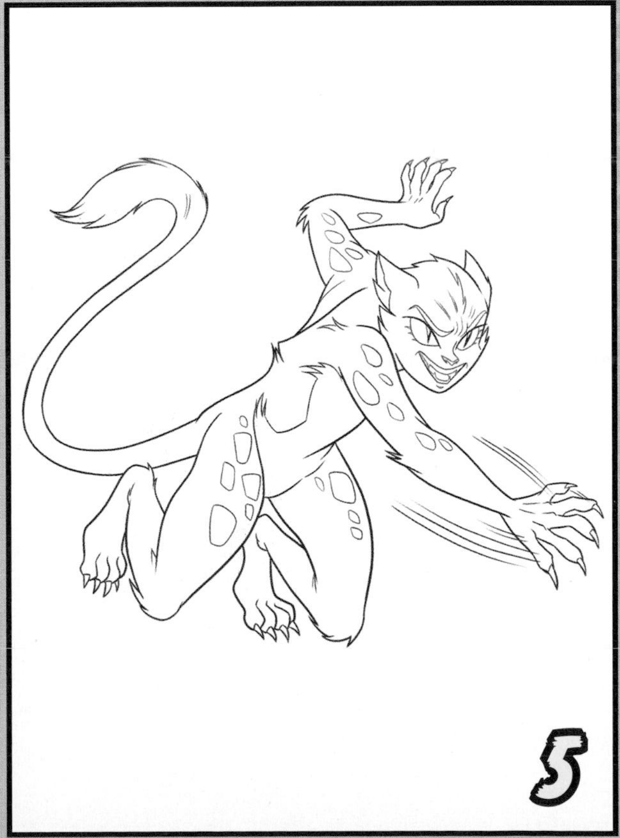
5

ARES

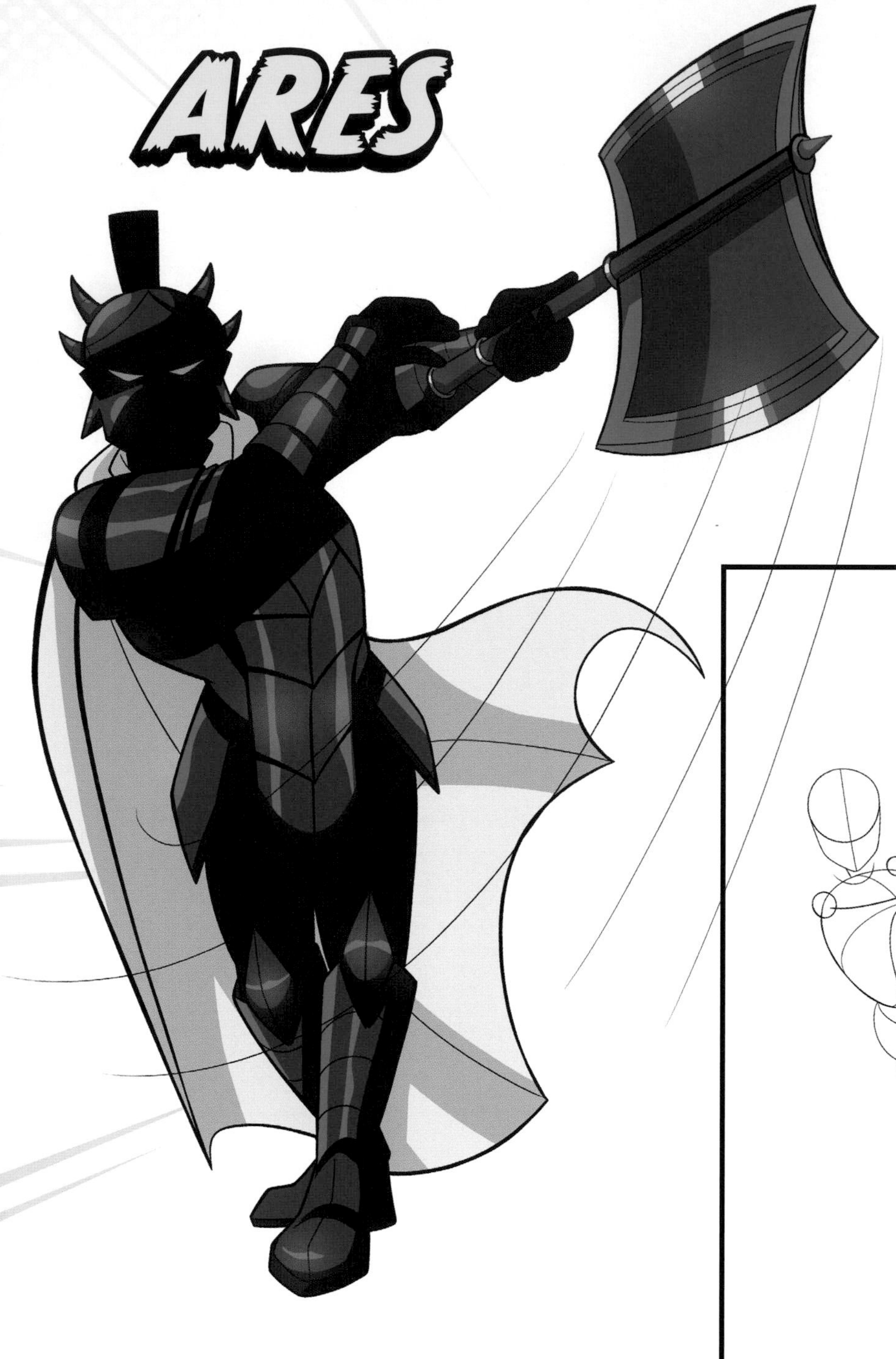

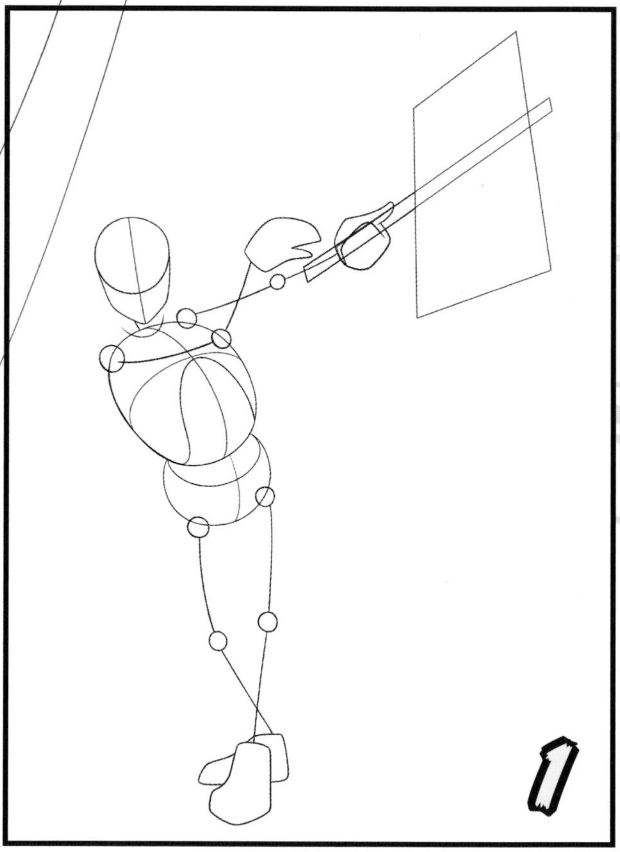
1

Ares always has an axe to grind. As the Greek god of war, he tricks mortals into fighting among themselves. And the more hate he creates, the more powerful he becomes. From superhuman strength and indestructibility to shape-shifting and teleportation, this malicious immortal has the means to make massive mayhem!

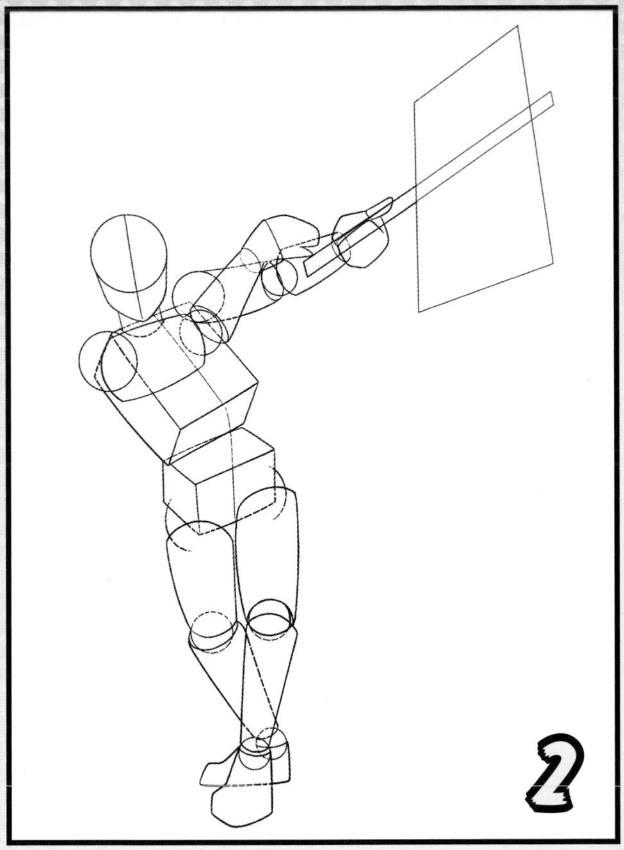
2

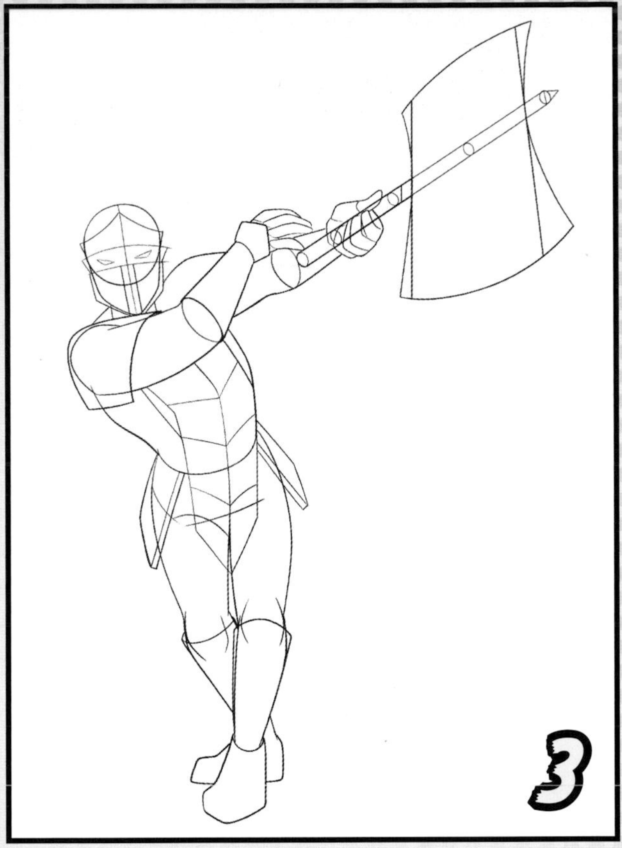
3

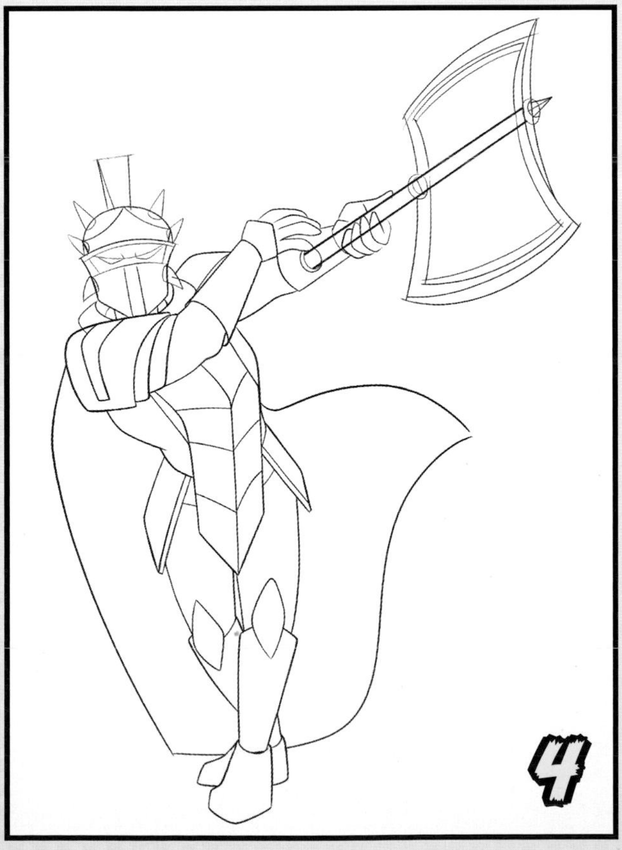
4

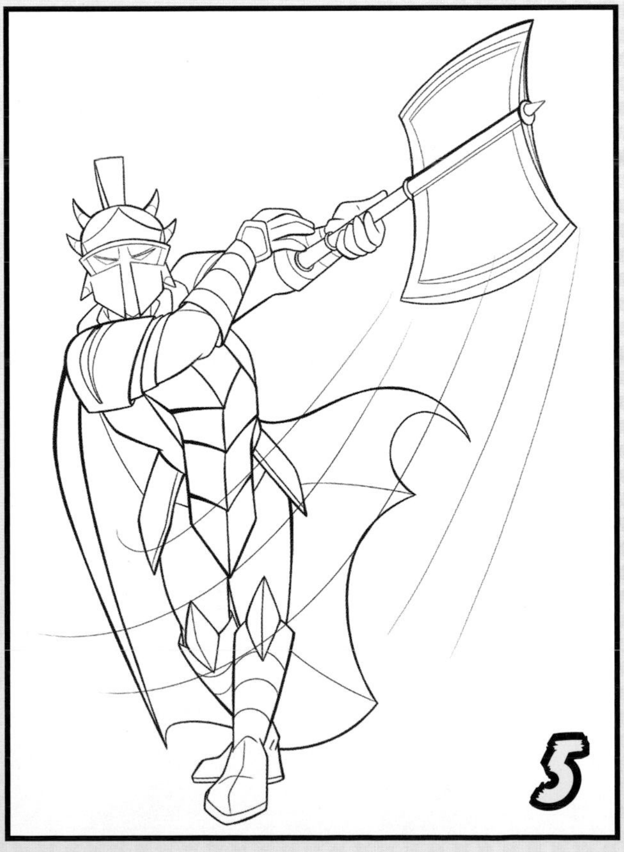
5

CIRCE

The sorceress Circe has a mischievous mission: Make life difficult for Wonder Woman. Using mind-bending spells, she can create evil illusions and teleport anywhere in the world. On top of that, Circe never gets *boared* of her signature move—turning opponents into pigs!

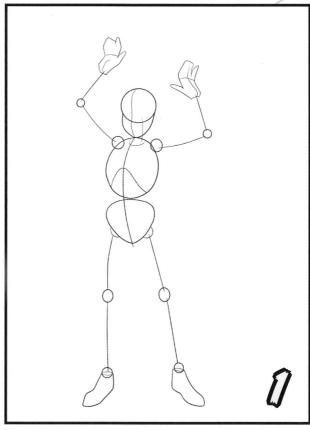

MANGA FACT

A manga character's eyes can say a lot about how they feel. Experiment with the shape of Circe's eyes and eyebrows to show different emotions.

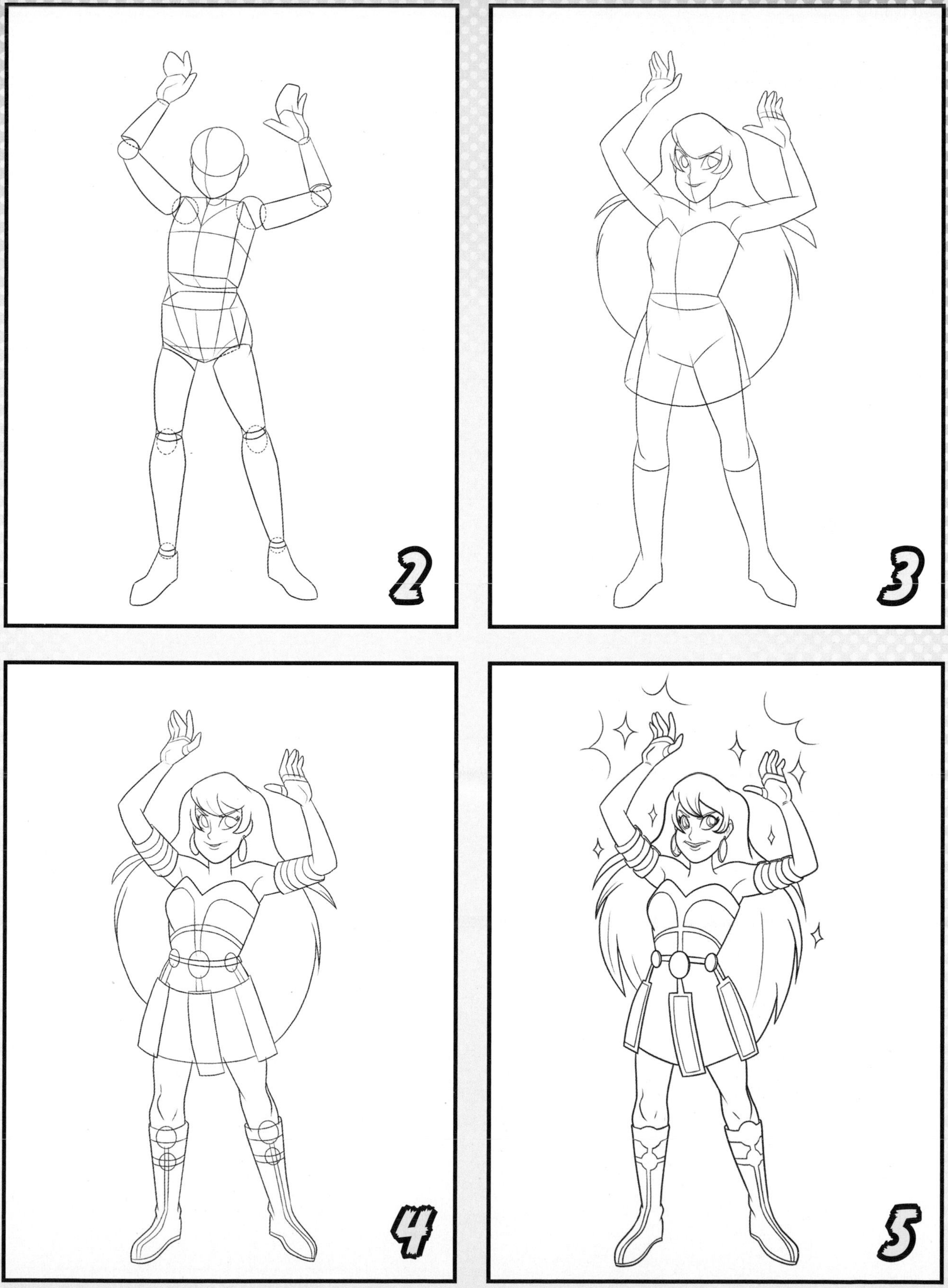
2
3
4
5

GIGANTA

It's fair to say Giganta stands head and shoulders above other crooks. The size-shifting Super-Villain can grow from normal human height into a towering titan in no time flat! And her might multiplies as she gets bigger. At her largest, Giganta is stronger than Wonder Woman and can crush anything she clutches!

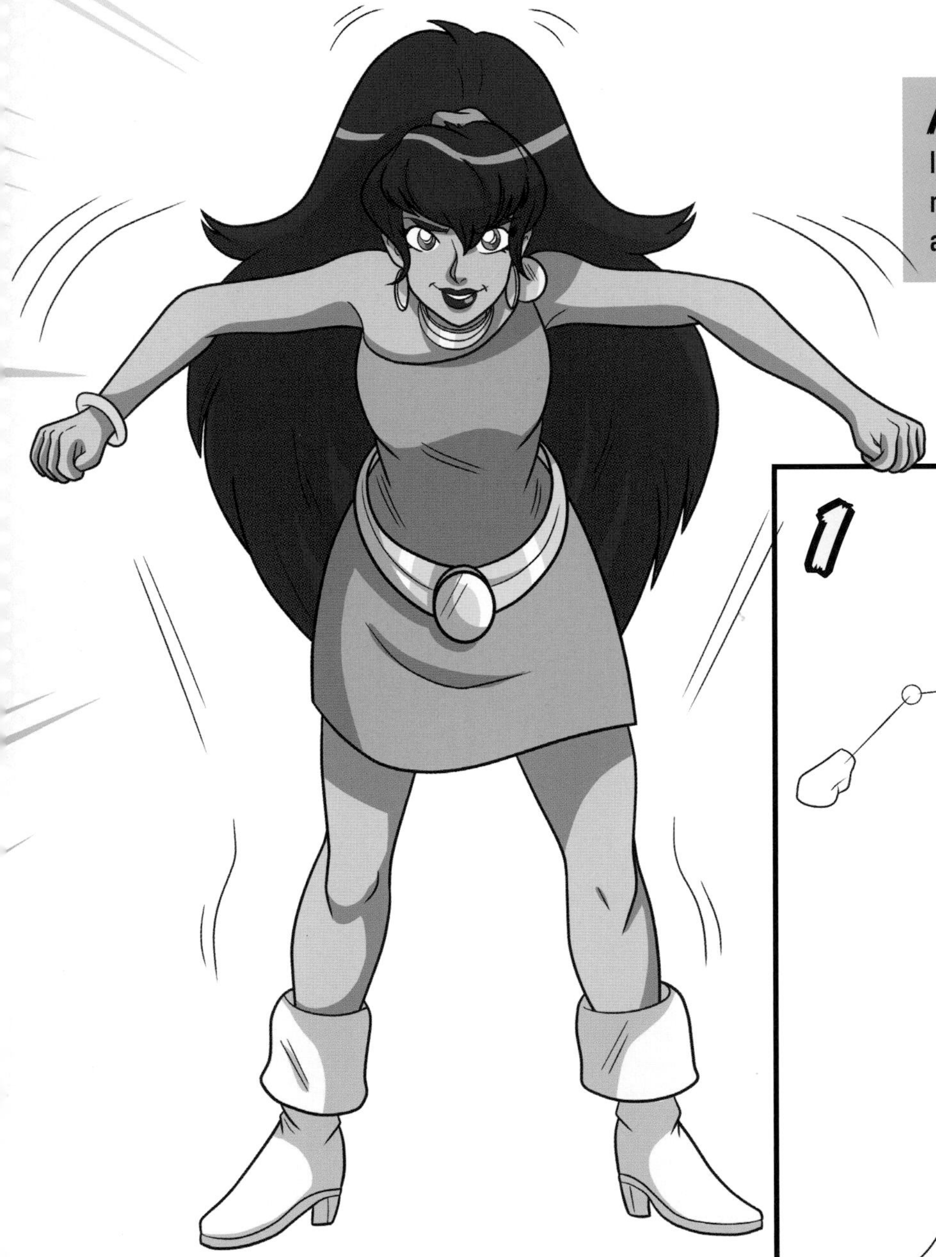

MANGA FACT

In 2021, Japan's manga industry took in more than $5 billion in sales of printed and digital materials!

1

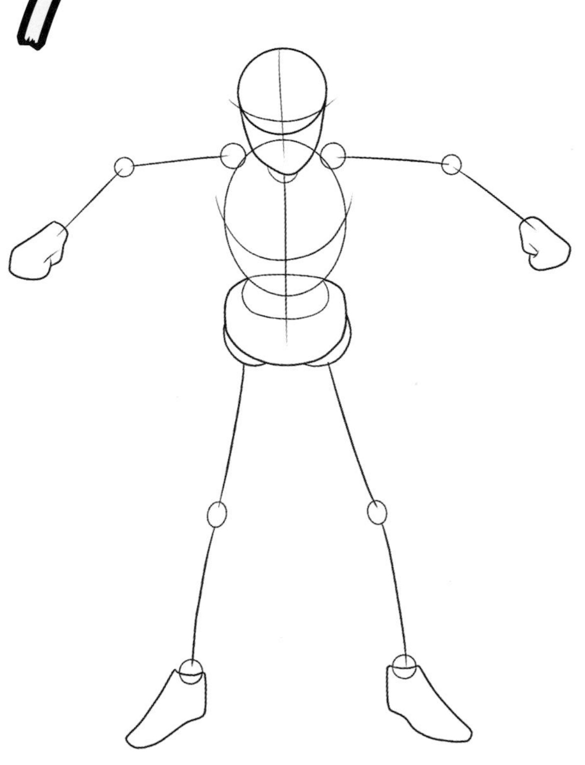

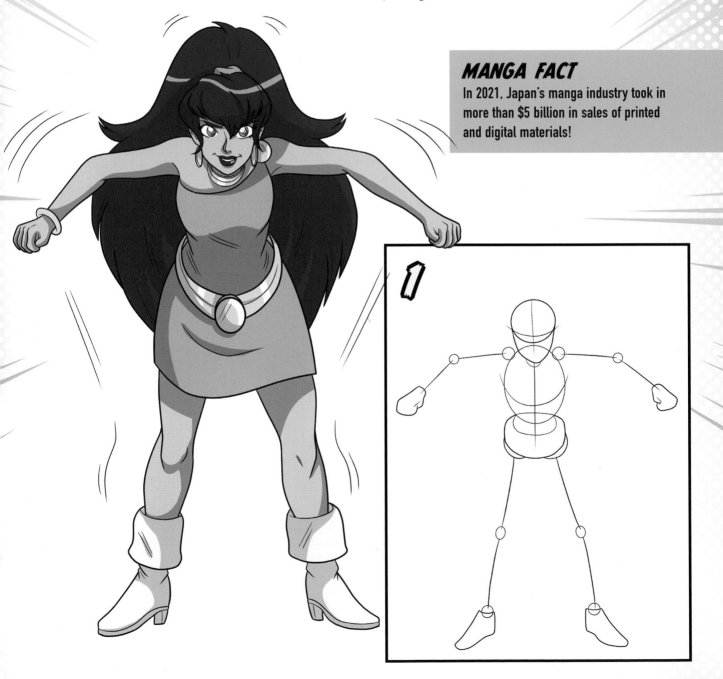

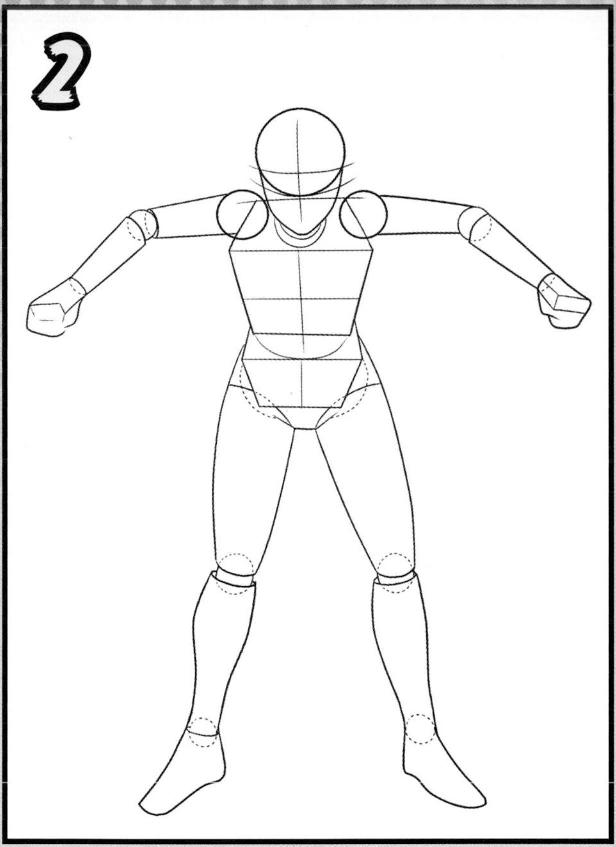
2

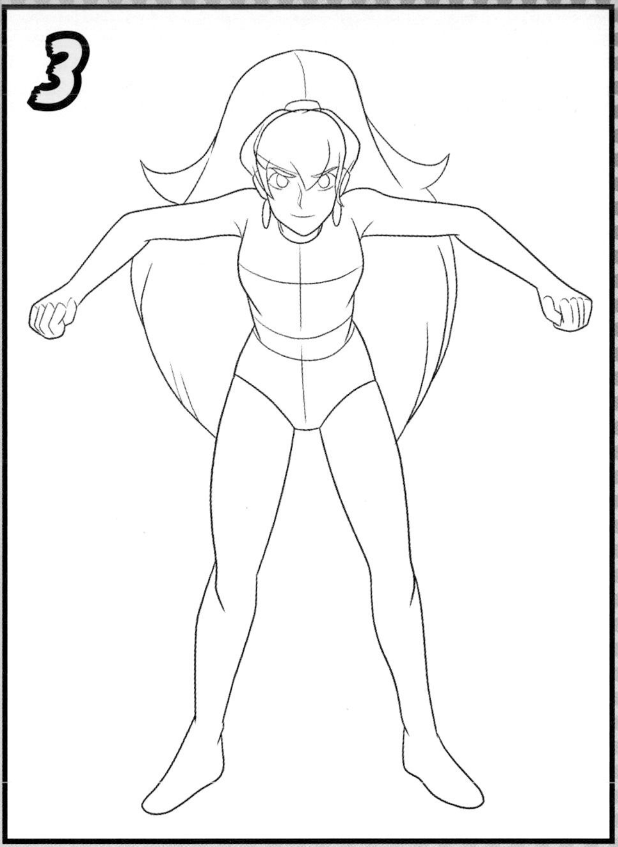
3

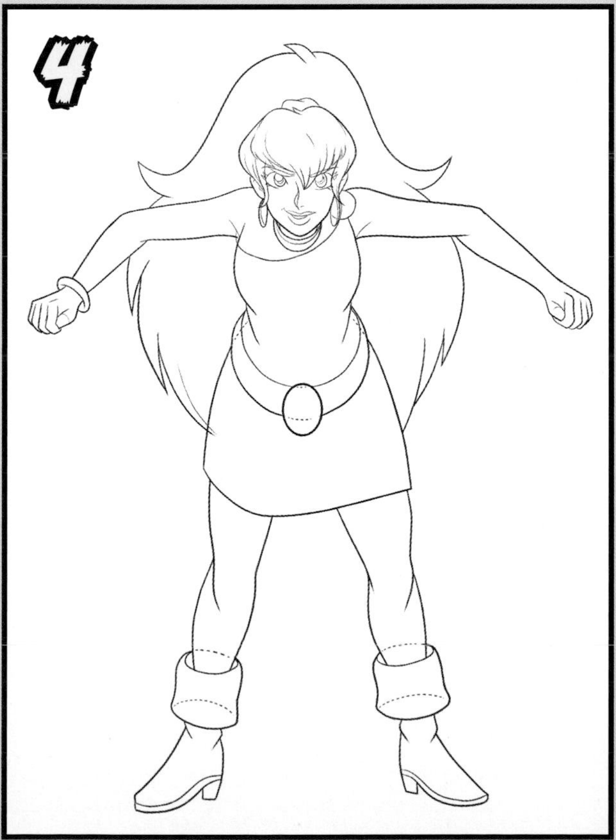
4

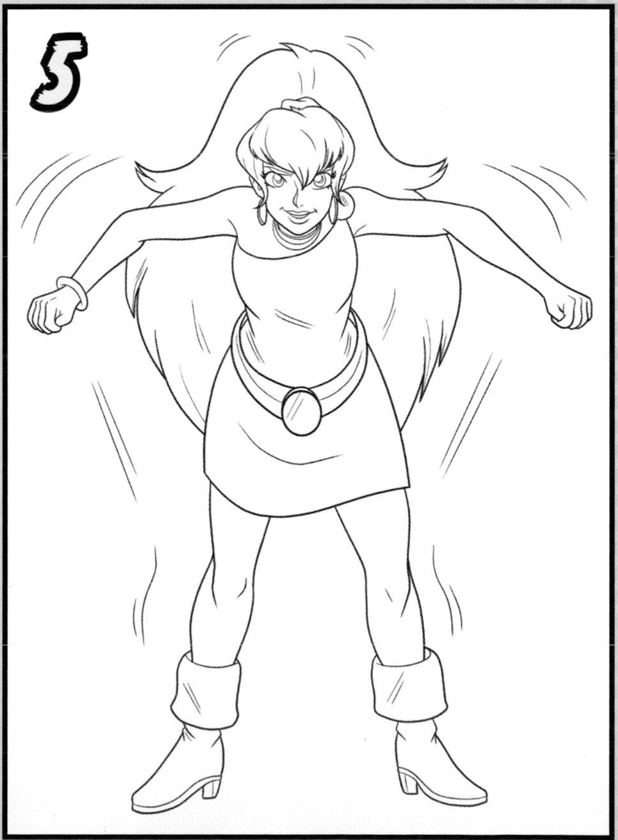
5

DEVASTATION

To defeat the Amazons, the Greek god Cronus decided to make a living weapon. Out of clay, he formed a twisted copy of Princess Diana. The result? A child named Devastation. With Wonder Woman's strength, durability, and speed, Devastation is determined to bend the Super Hero to her will!

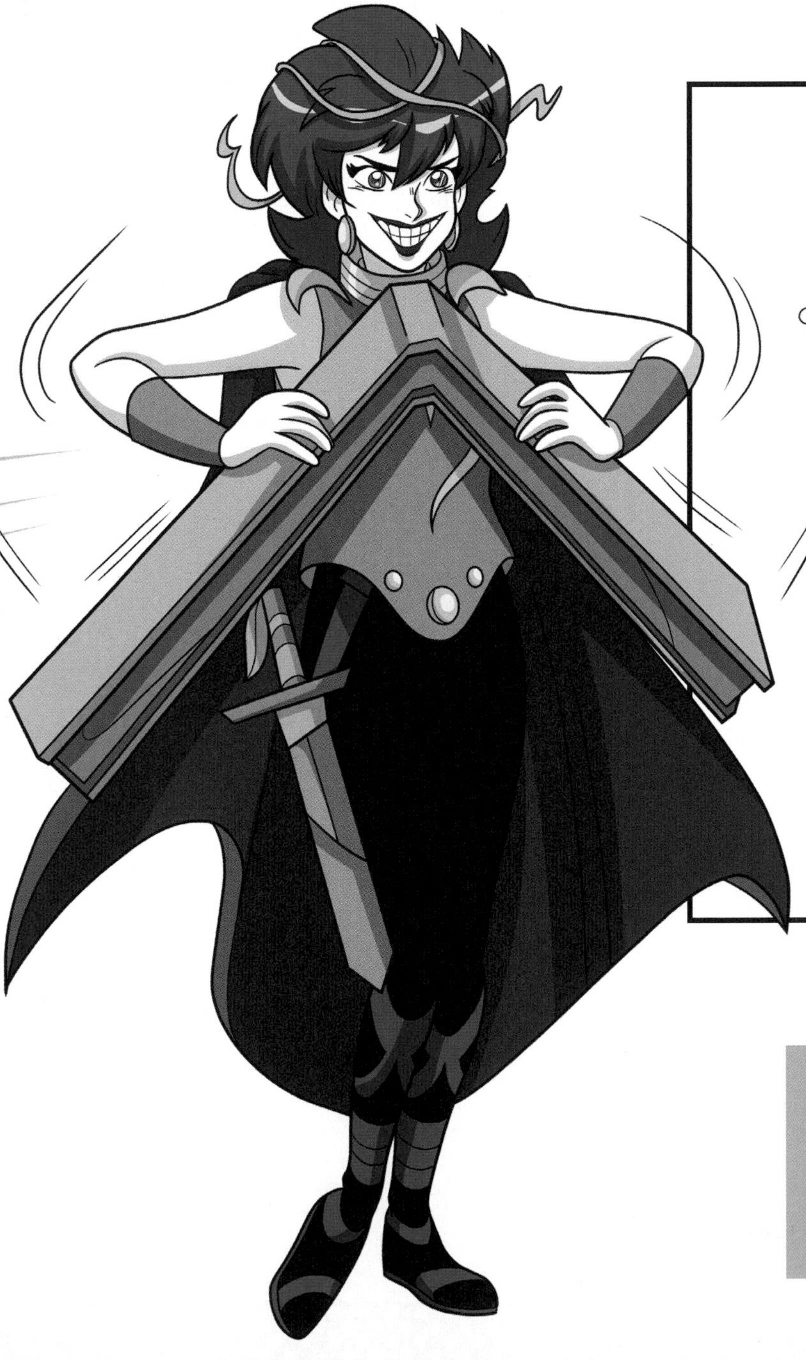

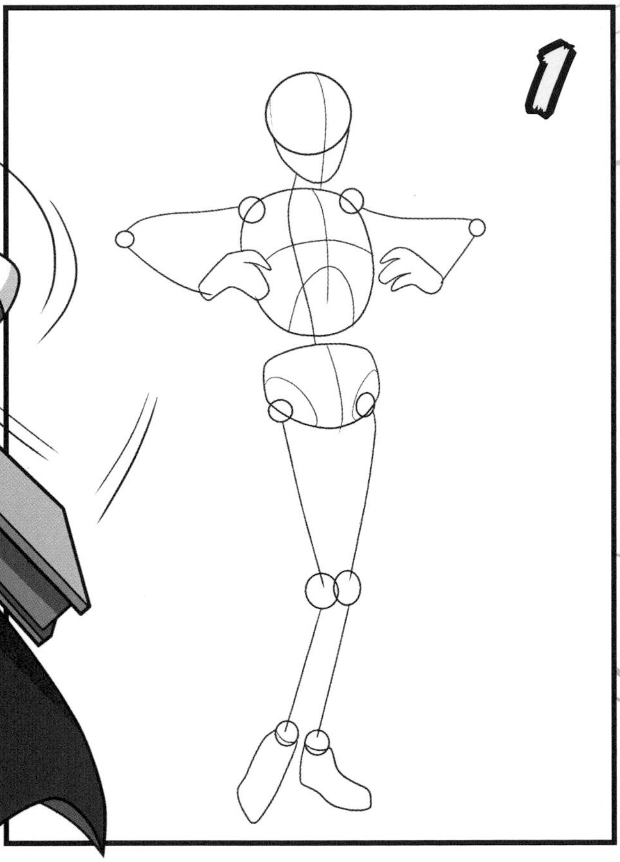
1

MANGA FACT

Manga and *anime* mean two different things. Anime is any animated story made in Japan. Manga is printed. But if a manga series is popular, it might be adapted into an anime.

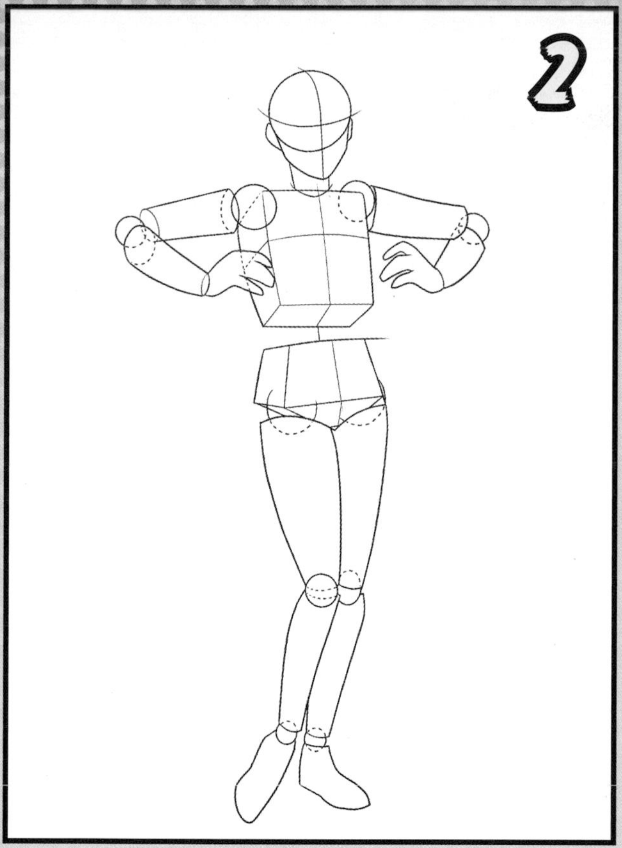
2
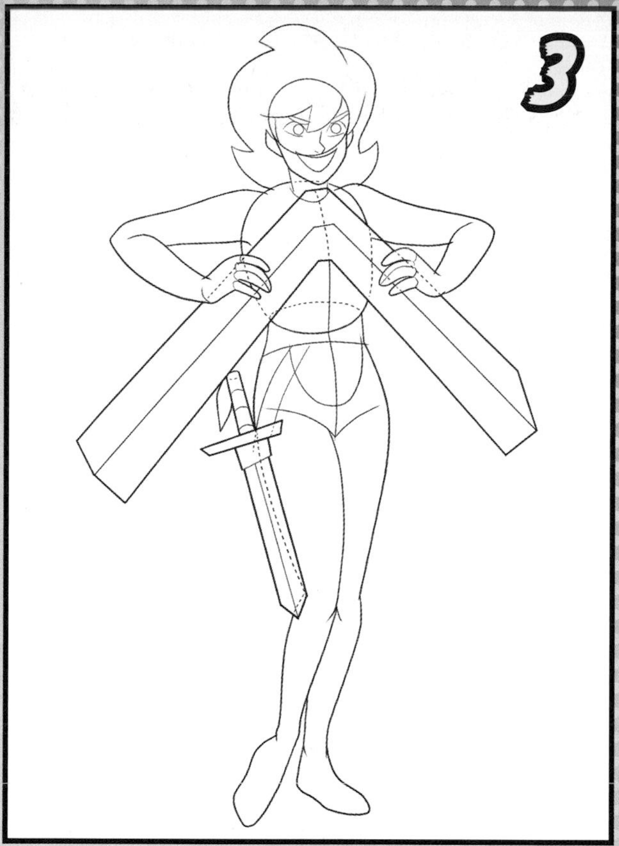
3
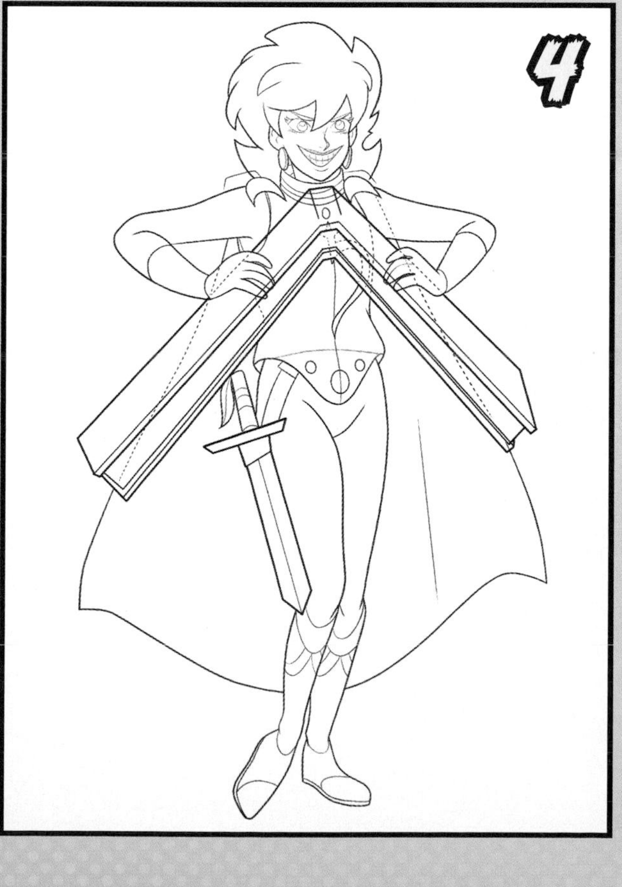
4
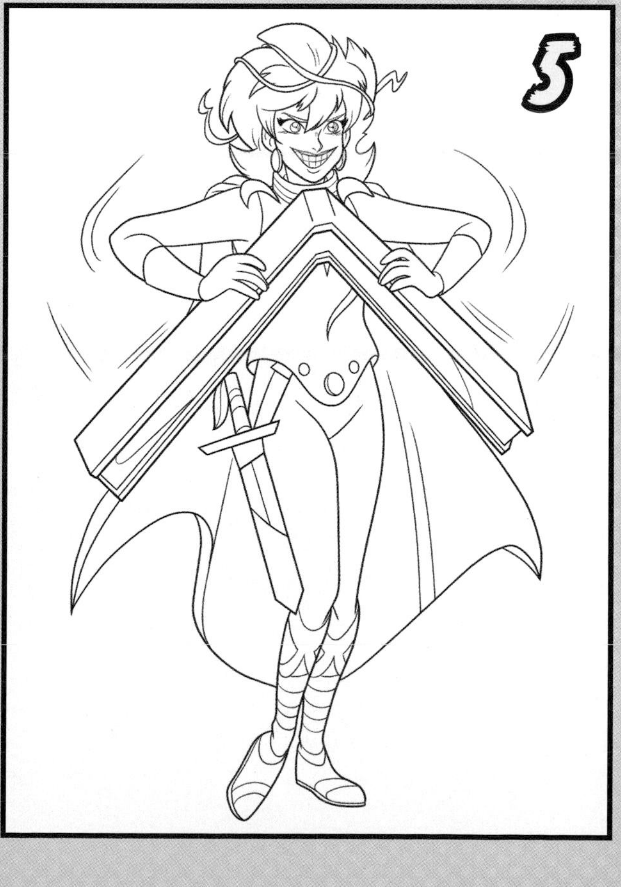
5

MORGAINE LE FEY

Stay out of the way of Morgaine le Fey! The evil sorceress from King Arthur's time is a masked menace. Telepathy, spell casting, and youth absorption—yeah, she can drain your youth to restore her own—are just a few of her talents. And if she's backed into a corner, beware! Morgaine's mystical energy bolts can blast you into the past!

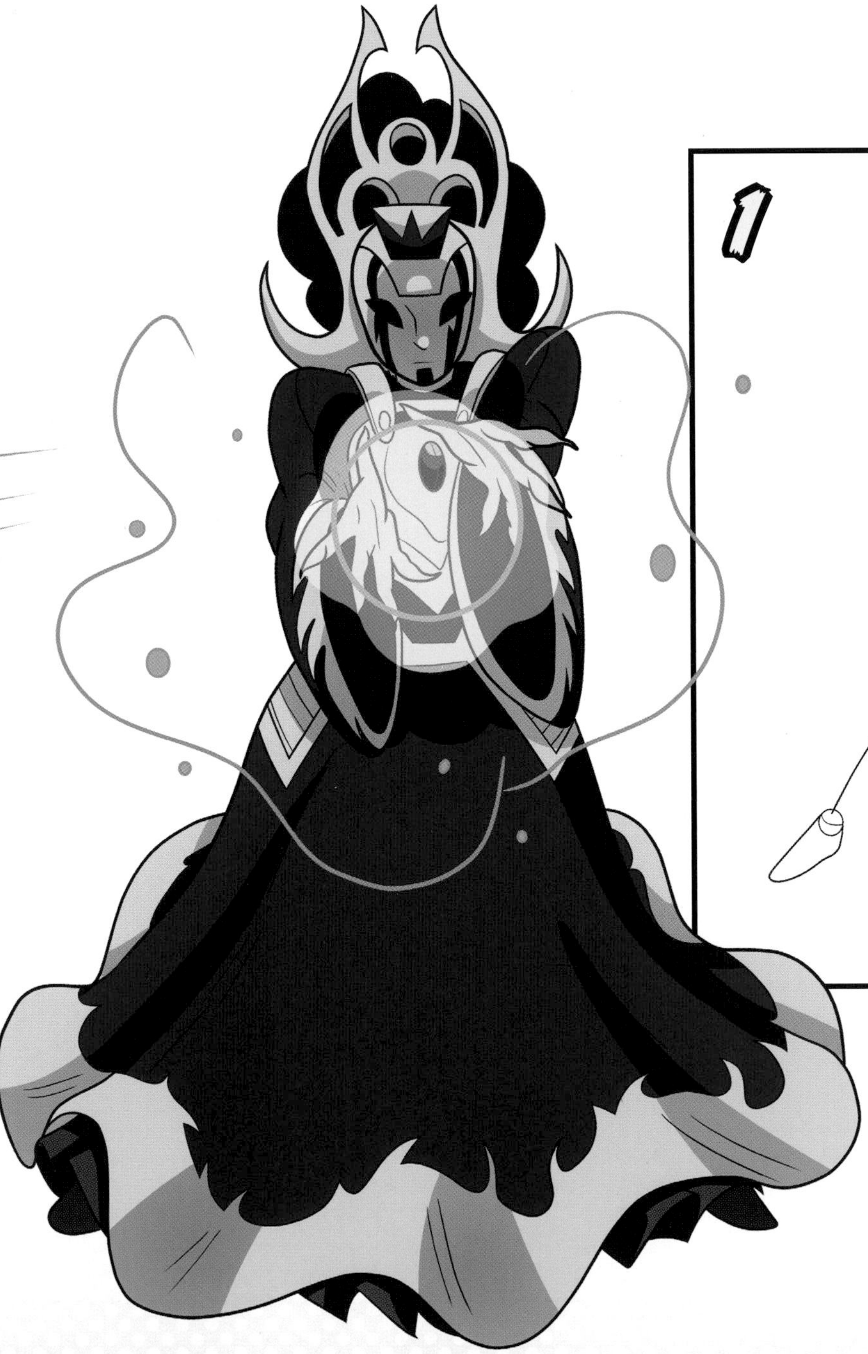

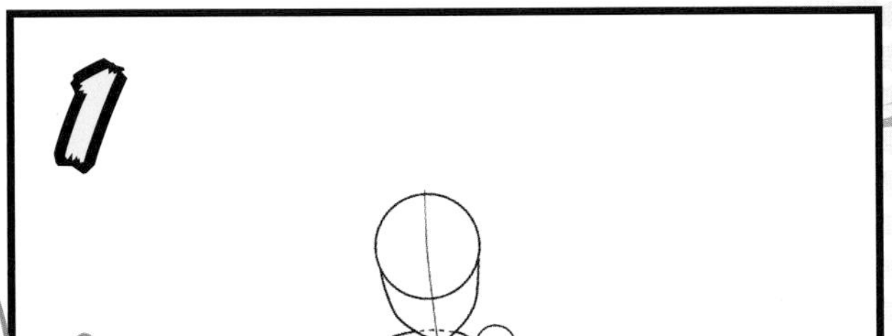
1

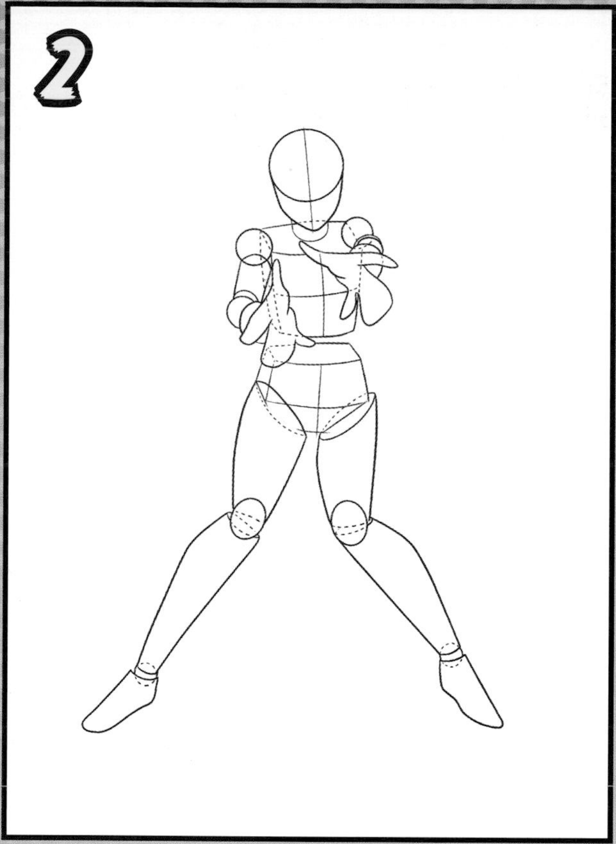
2
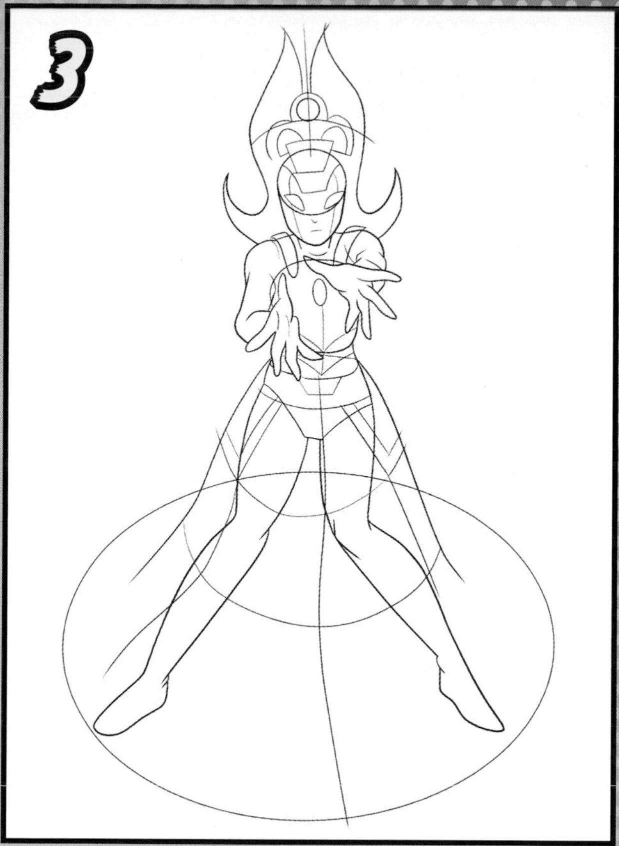
3
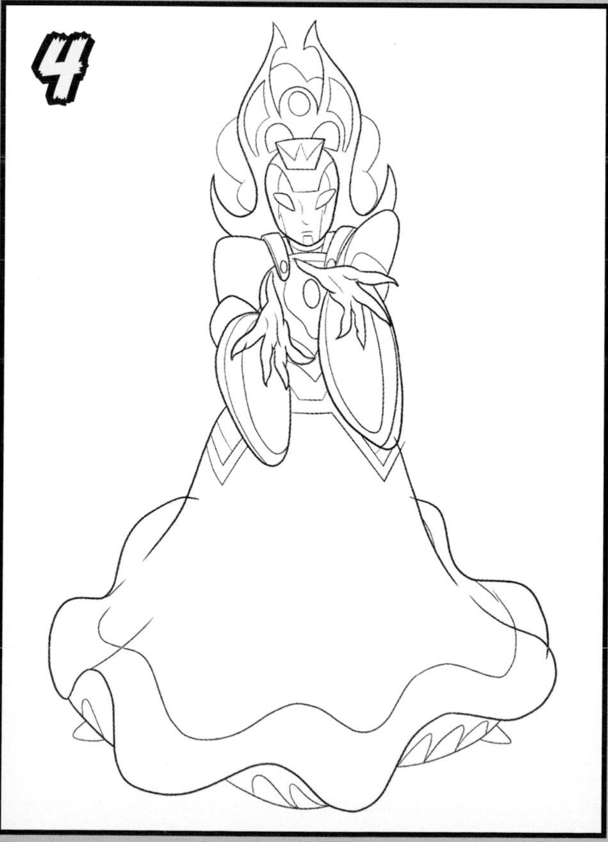
4
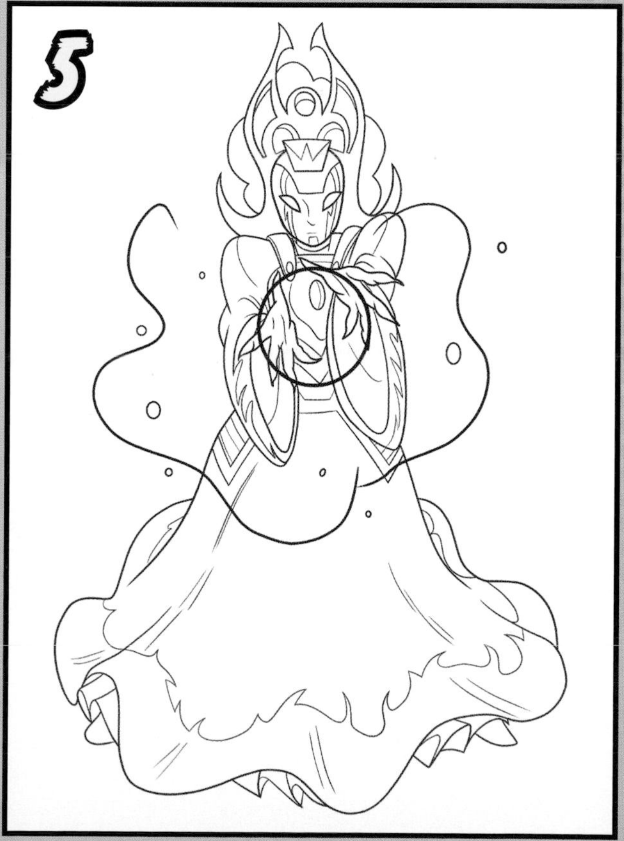
5

WONDER WOMAN VS. GORILLA GRODD

Uh-oh! Gorilla Grodd is up to no good in Gateway City! Can Wonder Woman survive the super-smart ape's attack? Or will her Amazonian shield buckle under the brutal bashing? YOU ARE THE MANGAKA. THE FATE OF THE AMAZING AMAZON IS IN YOUR HANDS!

MANGA FACT
Rumiko Takahashi is a legendary female mangaka who has created several best-selling series. Among her most well-known are *Ranma ½*, *Inuyasha*, and *Maison Ikkoku*.

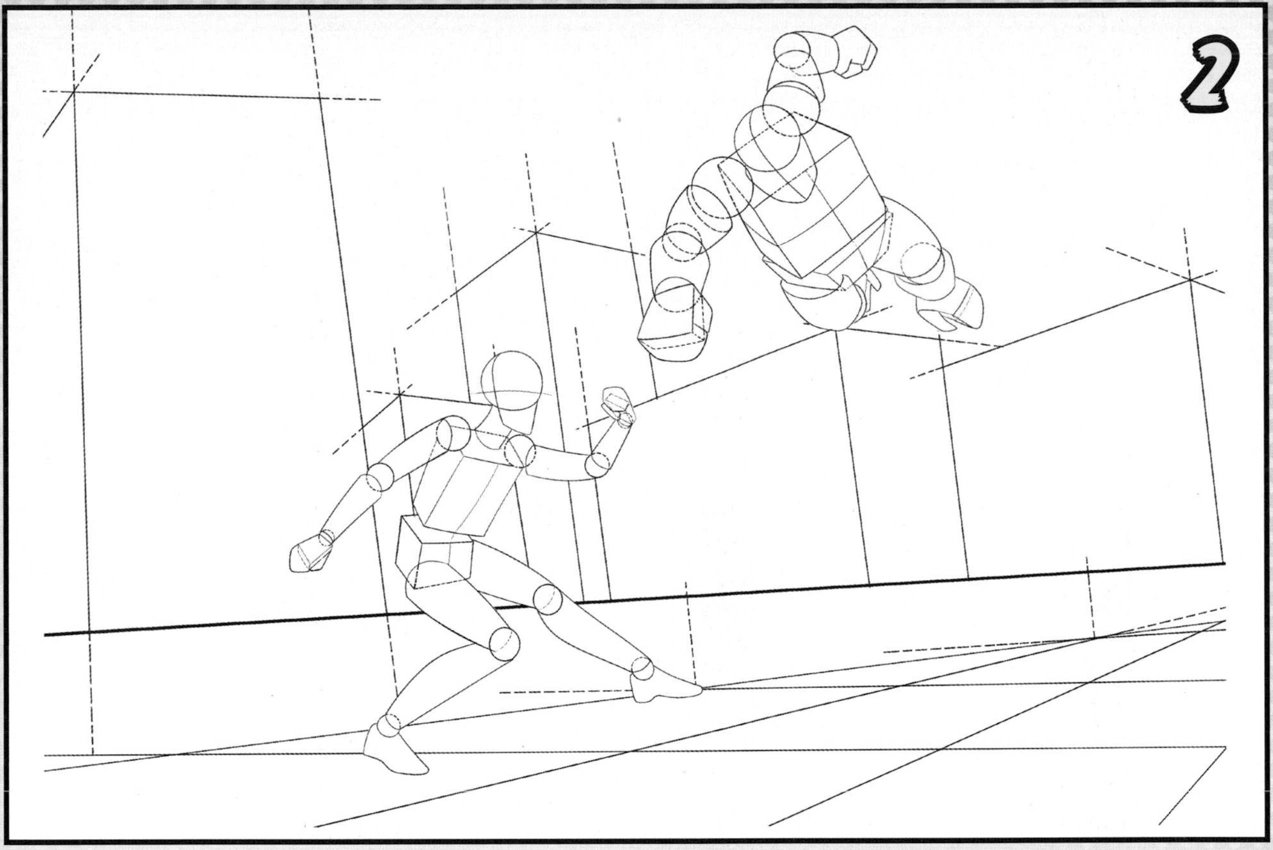
2

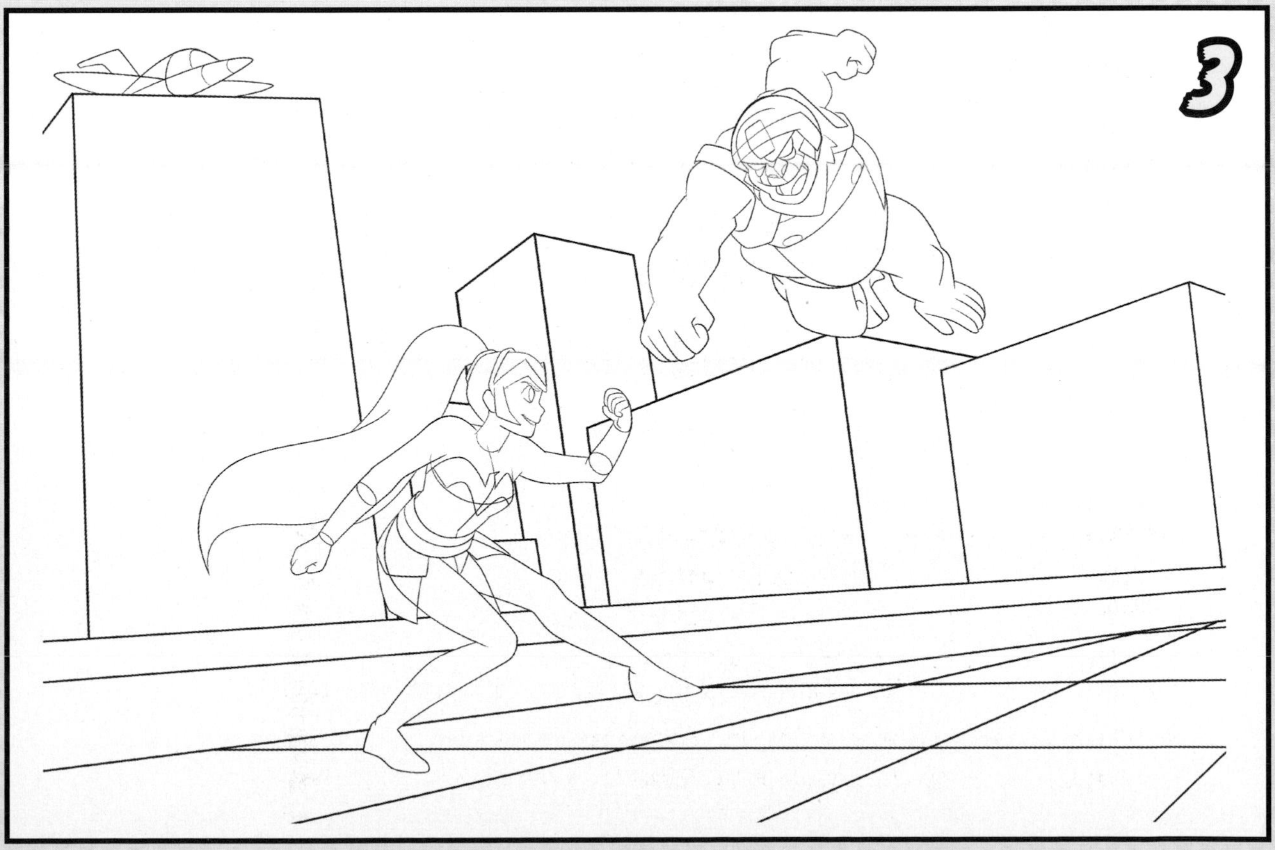
3

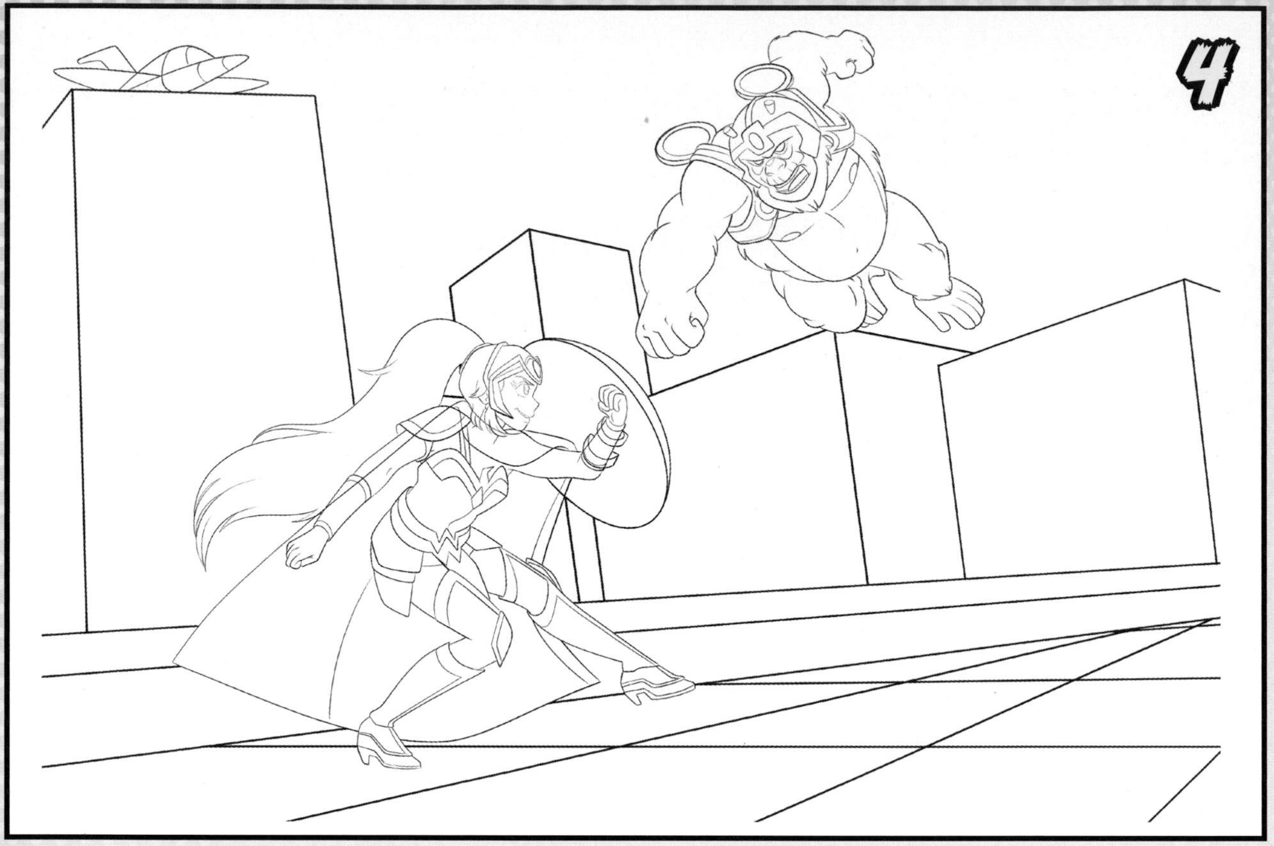
4

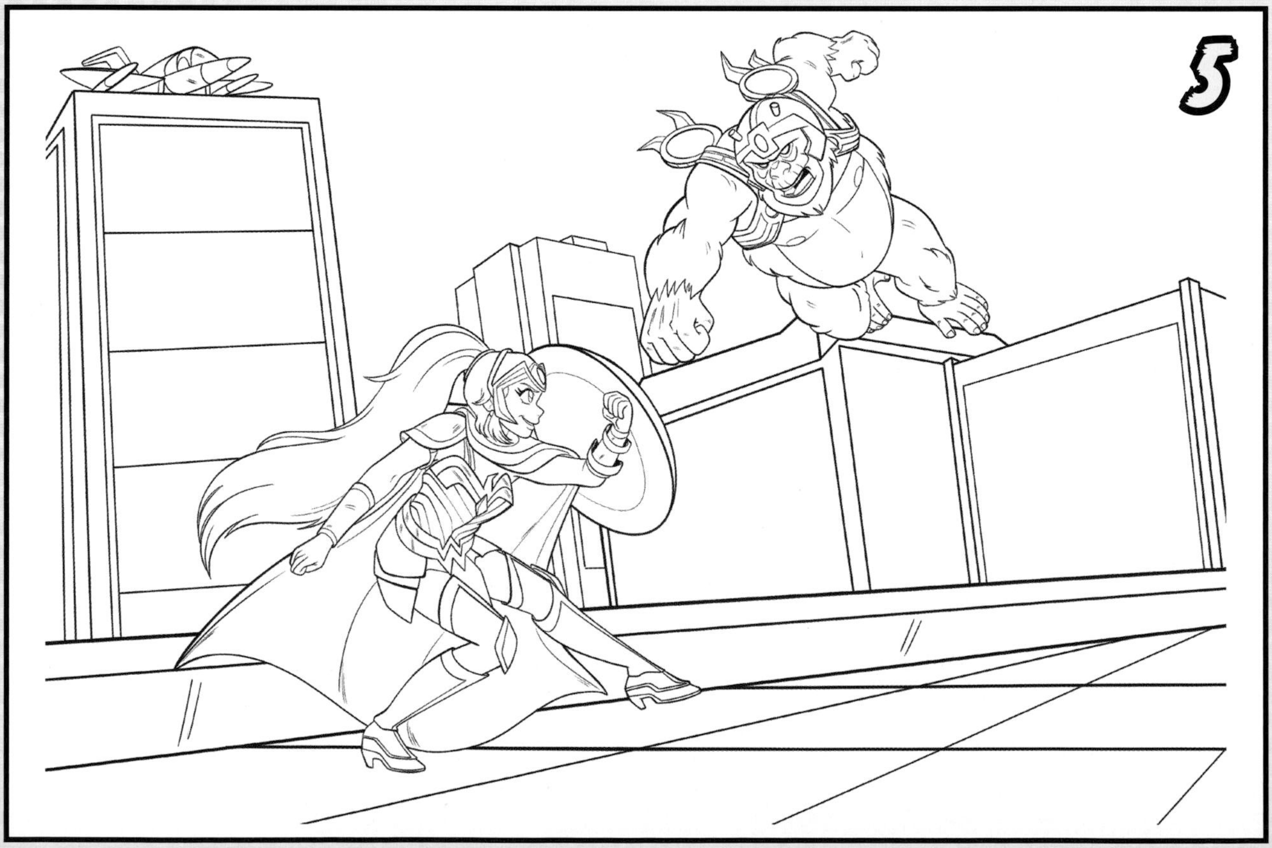
5

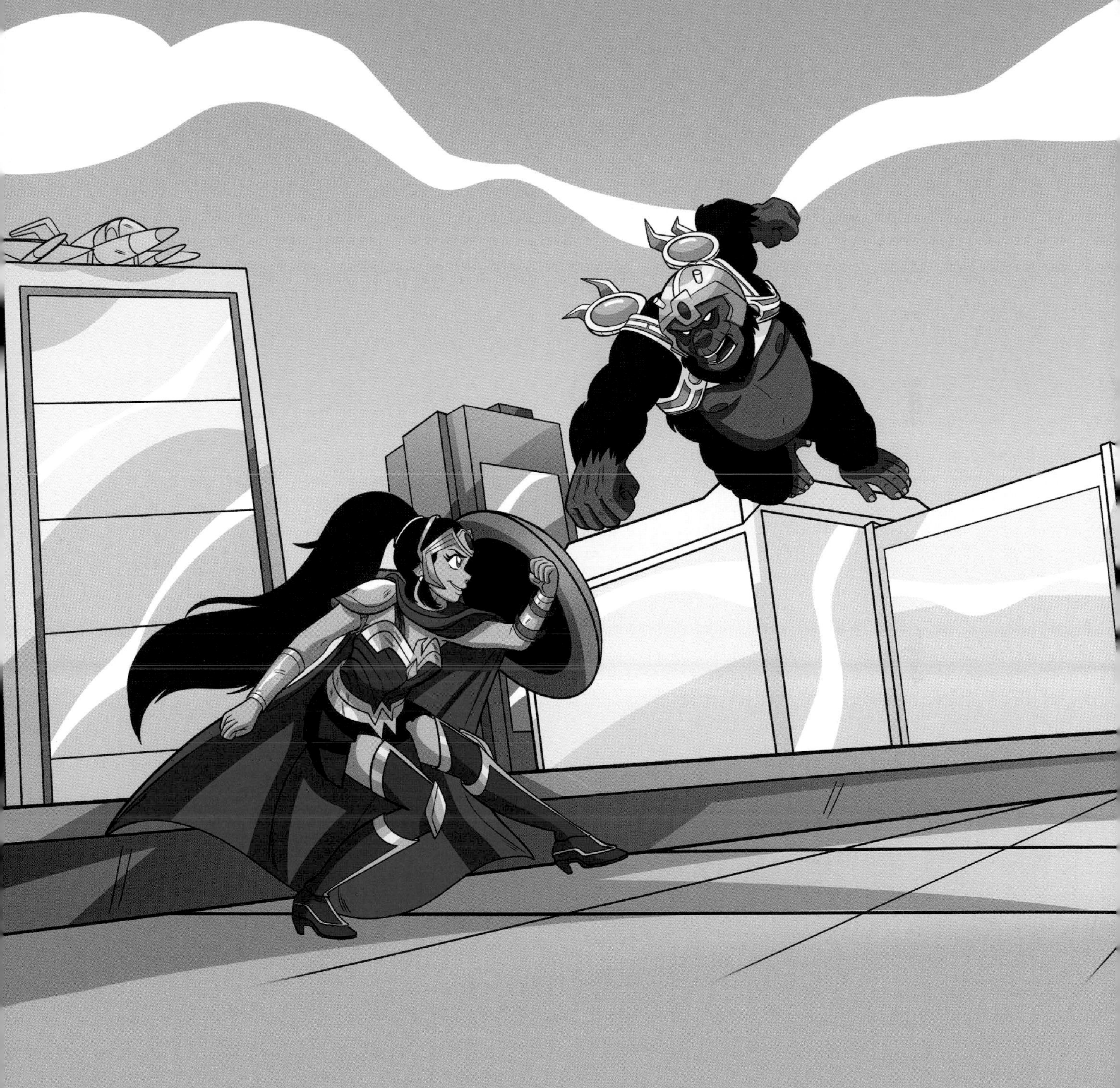

KRYPTO

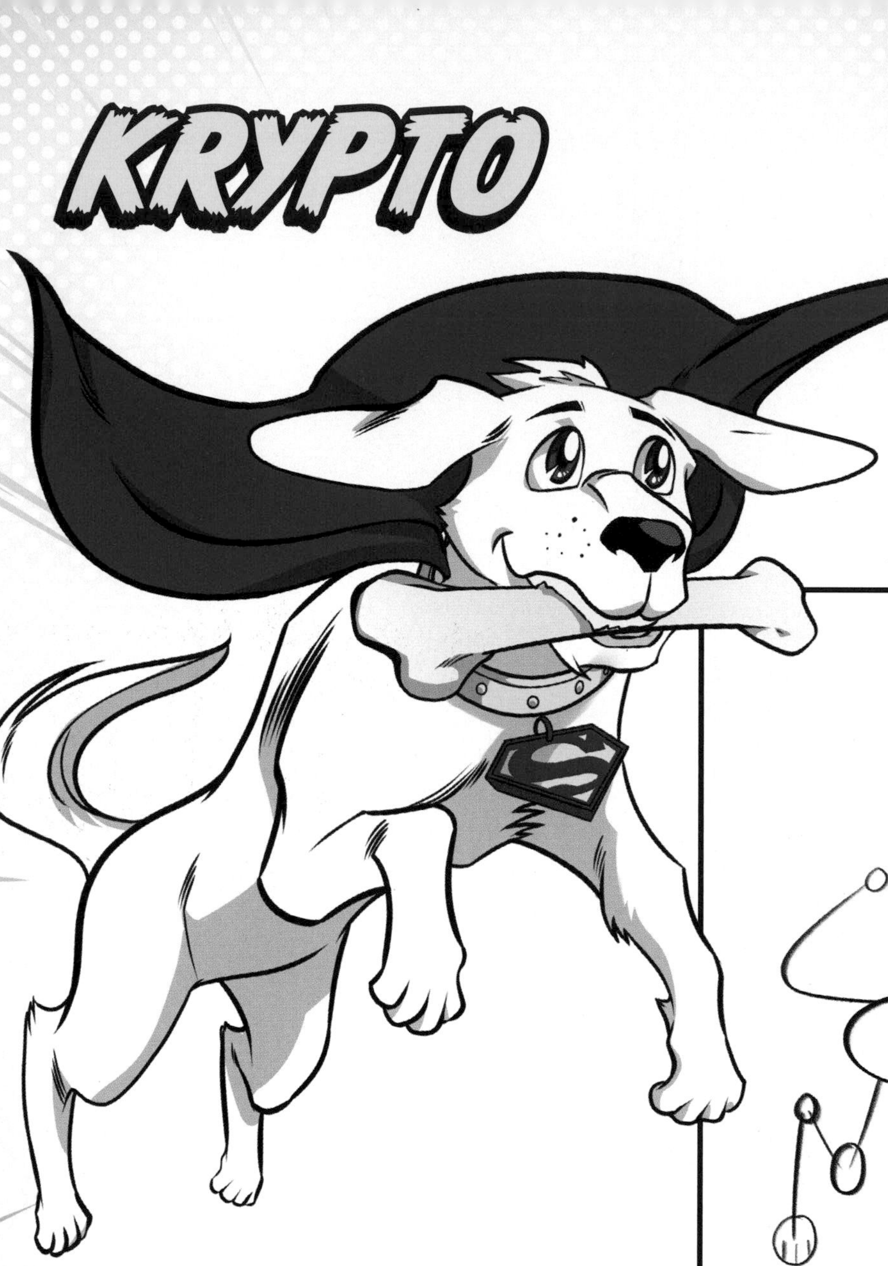

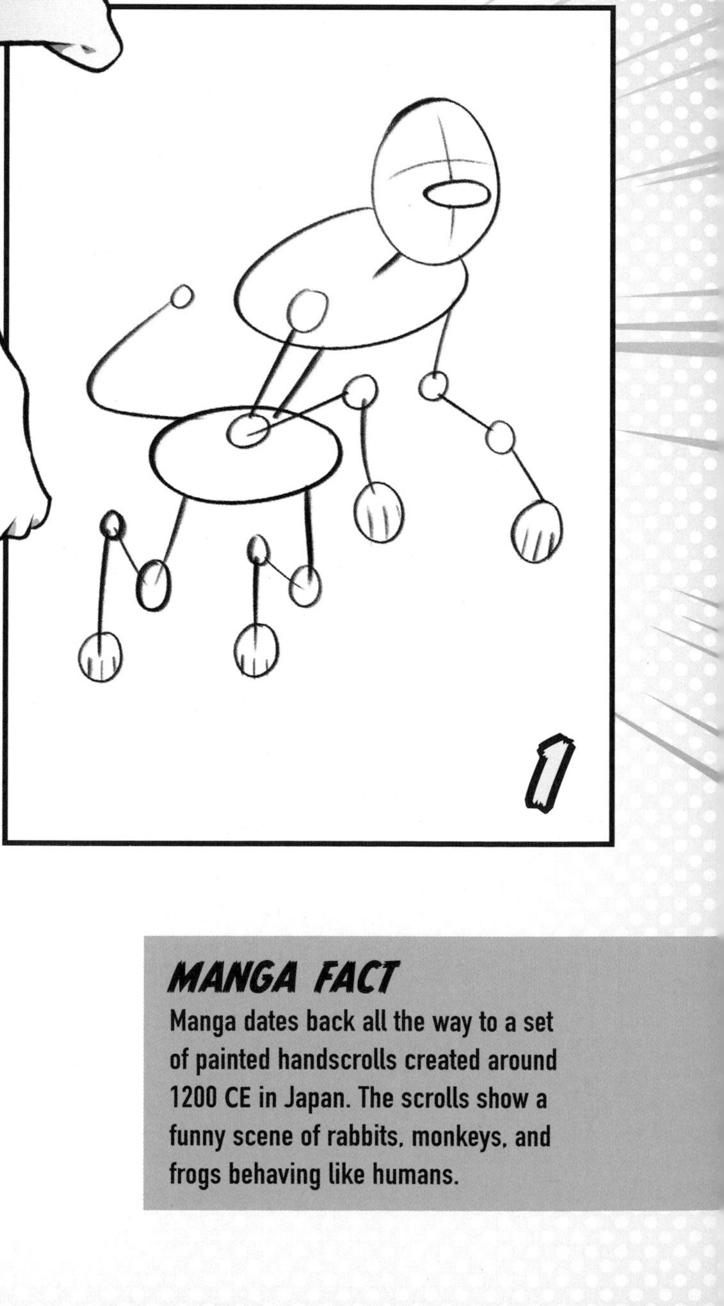
1

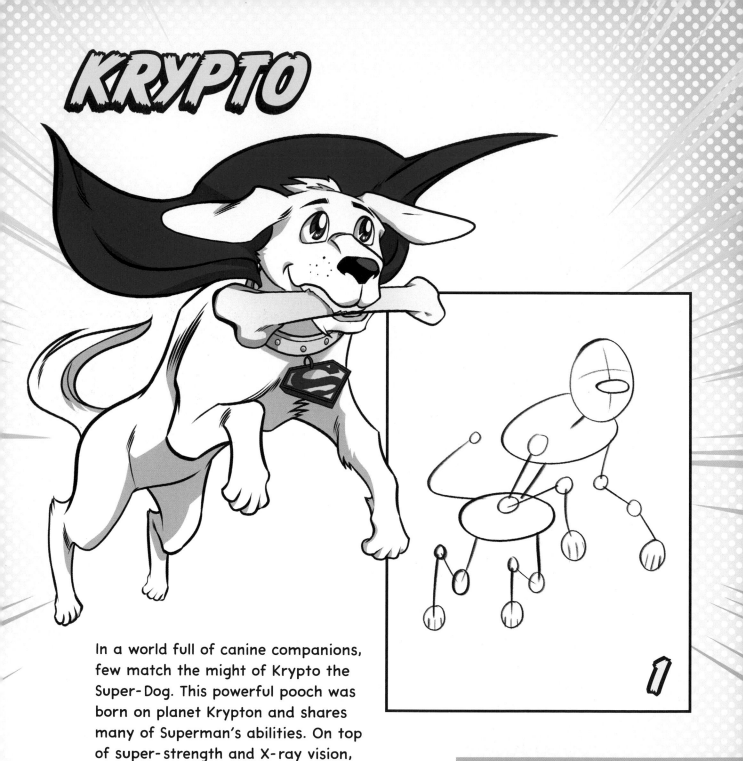

In a world full of canine companions, few match the might of Krypto the Super-Dog. This powerful pooch was born on planet Krypton and shares many of Superman's abilities. On top of super-strength and X-ray vision, Krypto also has souped-up senses of smell and hearing. So whenever the Man of Steel sends out a supersonic whistle, the Dog of Steel swiftly soars to his best friend's side!

MANGA FACT

Manga dates back all the way to a set of painted handscrolls created around 1200 CE in Japan. The scrolls show a funny scene of rabbits, monkeys, and frogs behaving like humans.

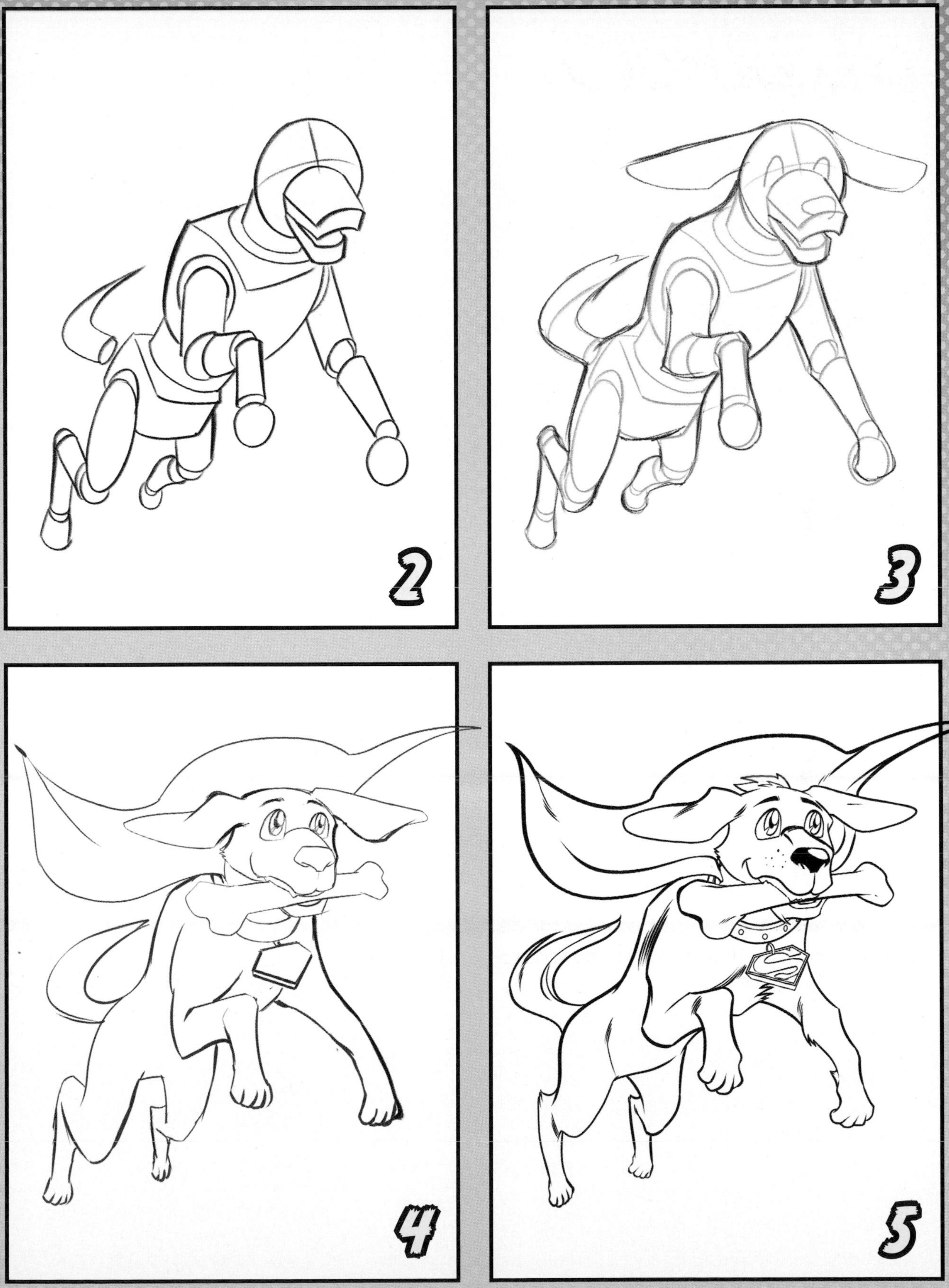
2
3
4
5

ACE

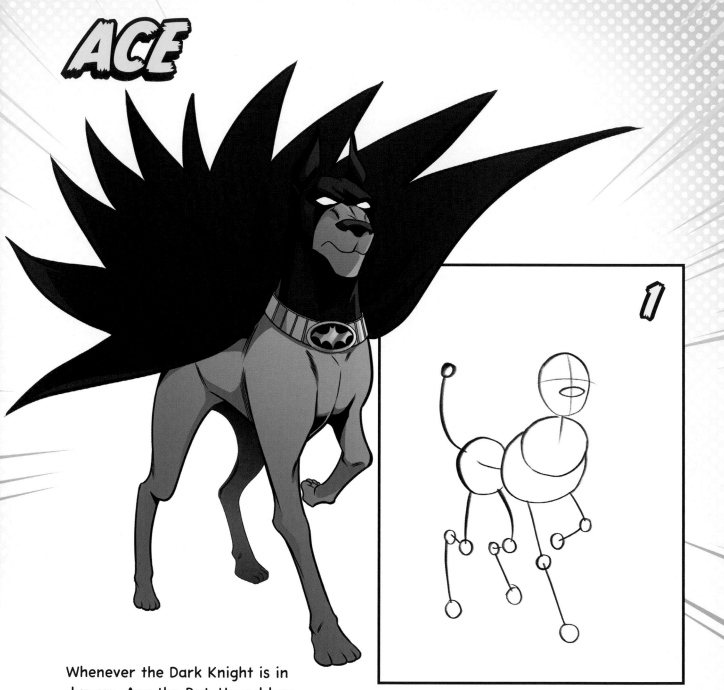

1

Whenever the Dark Knight is in danger, Ace the Bat-Hound has his back. This canine crime fighter isn't afraid to face a *ruff* crowd. But his most *scent*-sational ability? A nose for finding troublemaking ne'er-do-wells. With this sleuthing skill, Ace proves time and again that he's the perfect pal for Batman, the World's Greatest Detective.

MANGA FACT
Mangaka often study real-life objects in order to create believable characters. Want to put Ace in a new pose? Search online for dog photos to help get his body just right.

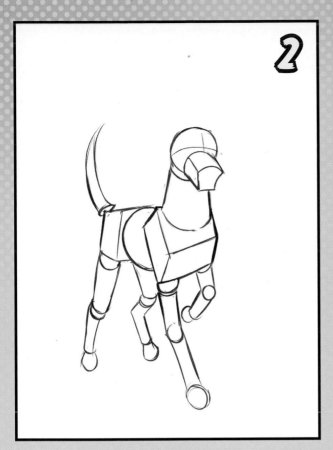

JUMPA

Every warrior princess needs a royal steed—and Wonder Woman is no exception. Luckily, the Amazing Amazon can saddle up Jumpa whenever she has a need for speed. This giant Kanga is a swift runner and powerful jumper. Whether running races on Paradise Island or leaping into battle, Jumpa is ready to spring into action!

MANGA FACT

Some manga animals are drawn with lifelike proportions. Others are stylized, with large heads and short legs. Play with your art style to see which you like best!

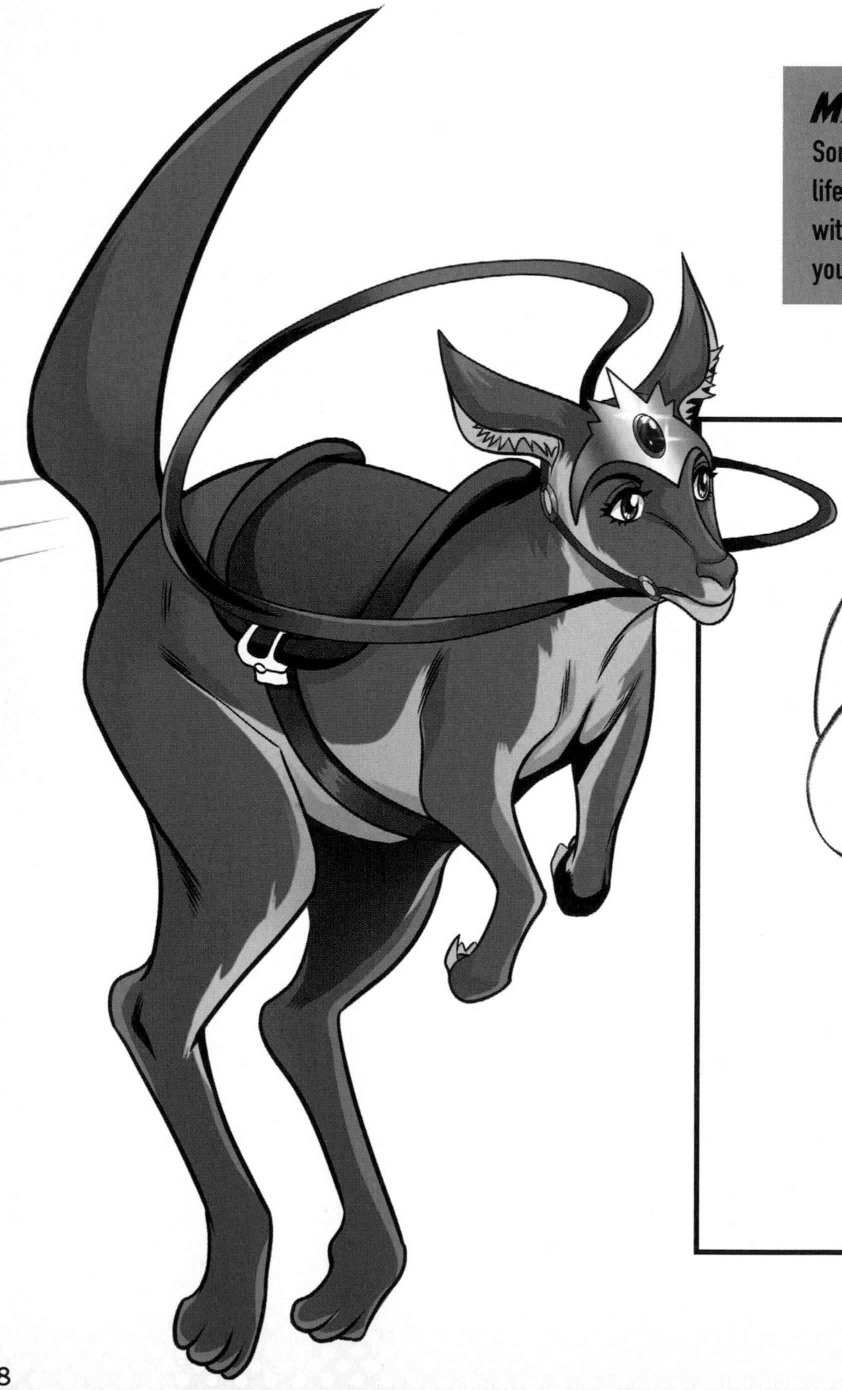

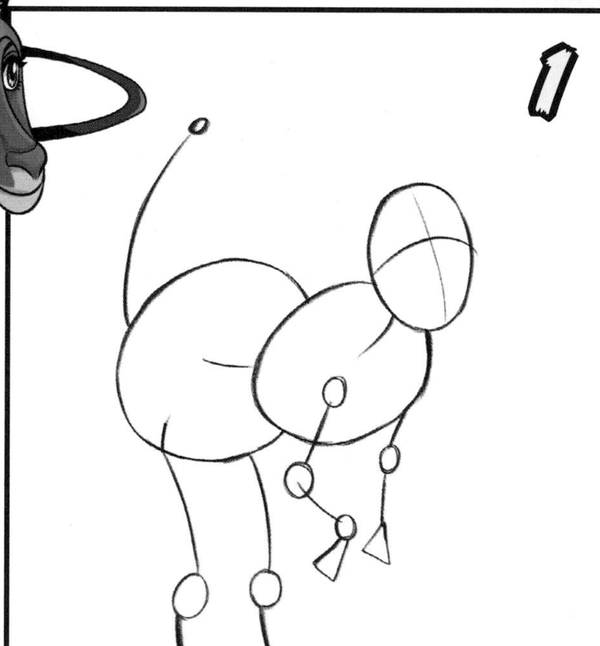
1

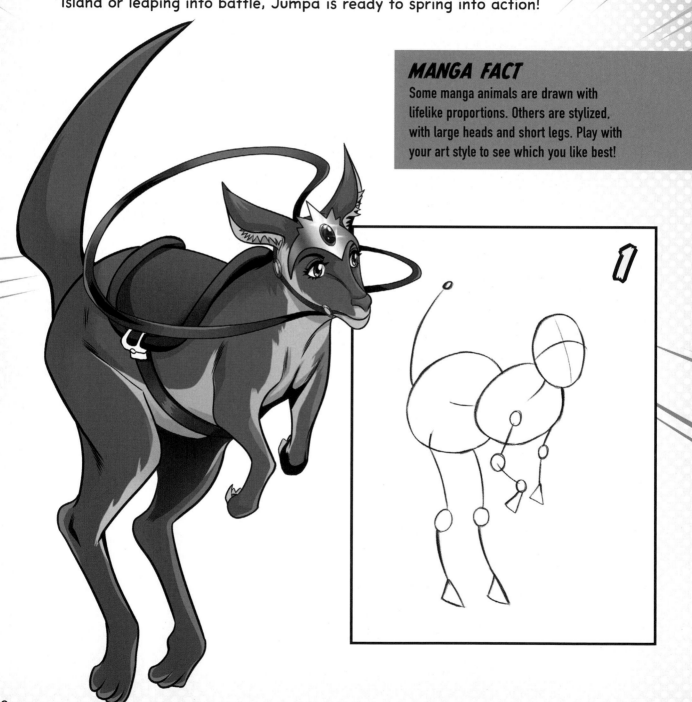

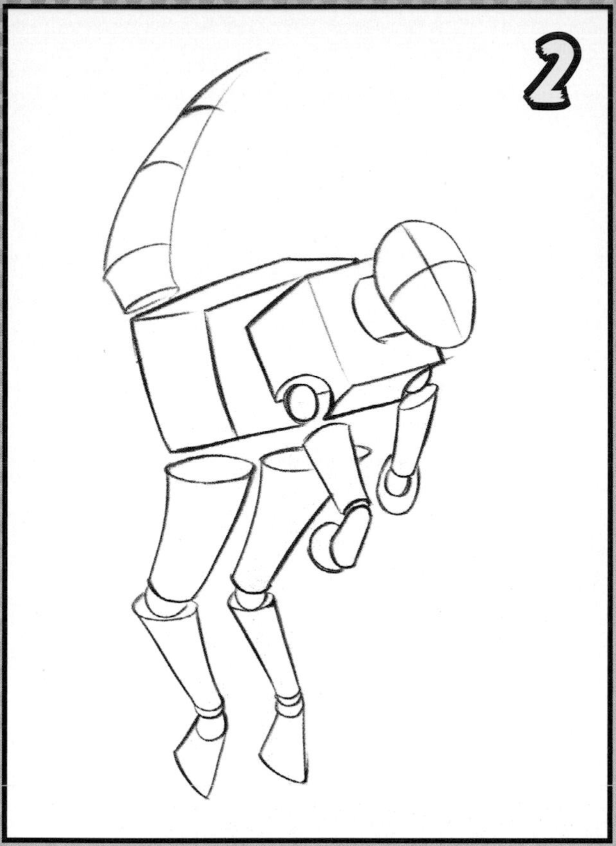
2
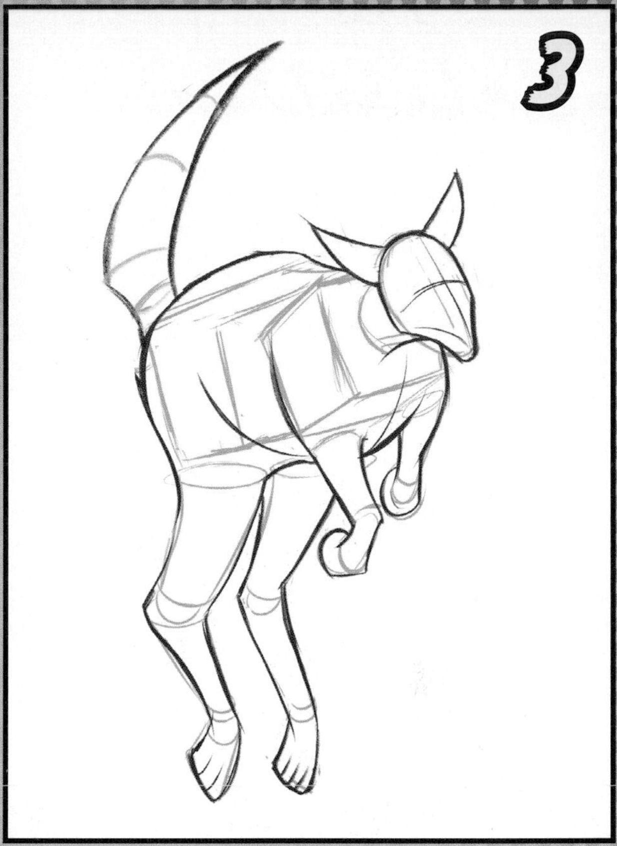
3
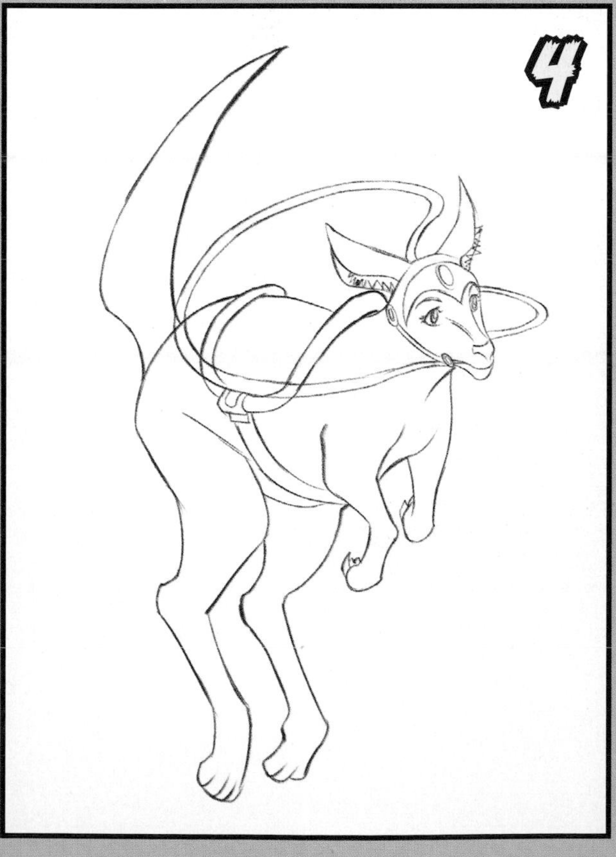
4
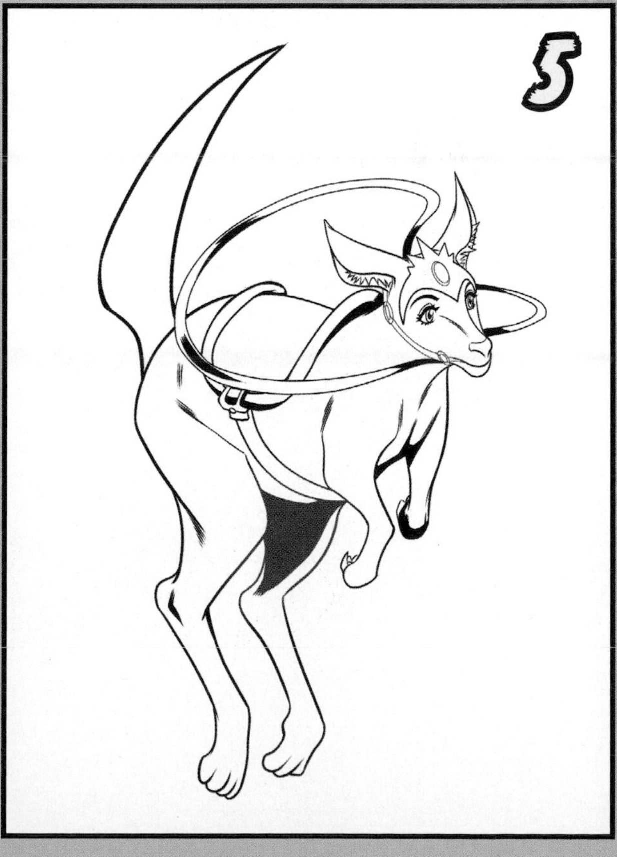
5

STREAKY

Streaky started out as Supergirl's normal pet cat. Then an experiment with X-Kryptonite changed everything! The radioactive rock gave Streaky *paw*-some superpowers. Heat vision, super-strength, super-speed, and flight are all at the command of this fearless feline. Now the Super-Cat dons a cape and S-Shield anytime he takes a swipe at a Super-Villain!

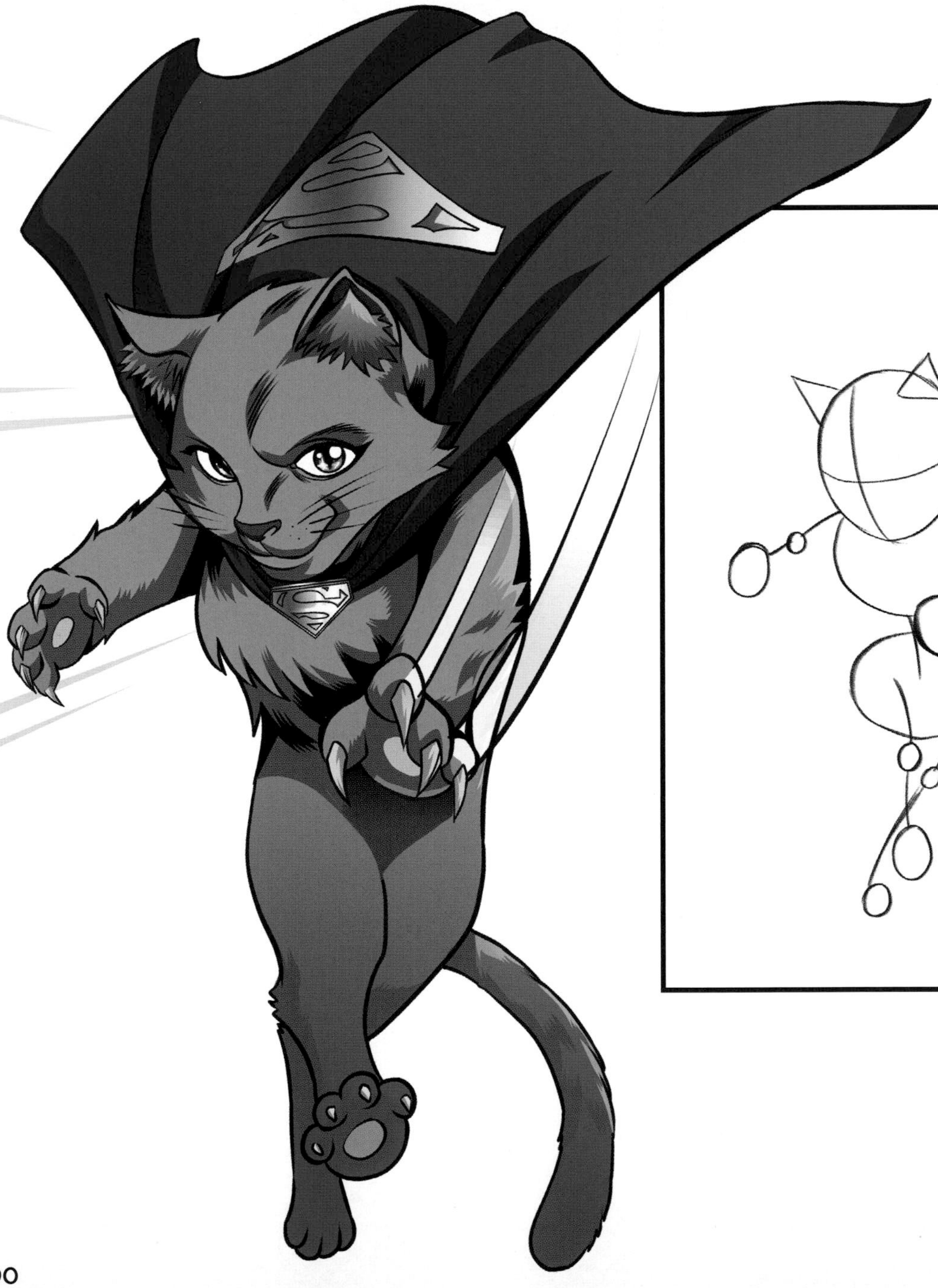

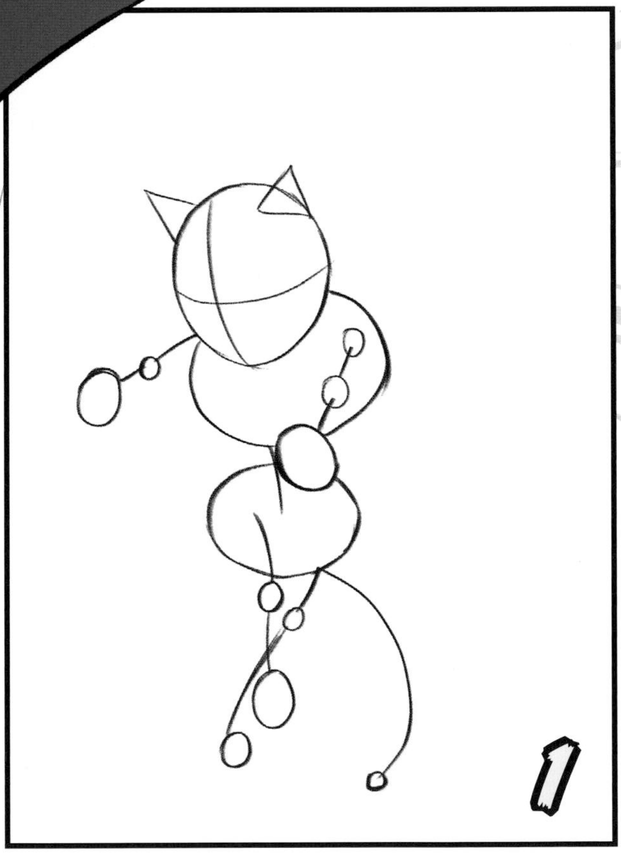
1

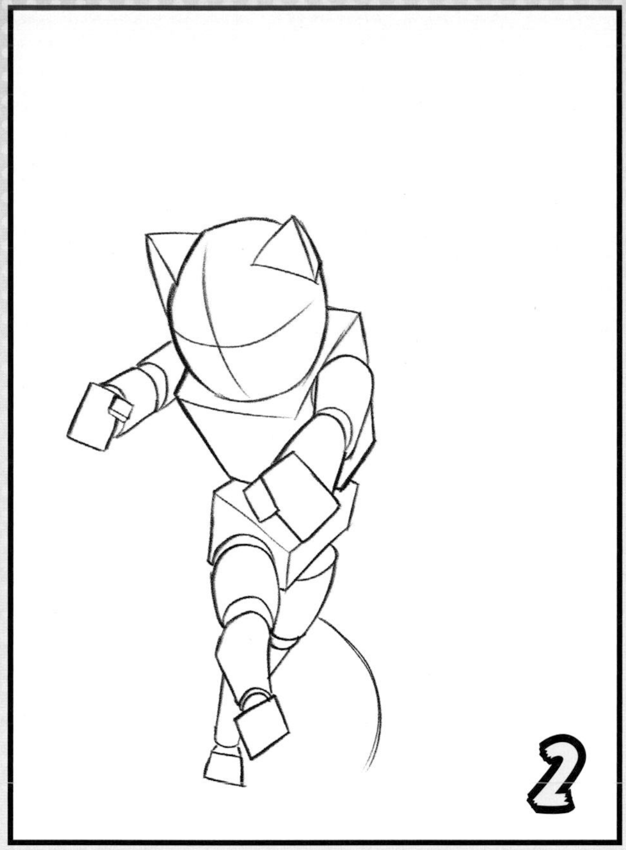
2
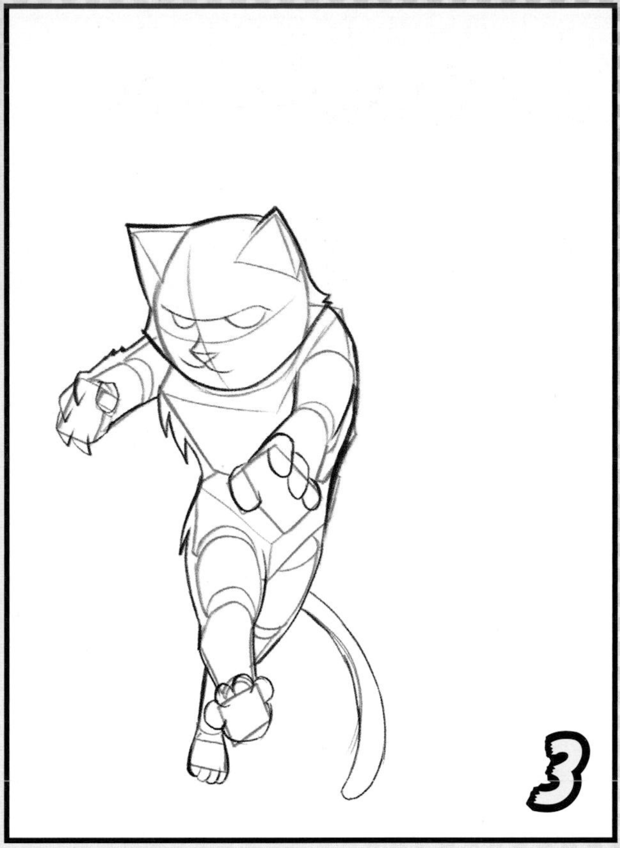
3
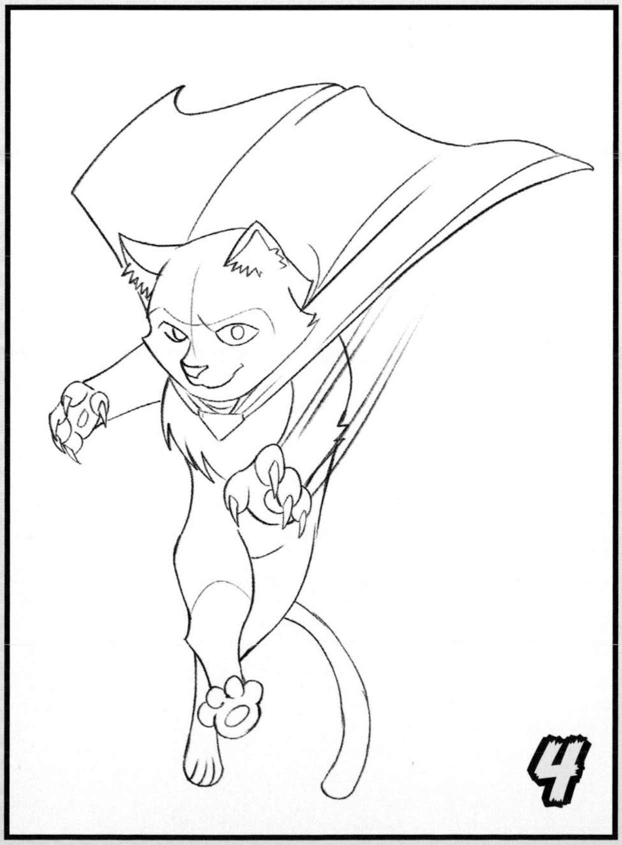
4
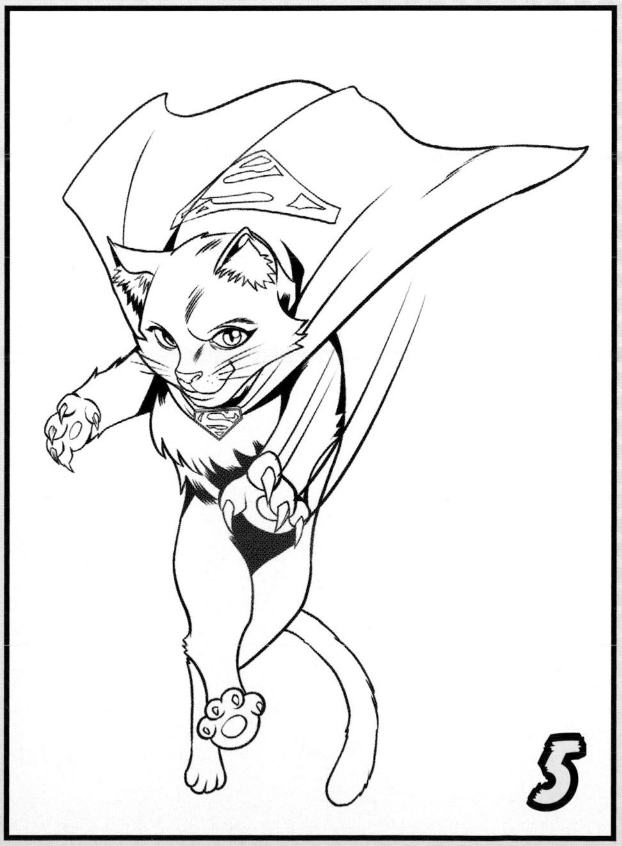
5

COMET

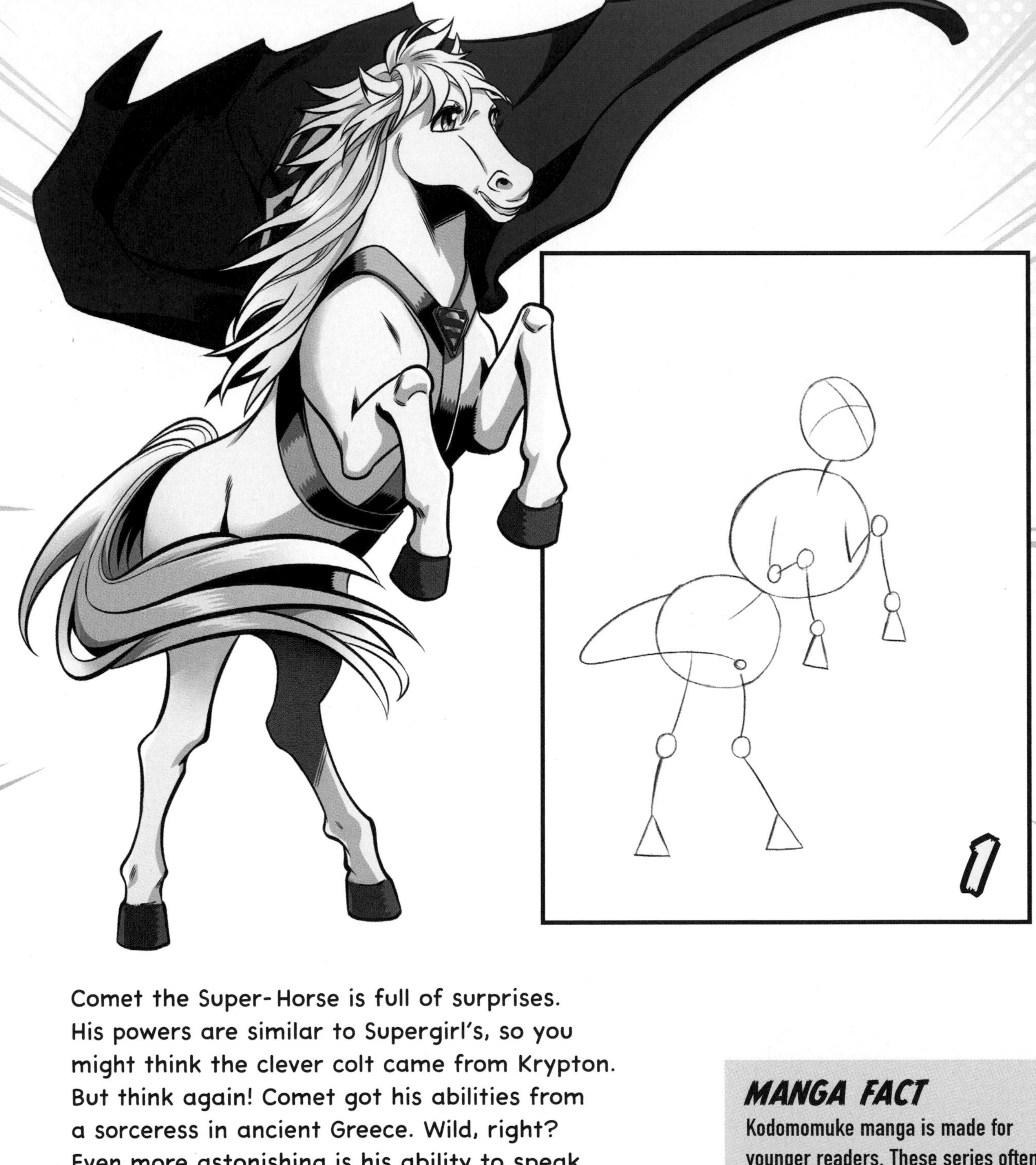
1

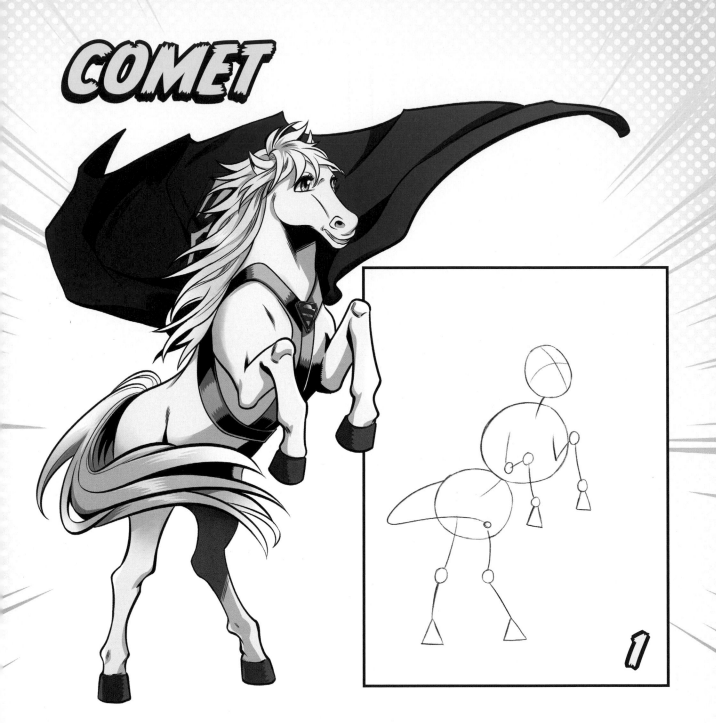

Comet the Super-Horse is full of surprises. His powers are similar to Supergirl's, so you might think the clever colt came from Krypton. But think again! Comet got his abilities from a sorceress in ancient Greece. Wild, right? Even more astonishing is his ability to speak to the Girl of Steel with his mind! Whoa, Nelly! Talk about a super-steed indeed.

MANGA FACT

Kodomomuke manga is made for younger readers. These series often have fun stories with cute characters and moral lessons. *Pokémon* is a popular kodomomuke series.

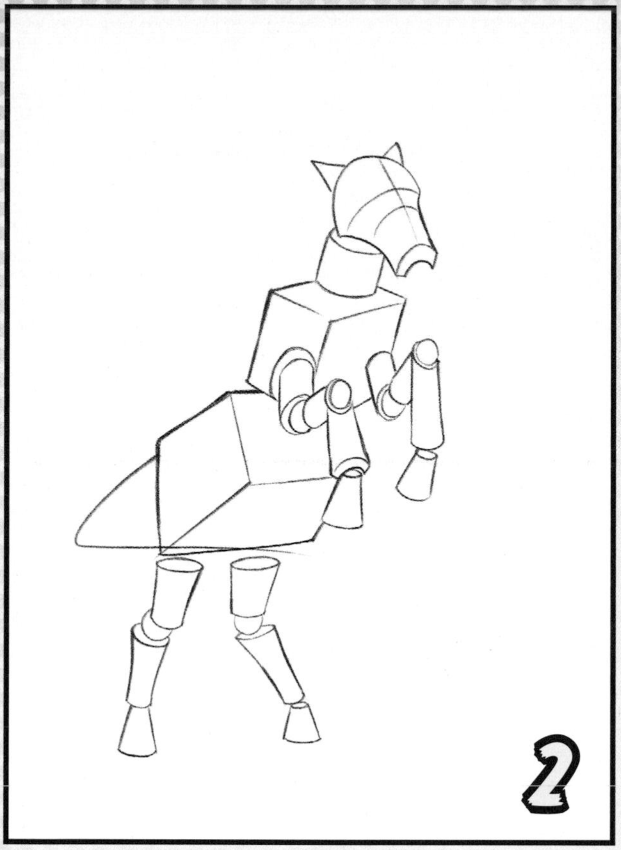
2
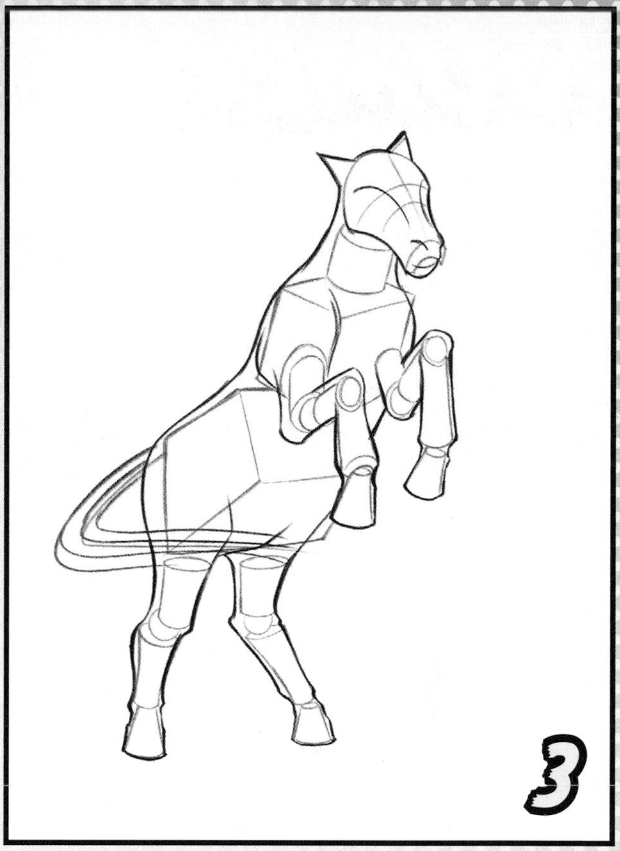
3
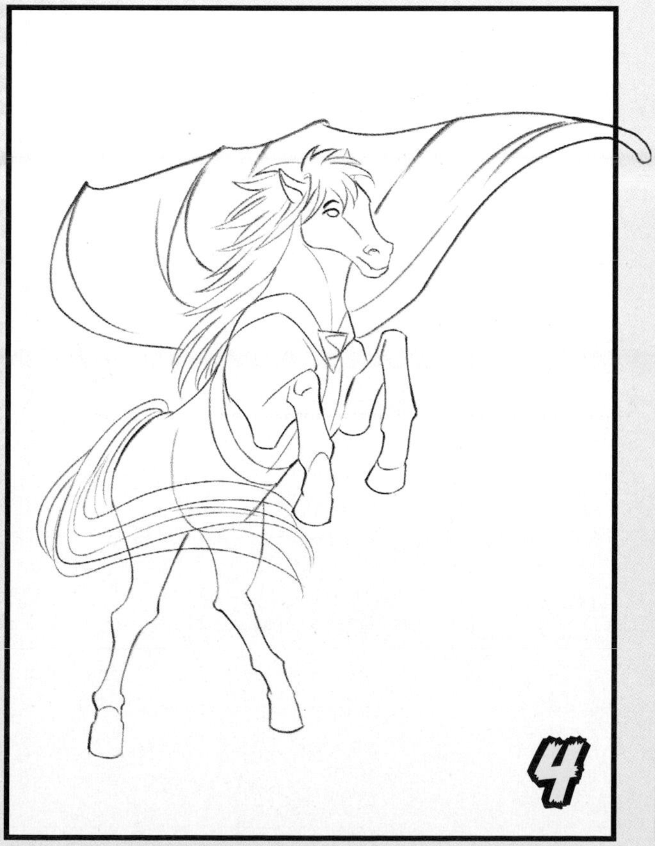
4
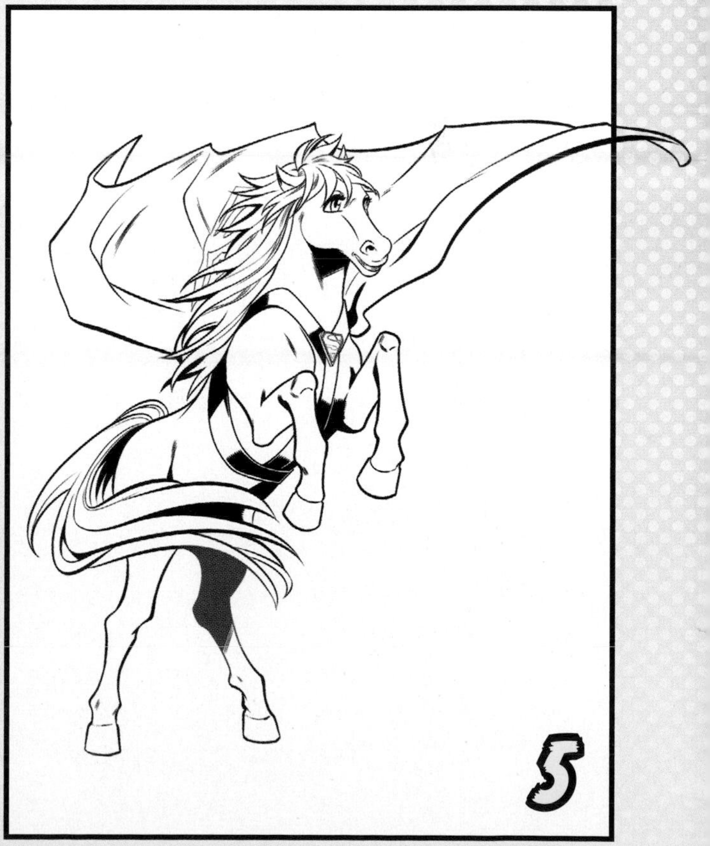
5

STORM

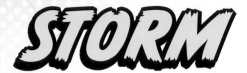

Whether cutting through currents or weaving through waves, Storm is a wonder to behold. But Aquaman's trusty steed packs more than aquatic horsepower. Just like the King of Atlantis, the super-smart seahorse can also speak to other sea creatures using his mind. With this talent, Storm can call on his friends to help burst the bubbles of black-hearted baddies!

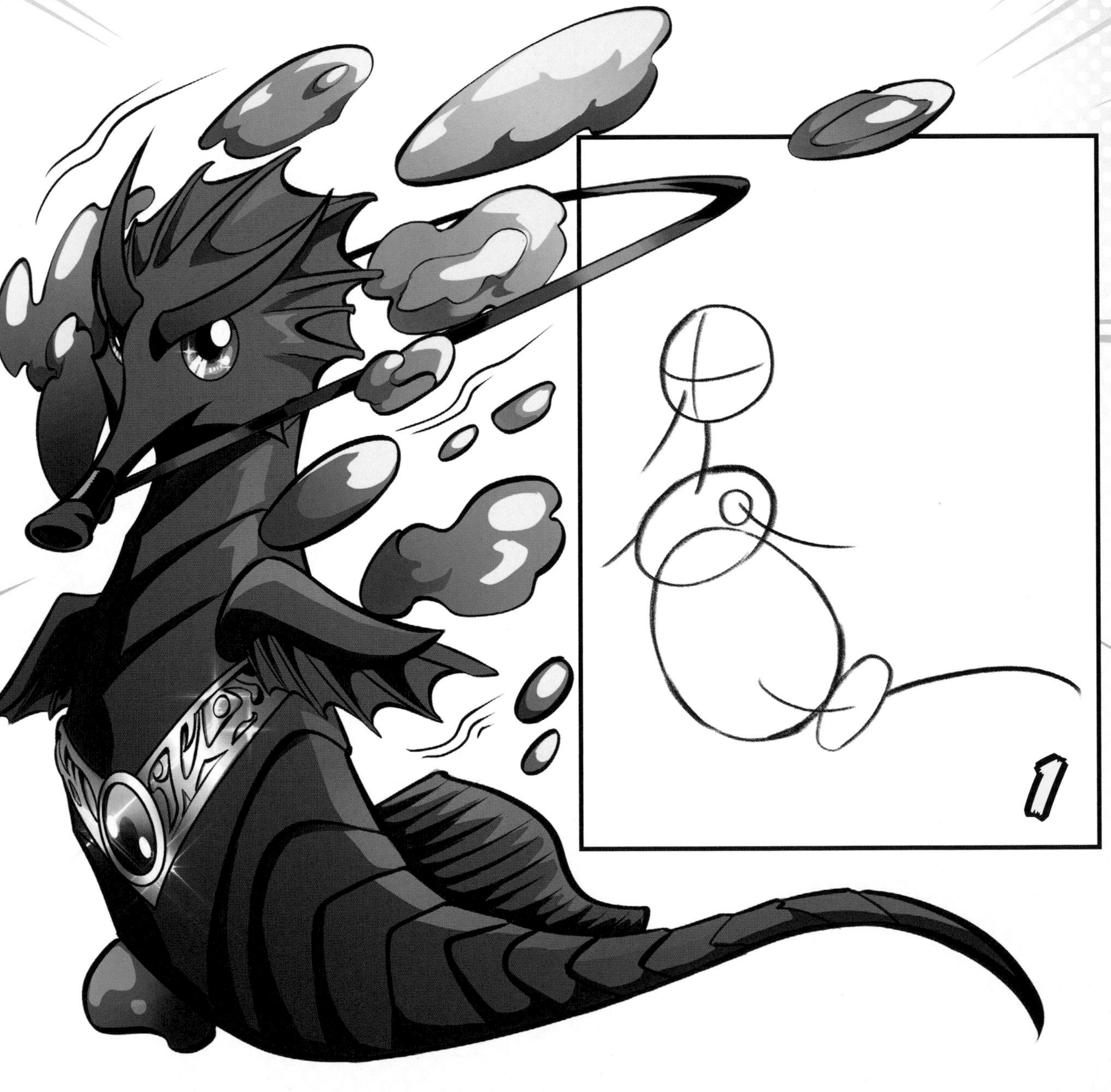
1

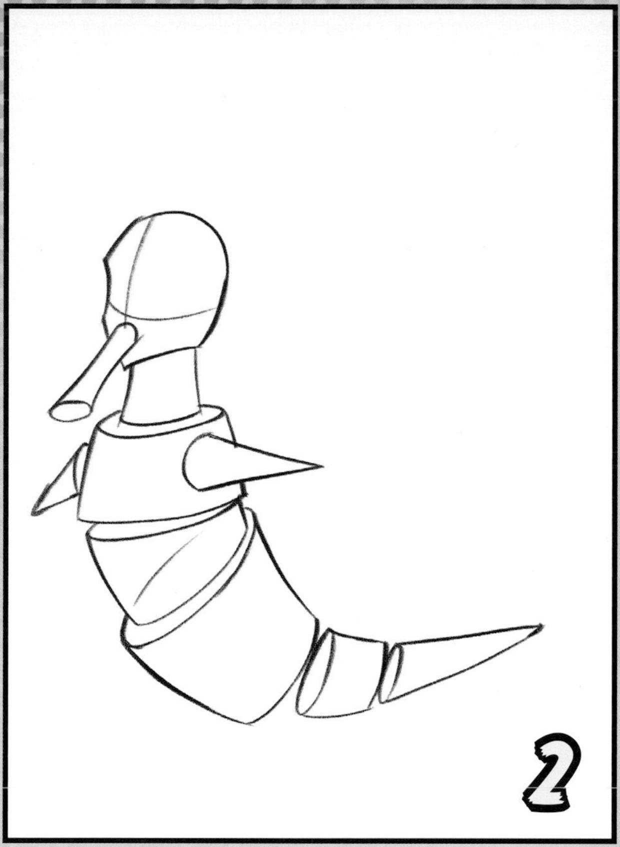
2
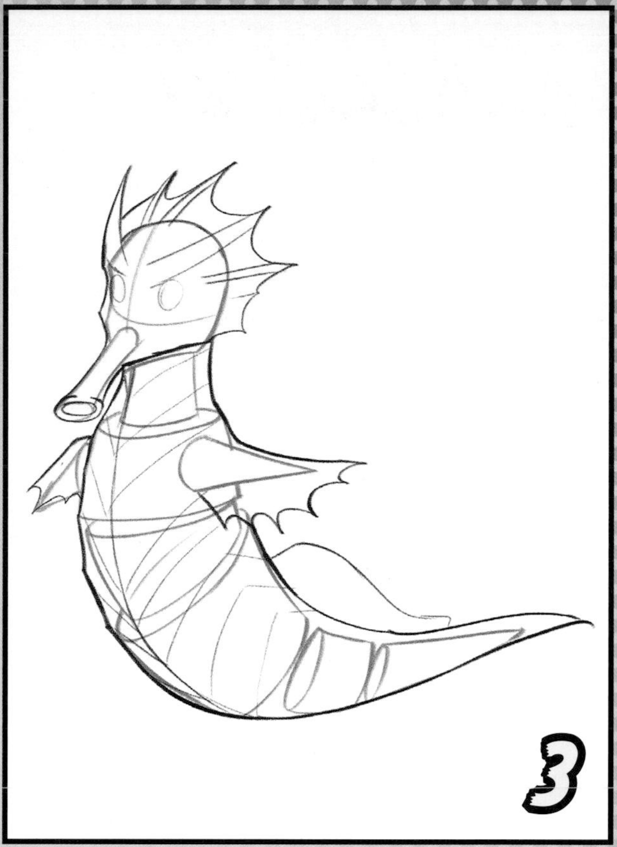
3
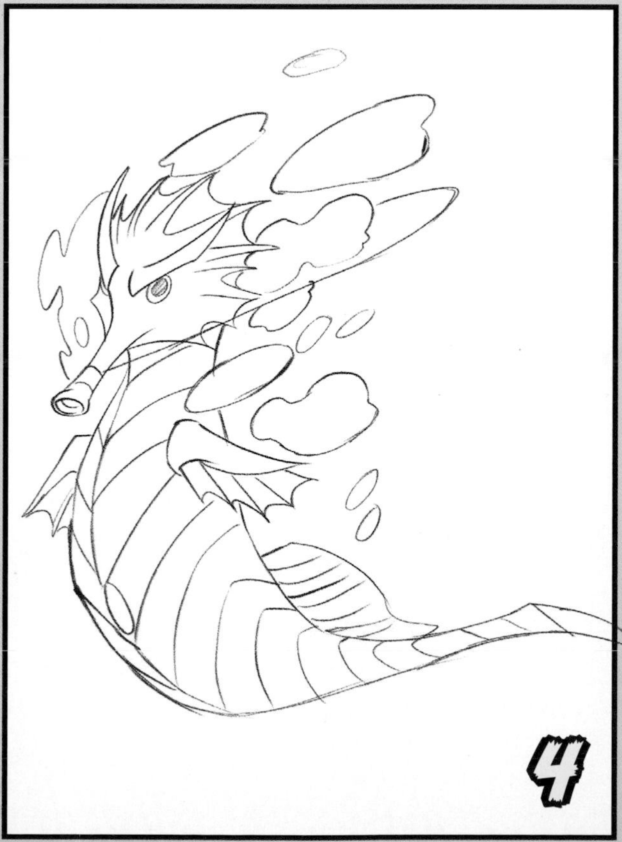
4
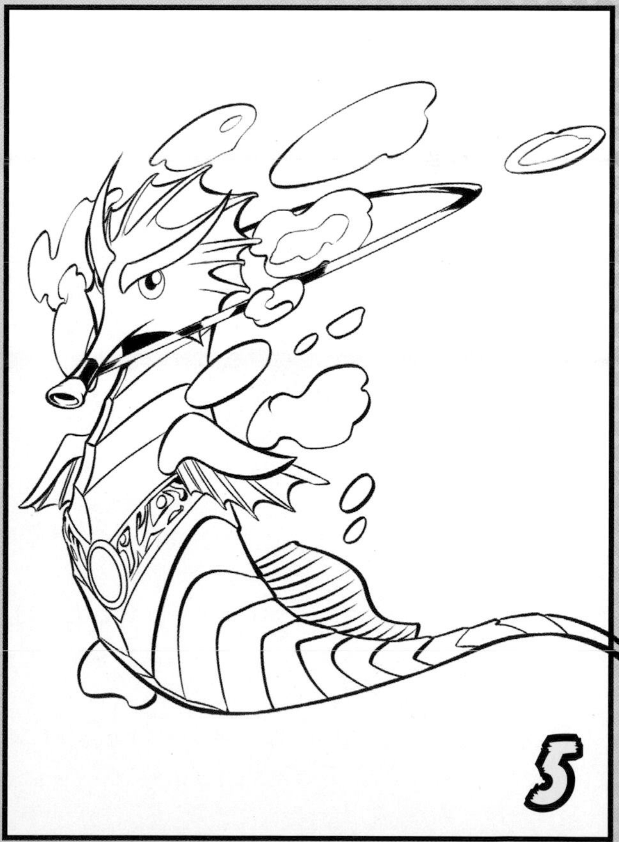
5

WHATZIT

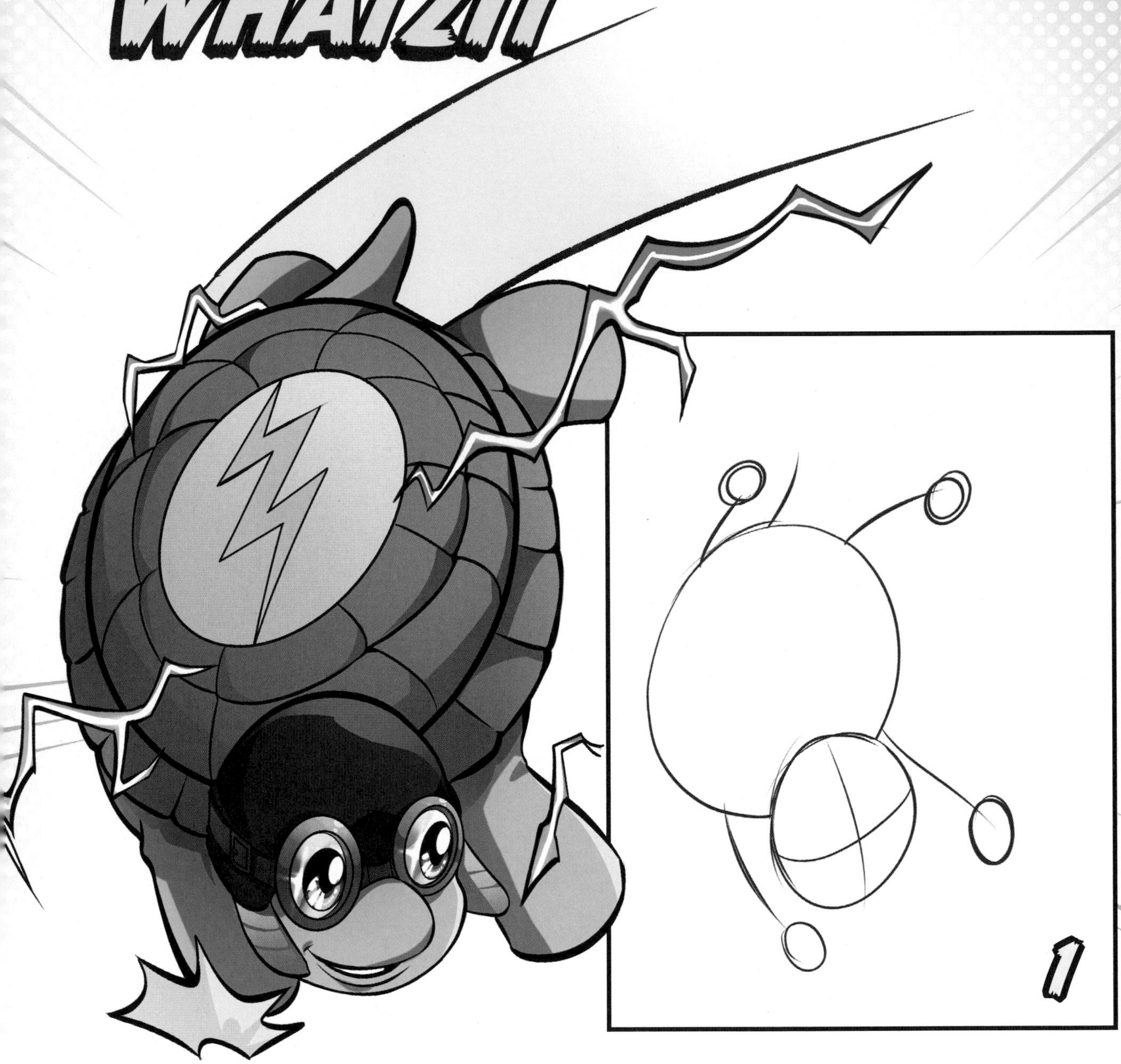
1

Merton McSnurtle is no ordinary turtle—he's The Fastest Turtle Alive! Better known as Whatzit, this fleet-footed friend of The Flash uses his powers to protect Central City. And what remarkable powers! His connection to the Speed Force is so strong, he can spin up tornadoes that leave enemies shell-shocked.

MANGA FACT

Whatzit's speed lines add a dynamic sense of motion. But these lines are also used in manga to emphasize a character's emotion, such as shock or excitement.

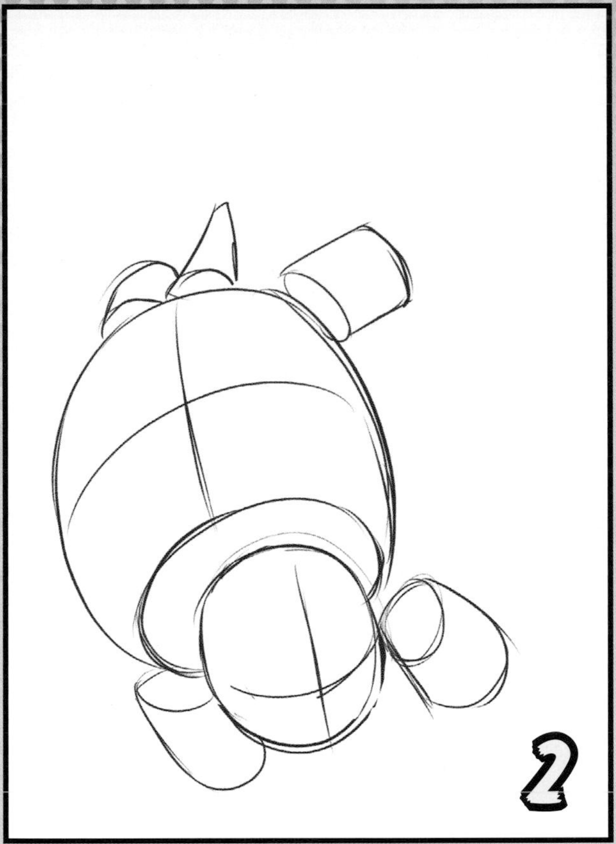
2

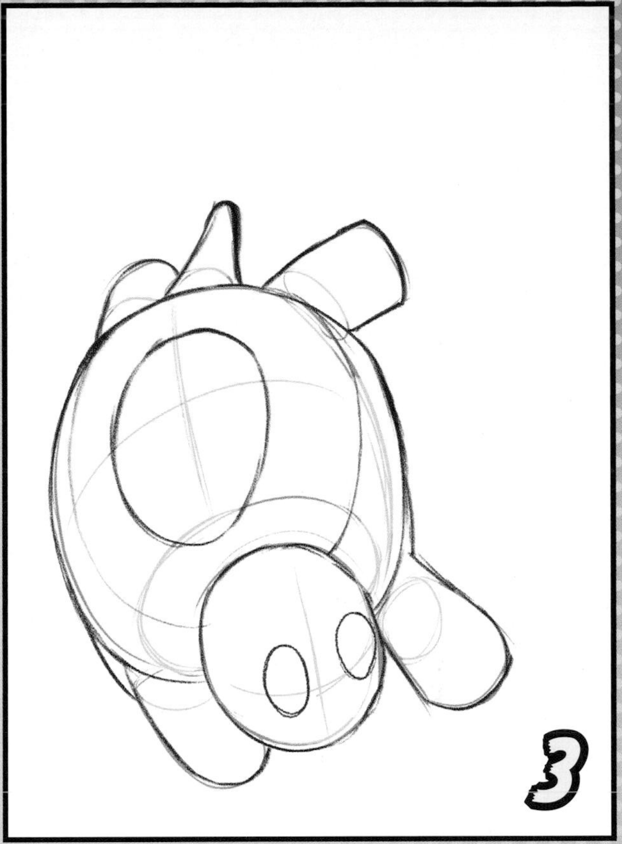
3

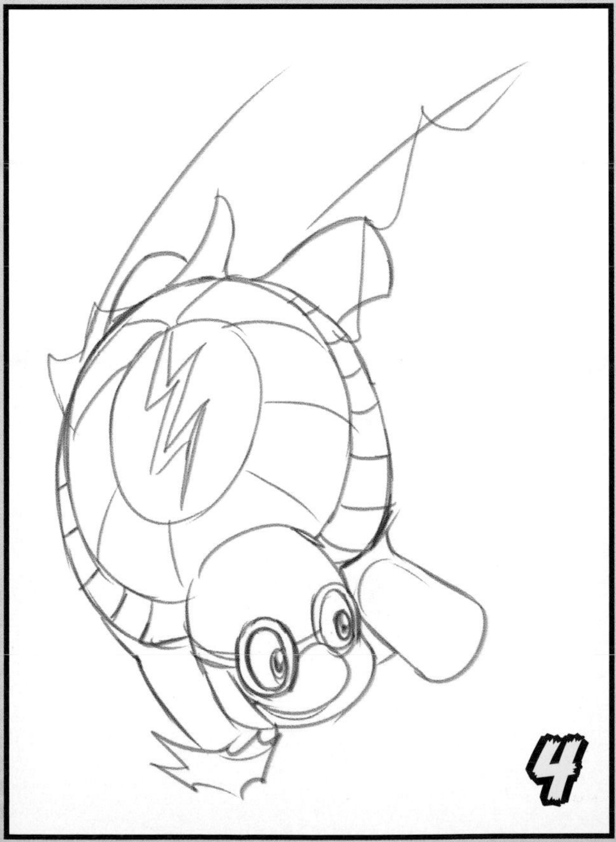
4

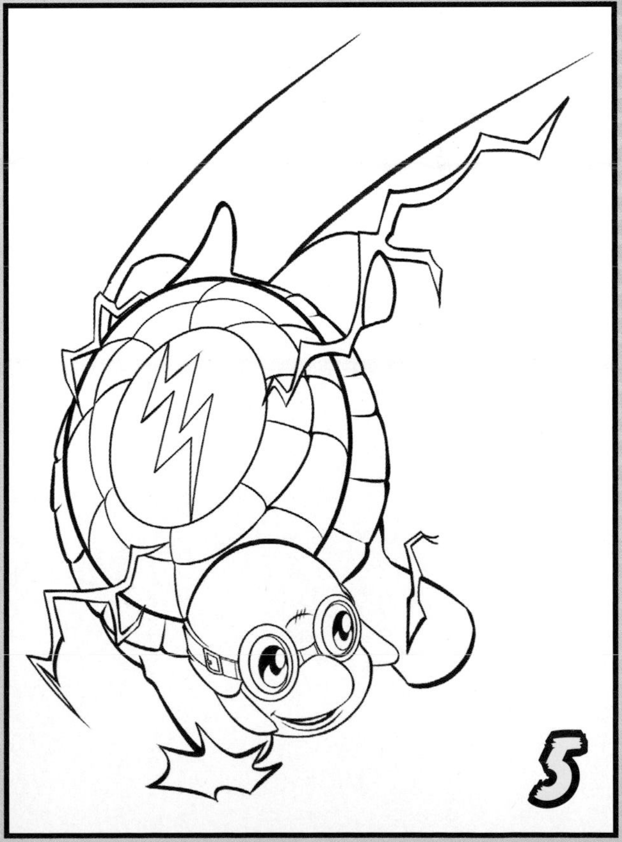
5

BEPPO

Beppo is one mischievous Super-Monkey. Before planet Krypton exploded, he stowed away in Kal-El's rocket ship. Little did he know that the baby would grow up to be Superman! But Beppo was bound for changes too. Once the two Kryptonians arrived on Earth, the yellow sun gave them both superpowers. Now Beppo soars up, up, and away to save the day!

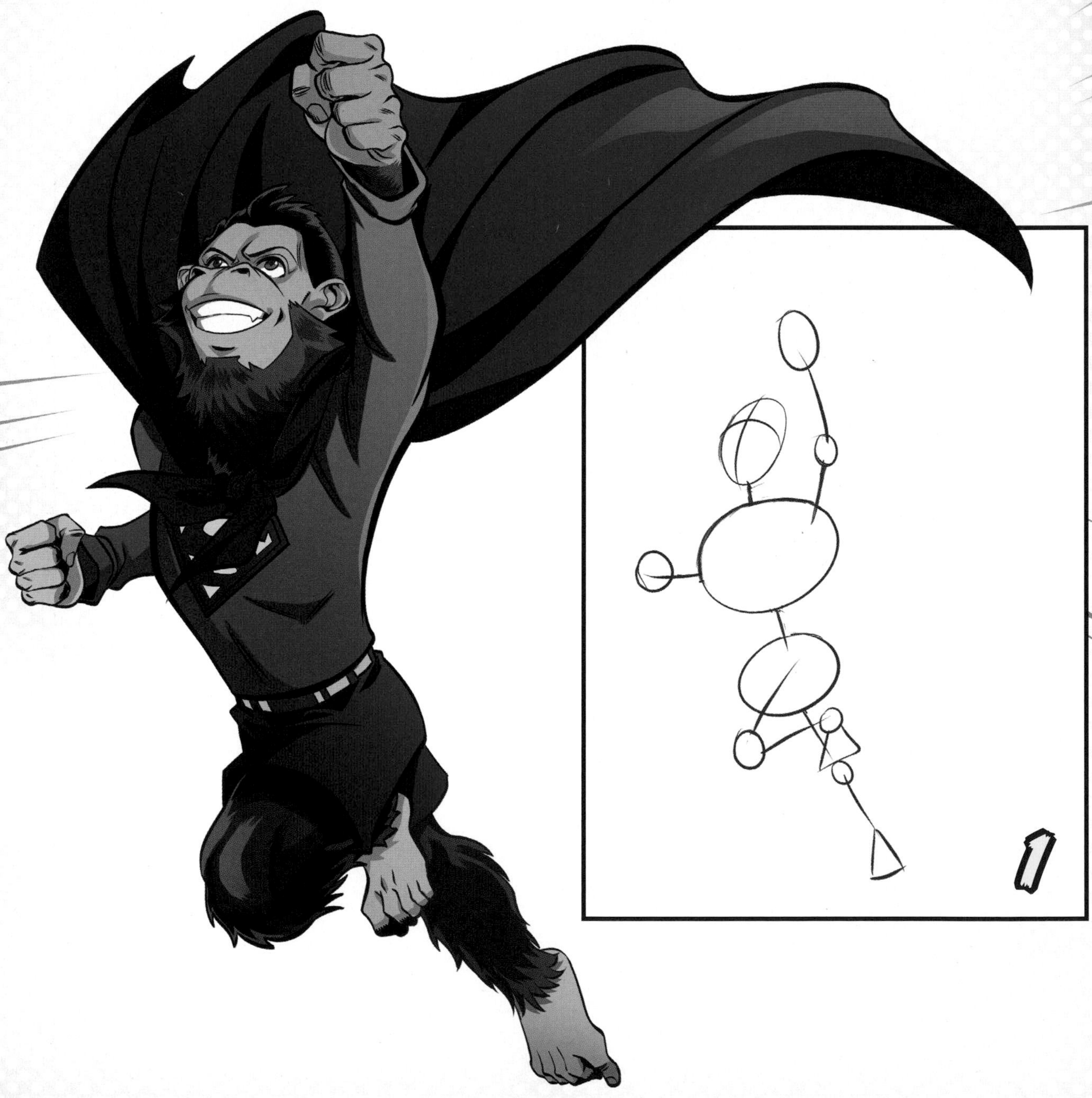
1

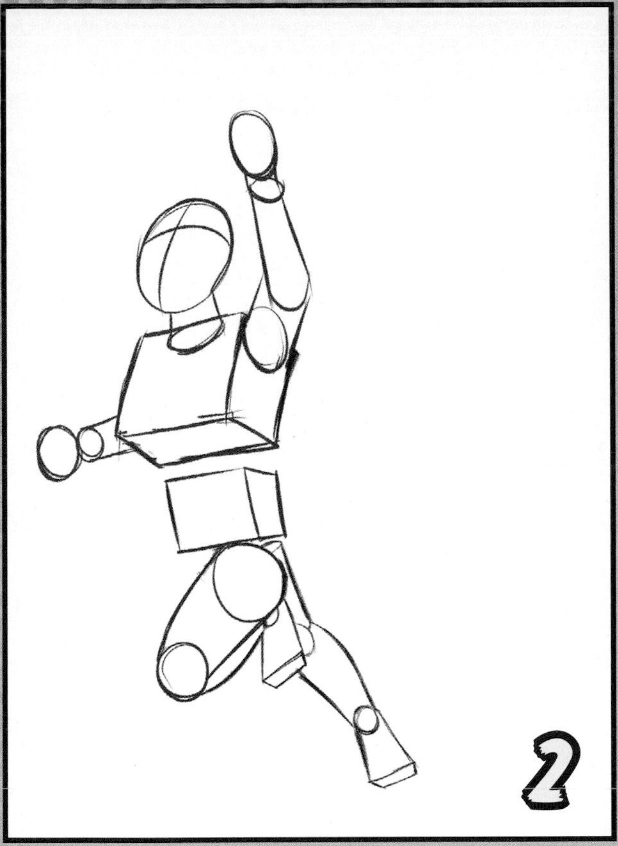
2
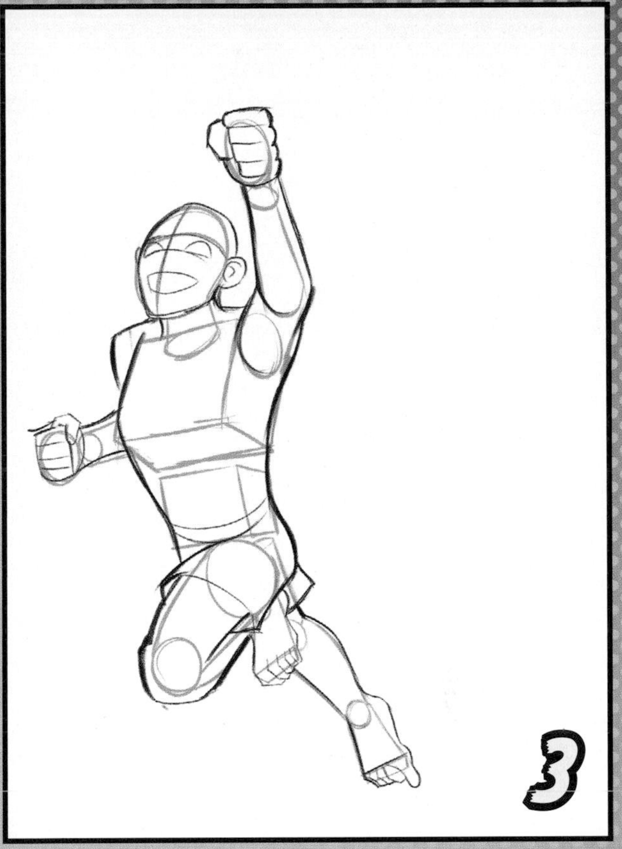
3
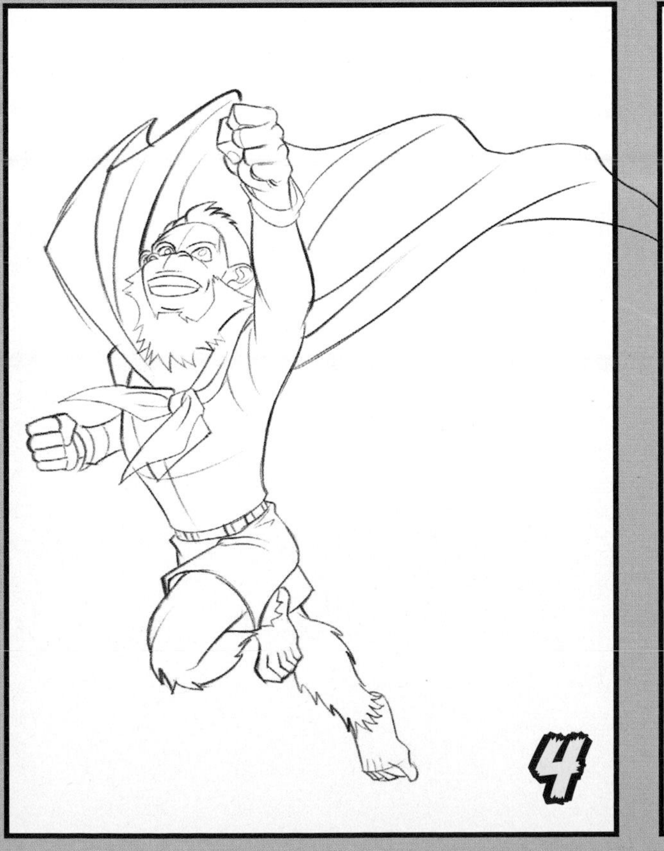
4
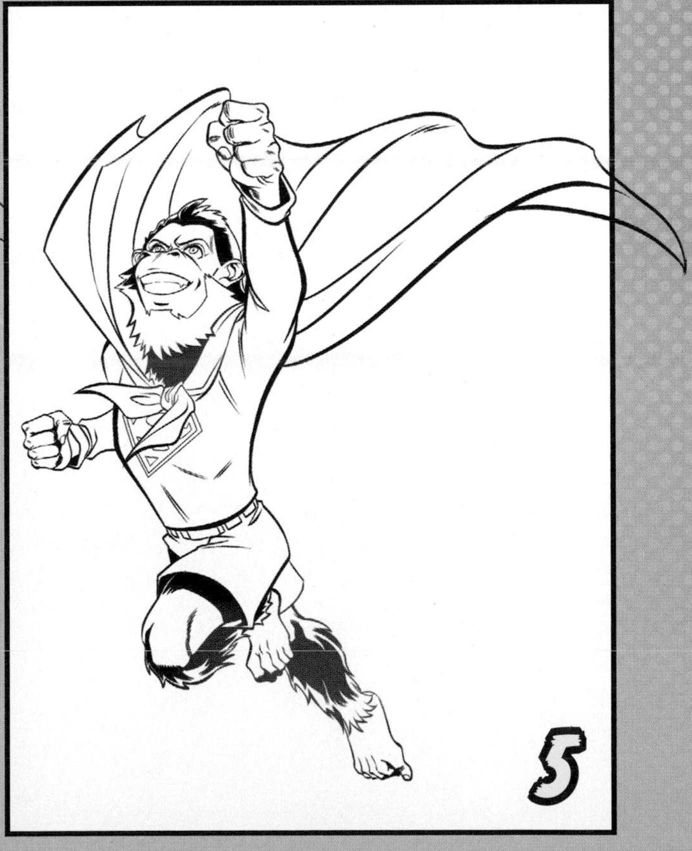
5

CRACKERS AND GIGGLES

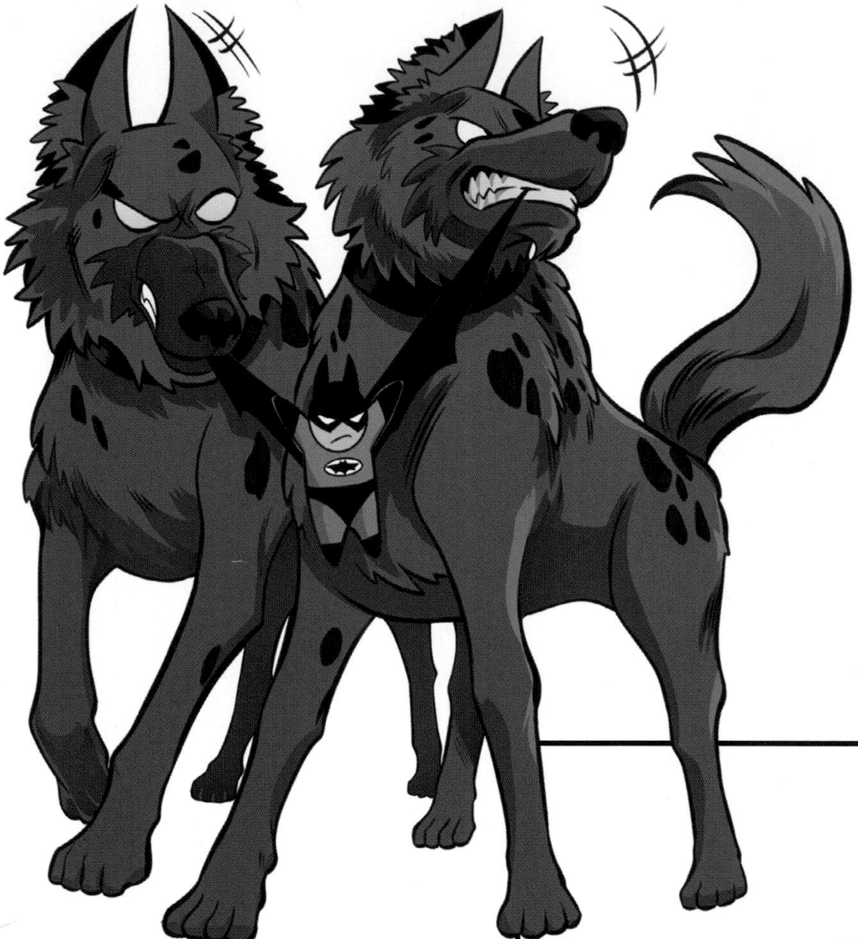

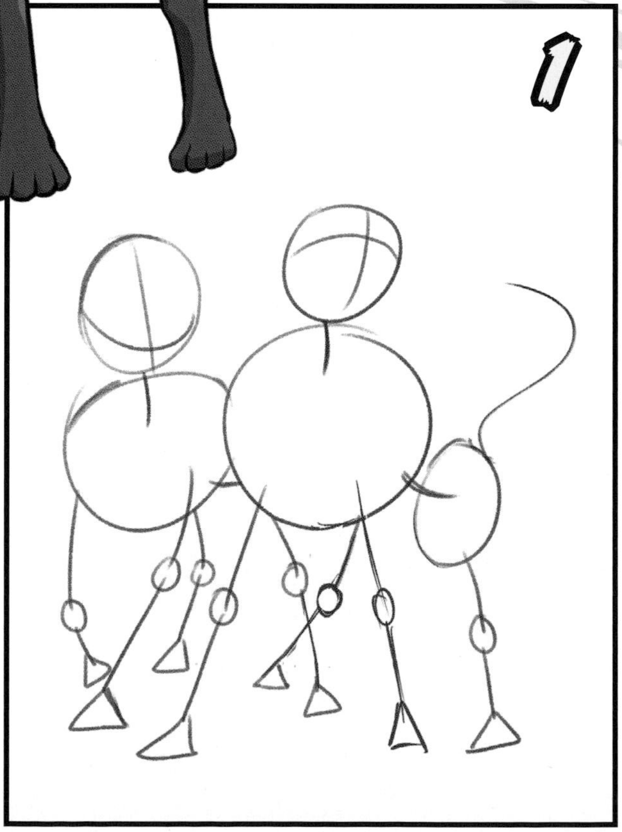
1

Few Super-Villain pets tickle the funny bone quite like Crackers and Giggles. Harley Quinn's two fiendish fur babies often show their loyalty by pulling pranks during her madcap capers. But don't let the hyenas' hilarious hijinks fool you. Given the chance, they would love to take a bite out of Batman!

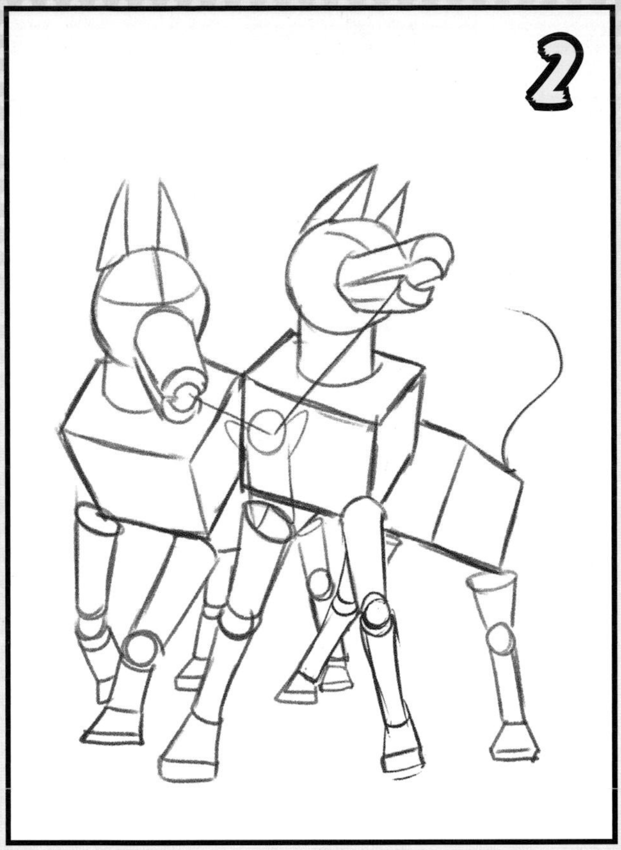
2
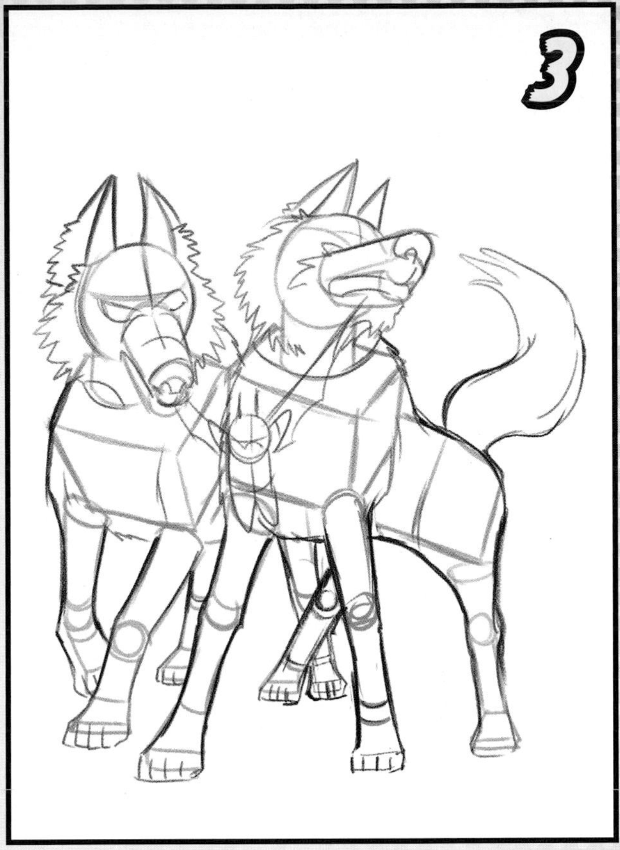
3
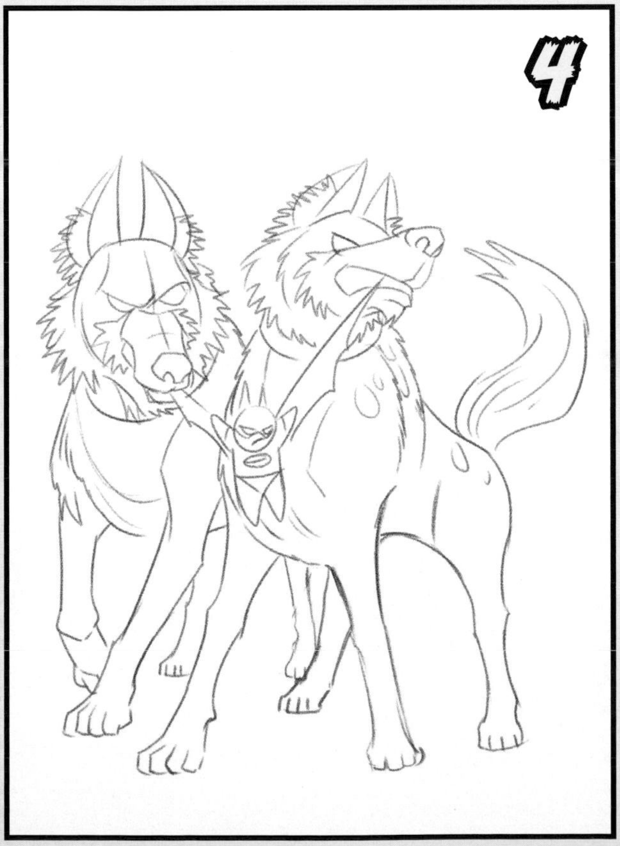
4
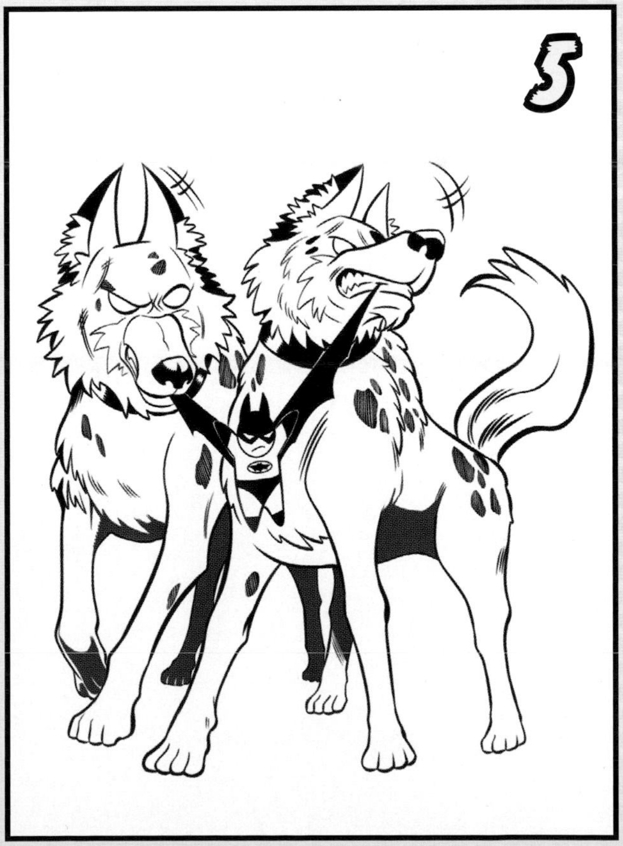
5

IGNATIUS

Leave it to Lex Luthor to have a pet as cold-blooded as himself. Ignatius is an iguana you don't want to meet on the dark streets of Metropolis. This vile reptile is superintelligent and a master of technology. Take extra care if the crook has a chunk of Kryptonite in his clutches. He'll use it to KO any Kryptonian he comes across!

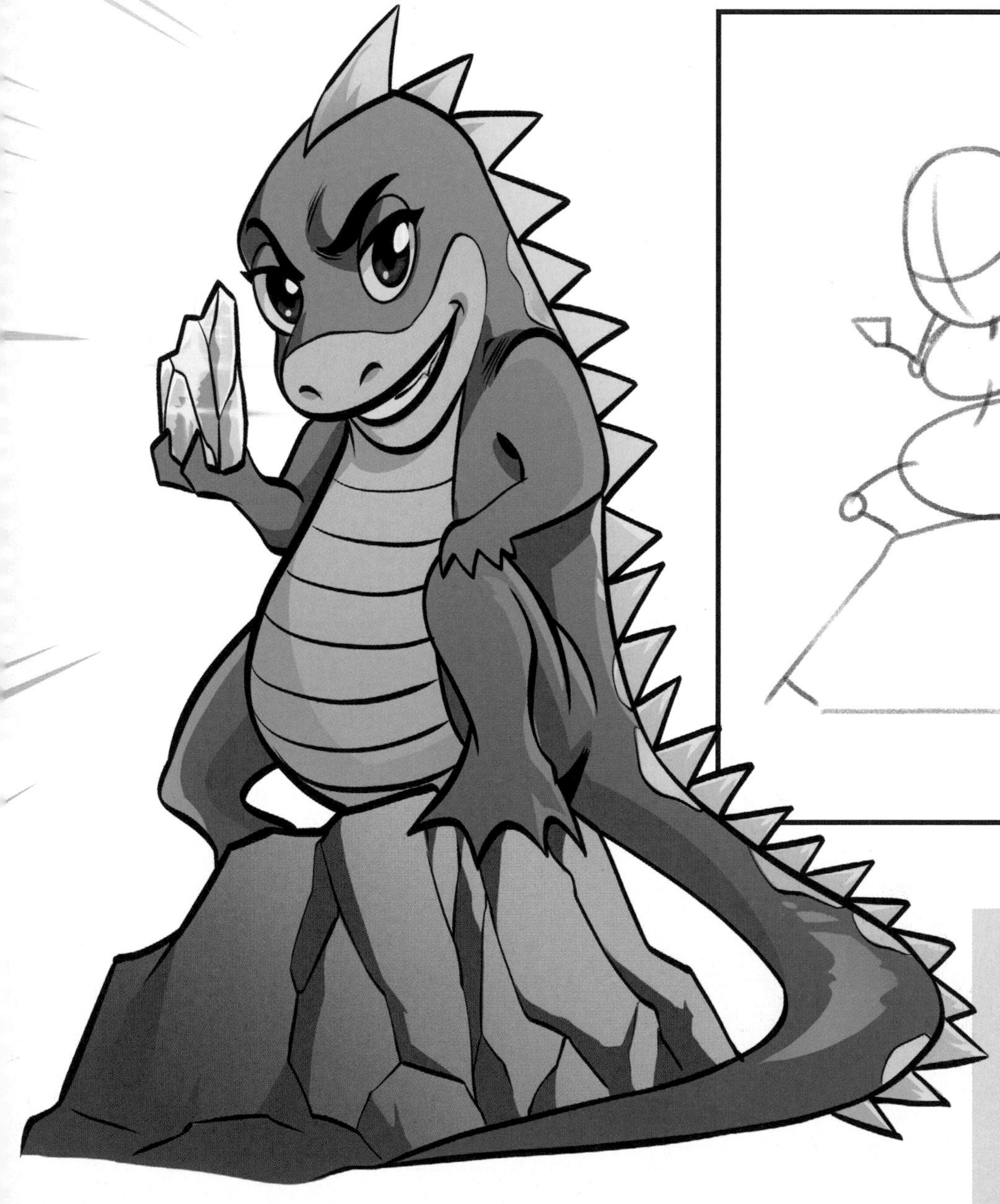

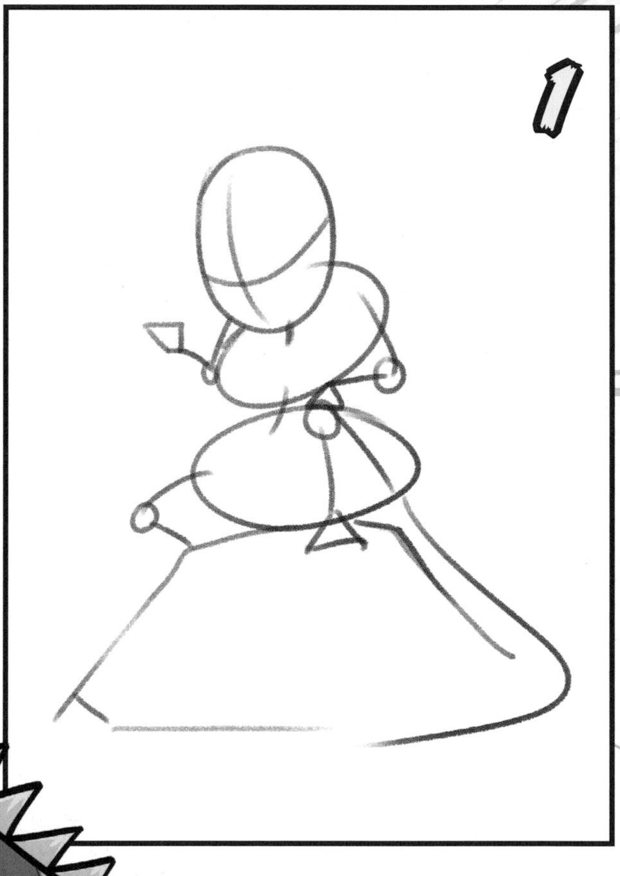
1

MANGA FACT

Manga animals don't always wear clothes. So their personalities often shine through physical features instead. Capture Ignatius's wickedness by showcasing his slithery tail, sharp spines, and evil grin.

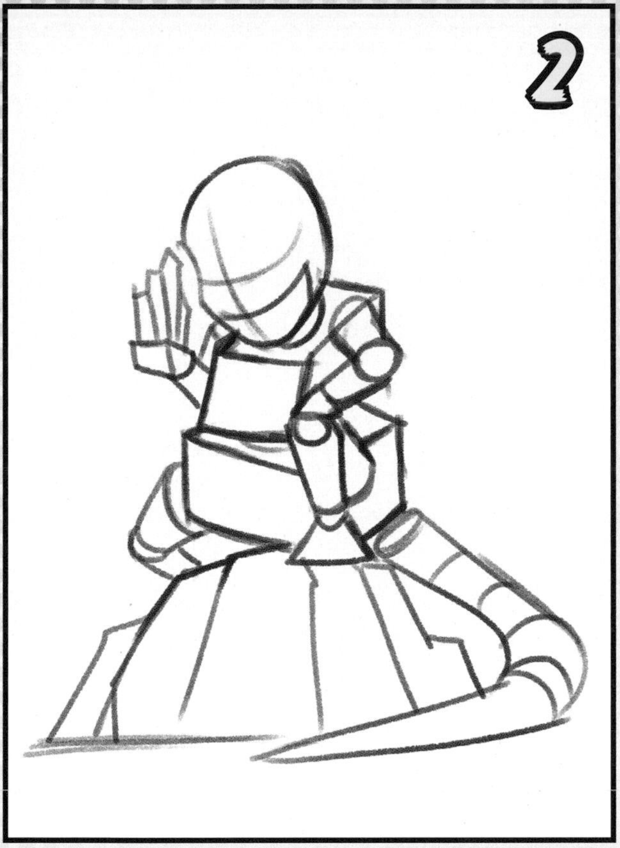
2
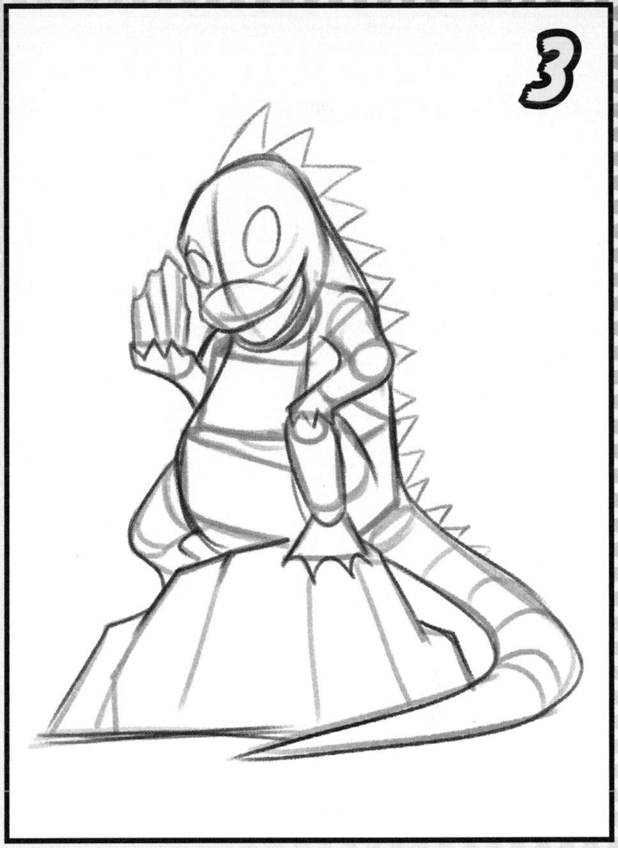
3
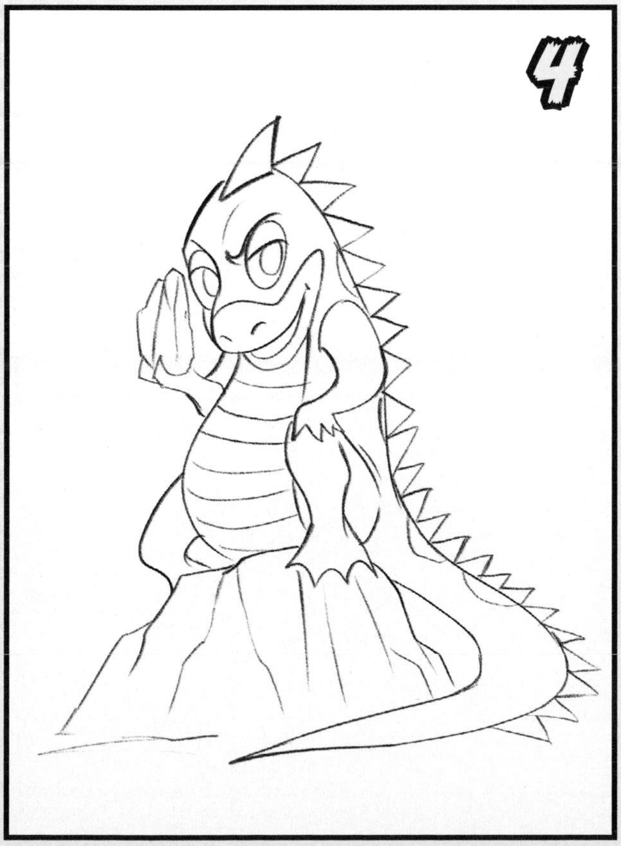
4
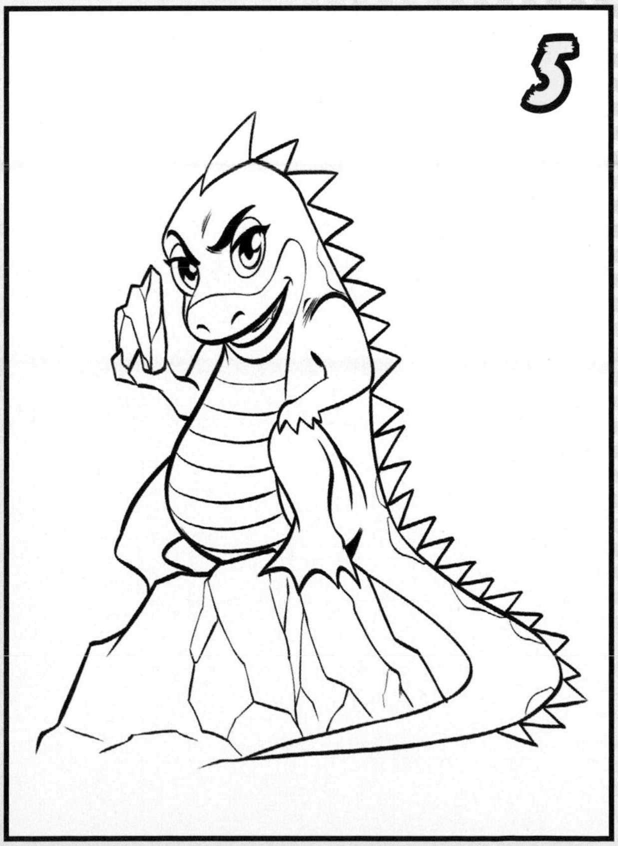
5

DOGWOOD

When Poison Ivy wanted a pet, she did what any floral felon would do. The Queen of Green used her skills to combine a dog with a plant! The result was the dastardly Dogwood. The horrible hybrid can control trees with his mind and has a bite that's worse than his bark!

MANGA FACT

Japan has manga cafés, or manga kissa. Here people can enjoy coffee and other beverages while reading their favorite manga borrowed from the café's large library.

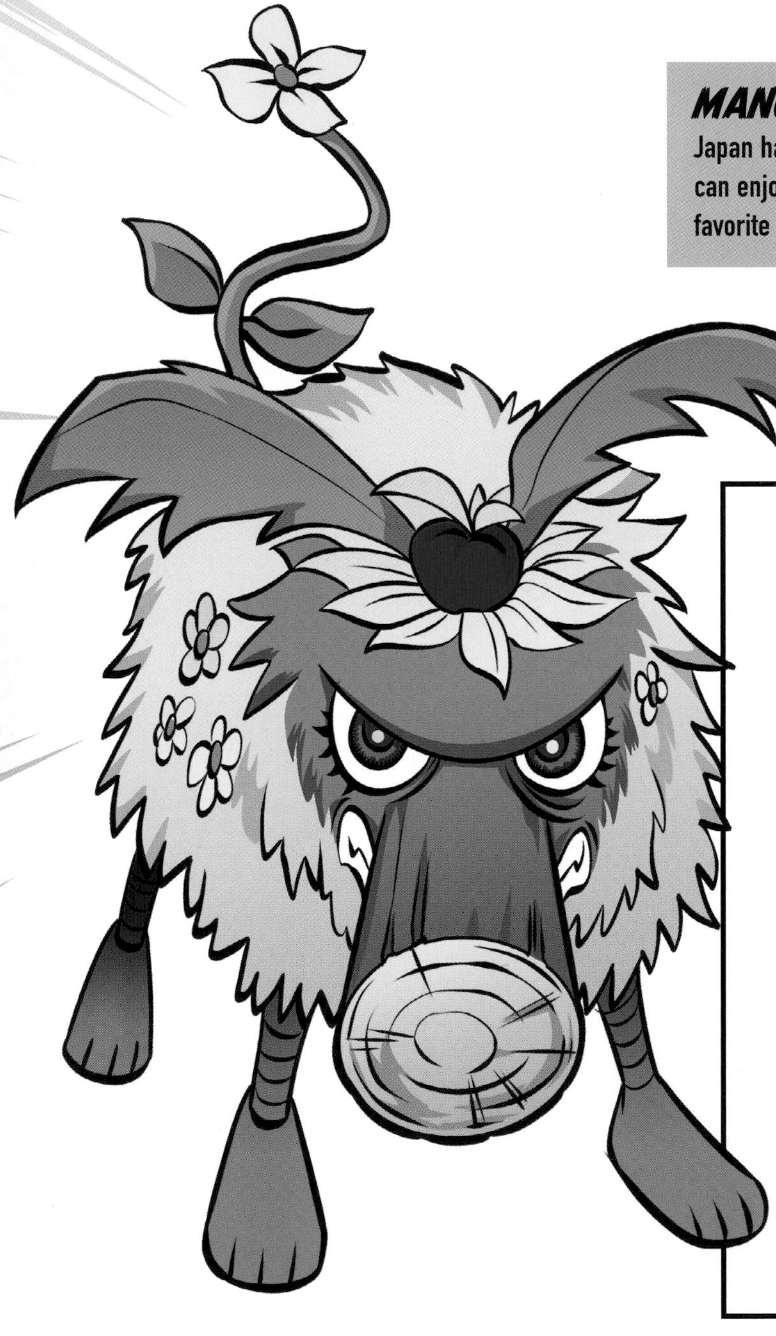

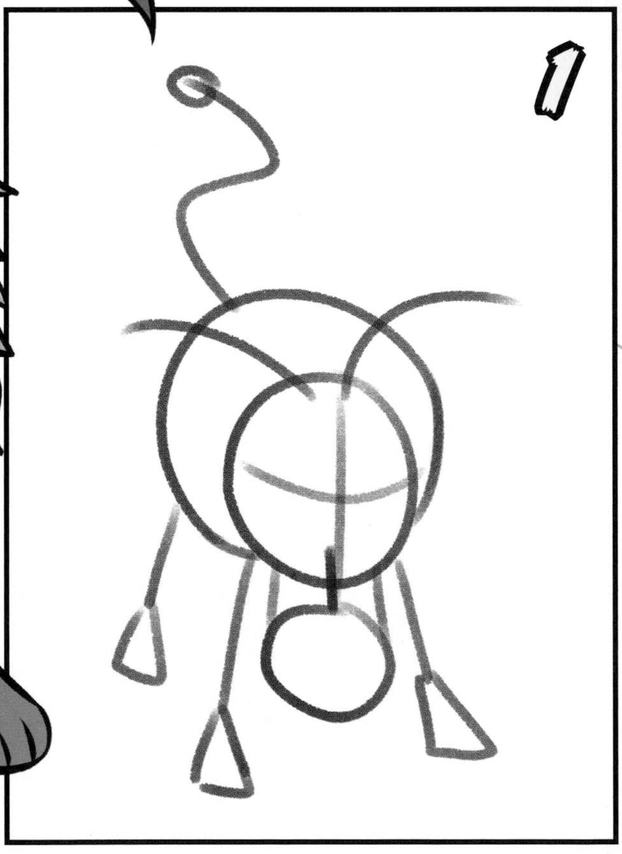
1

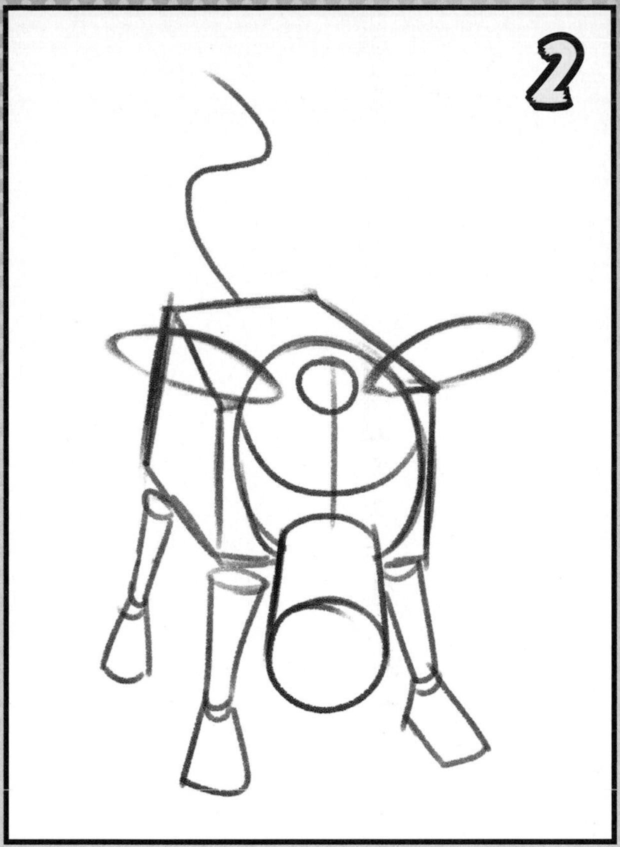
2
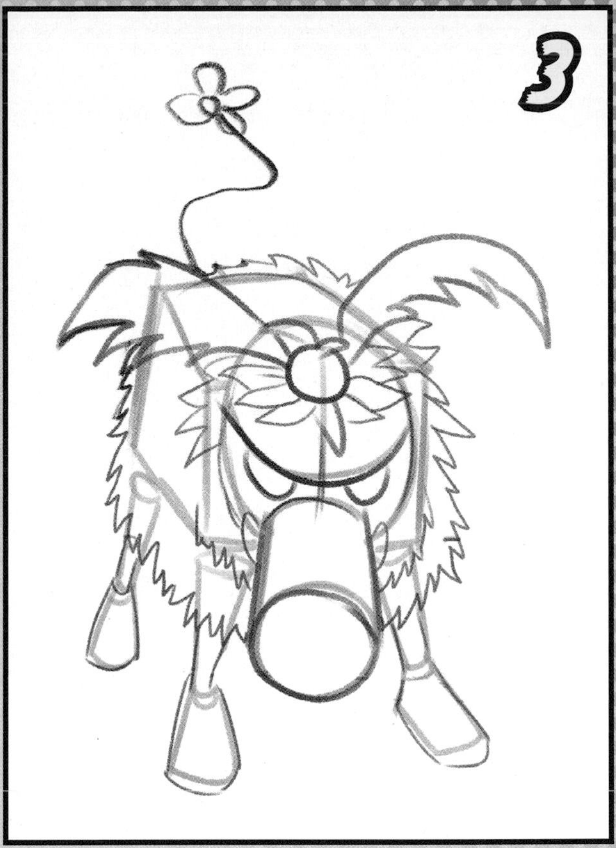
3
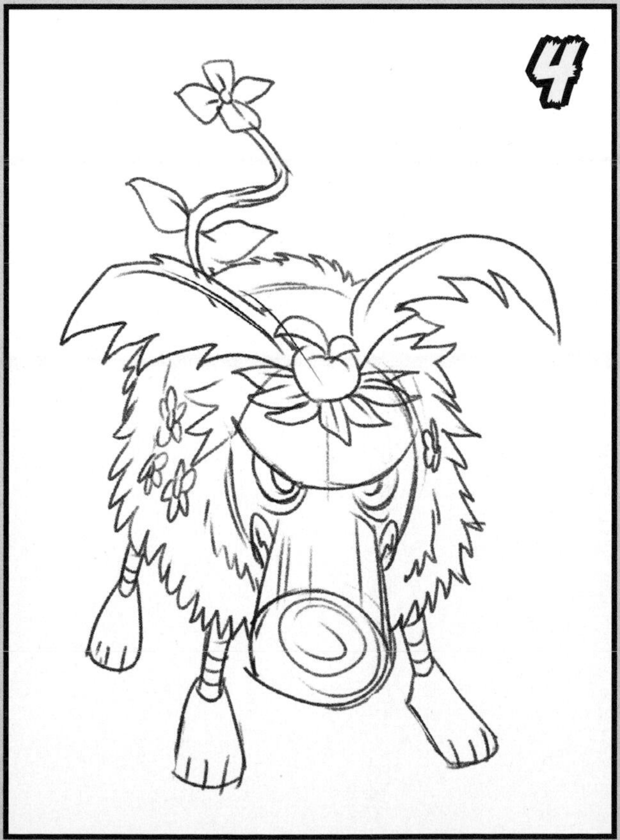
4
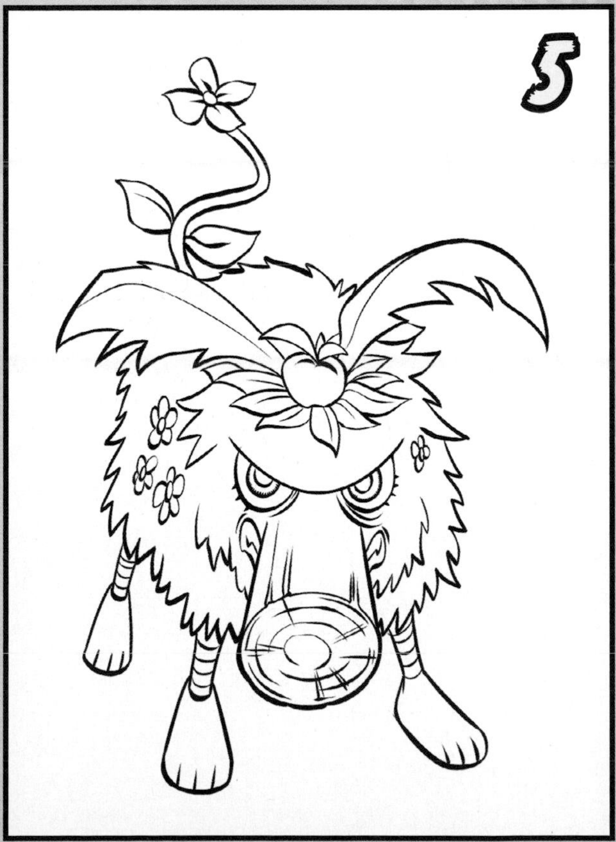
5

B'DG VS. DEX-STARR

High above Earth, a wild battle of wills rages! Green Lantern B'dg uses his green power ring against the red power ring of Red Lantern Dex-Starr. Can the space squirrel corral the corrupt kitty in the coils of justice? Or will the feline fiend cut through the Super Hero's last line of defense? YOU'RE THE MANGAKA. THE FATE OF THE PLANET IS IN YOUR HANDS!

MANGA FACT
Legendary manga creator Osamu Tezuka featured many animals in his stories. One of his most famous is Unico. This super-cute unicorn starred in his own manga from 1976 to 1979.

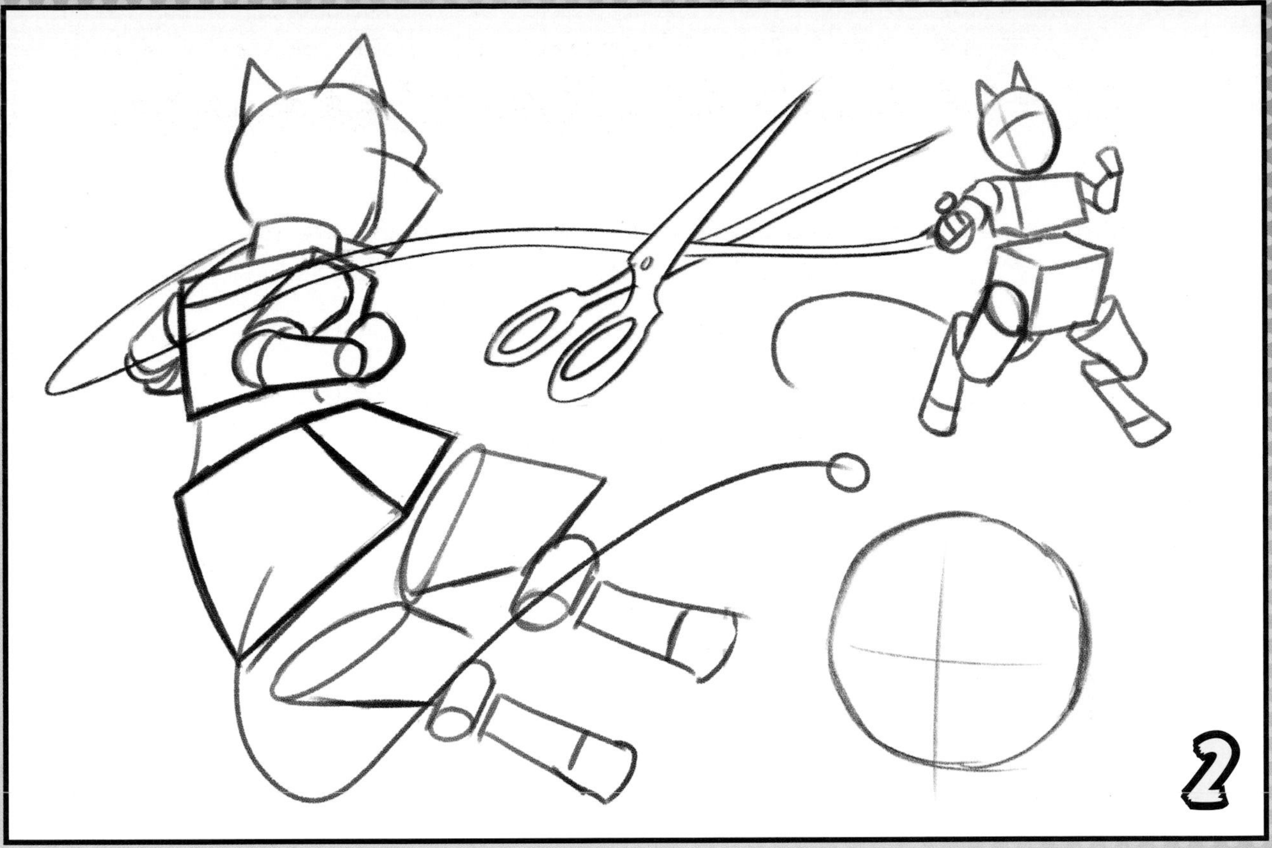
2
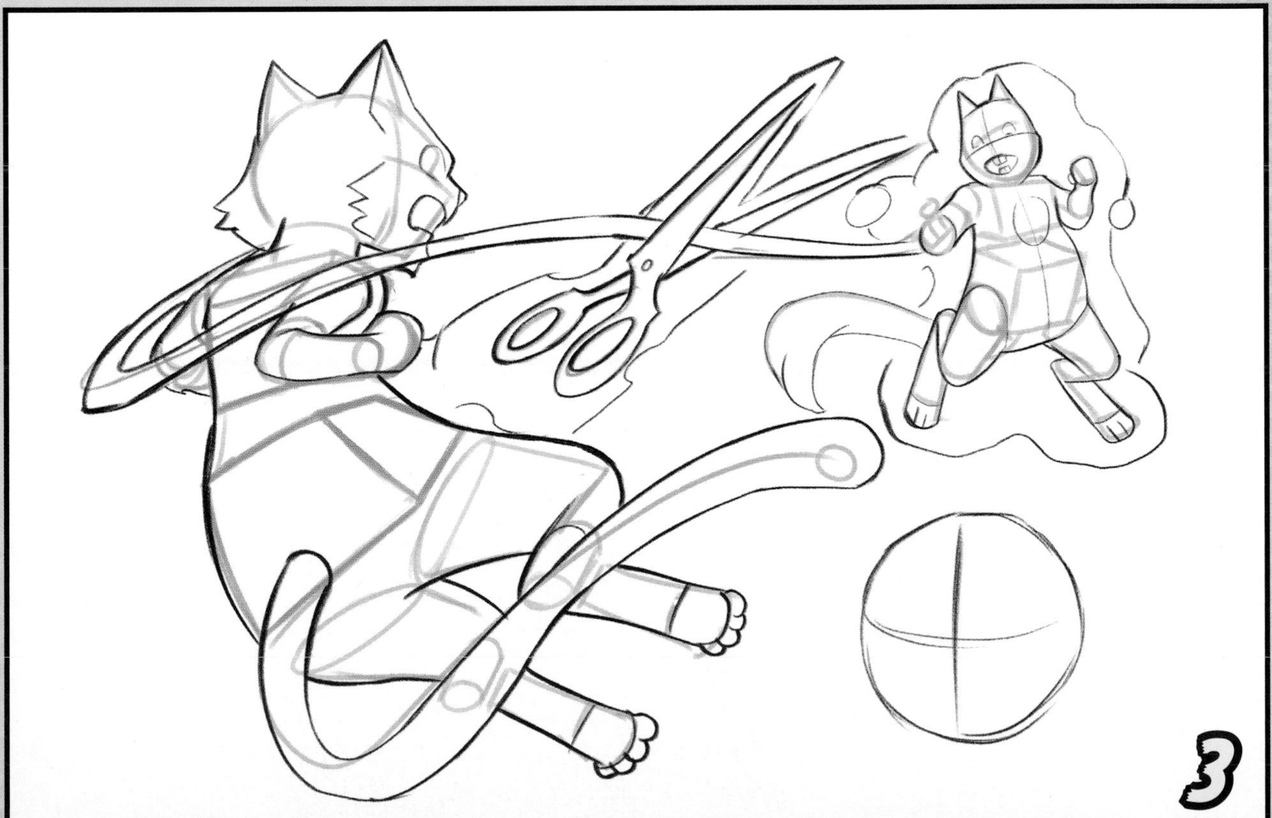
3

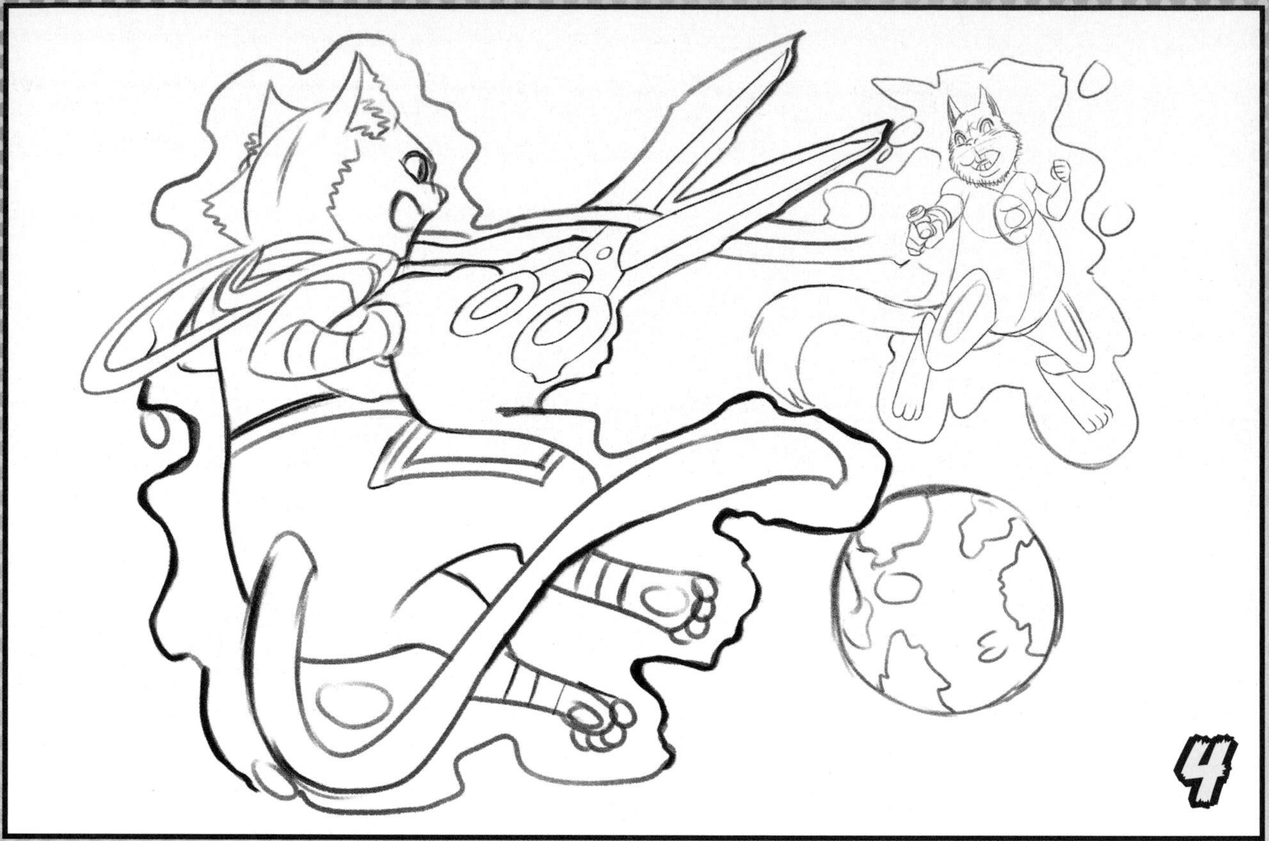
4

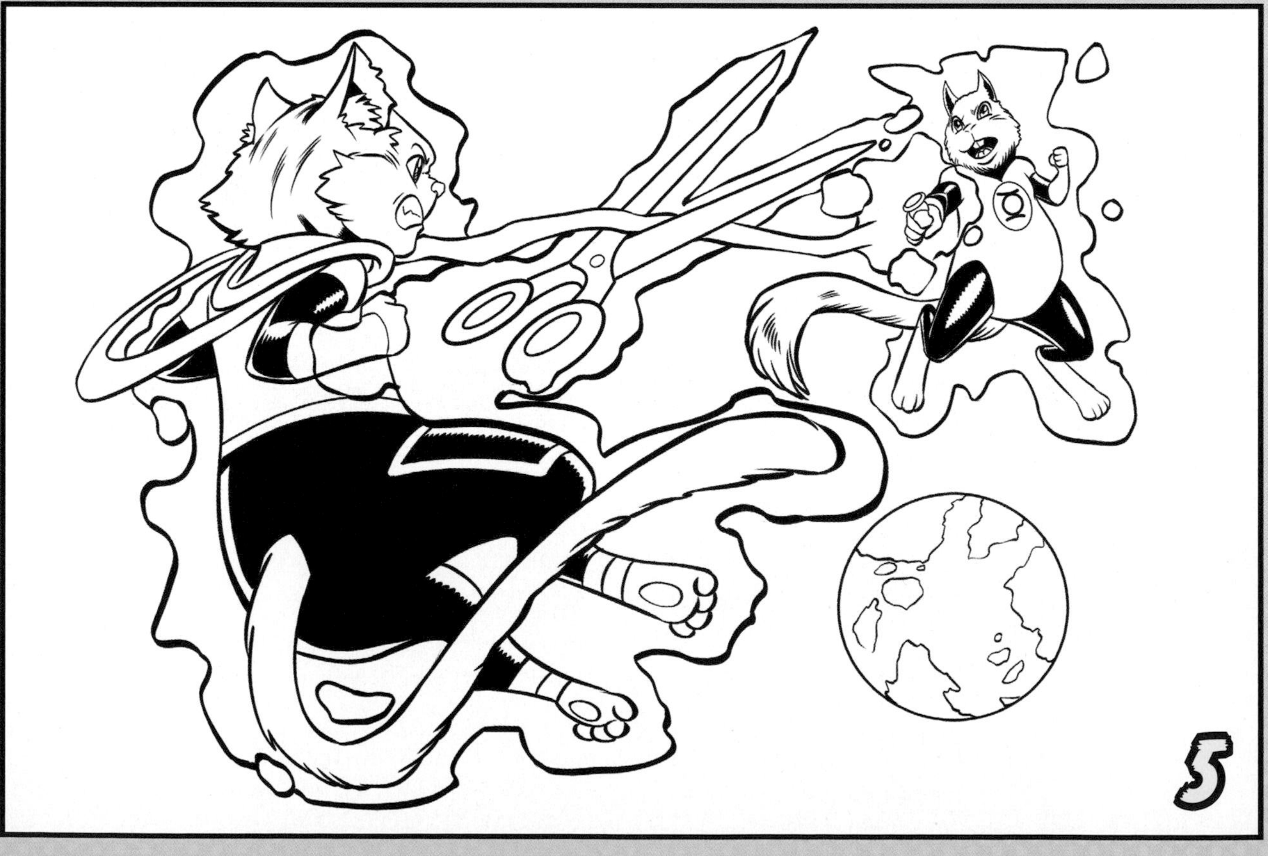
5

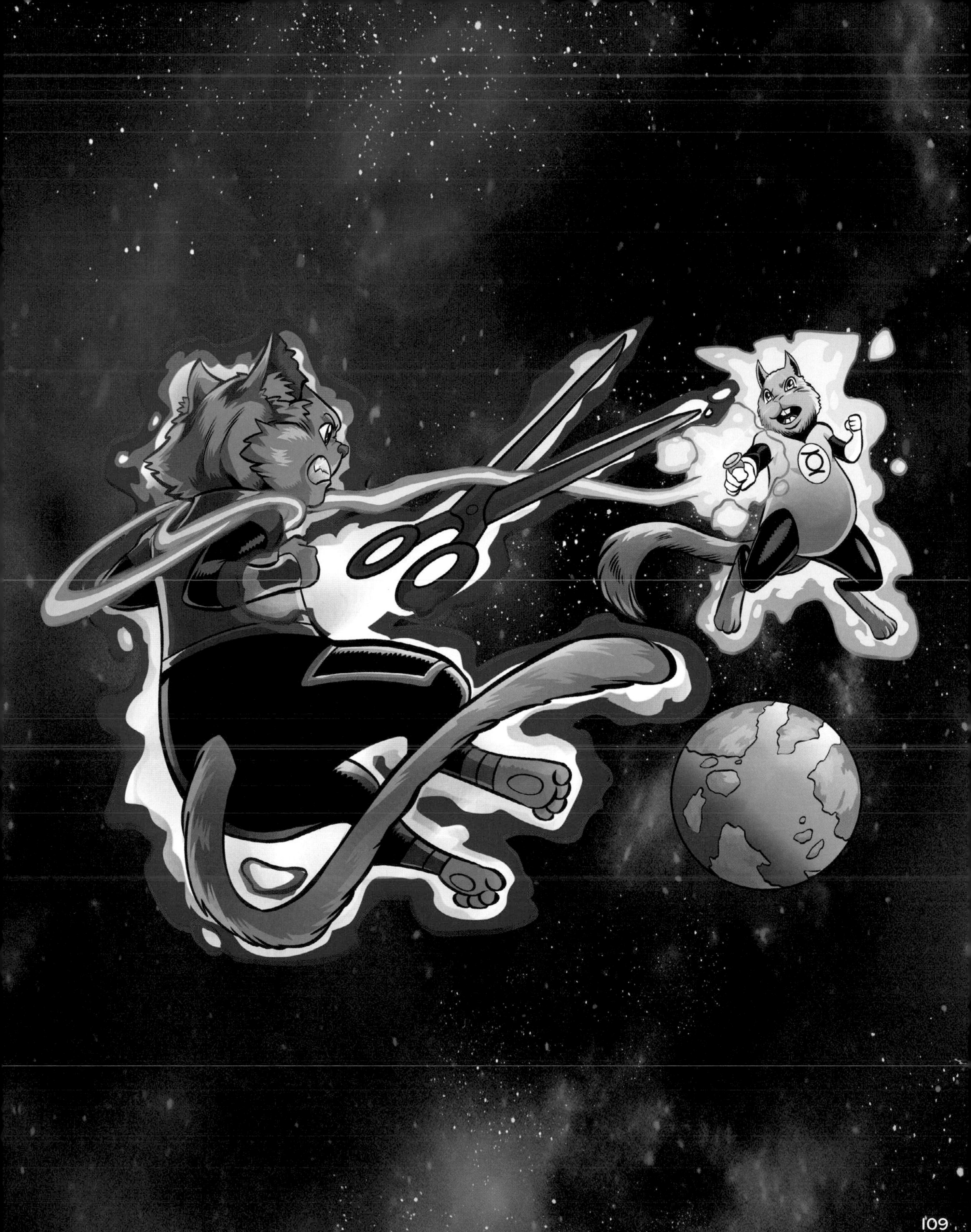

PANEL PRACTICE

Practice makes perfect! Use the following panels to sketch characters. Or, test your mangaka skills and create a complete adventure!

If you're creating a story, write it out first. Then sketch in the action. Leave room for any word balloons. Keep backgrounds simple so that the focus is on the characters. Use speed lines to add excitement. Once you're happy with how things look, polish up your drawings to finish your mini manga!

NEED STORY INSPIRATION? TRY THESE IDEAS:

- Write a classic hero versus villain matchup: Batman versus The Joker, Superman versus Lex Luthor, or Wonder Woman versus Ares.

- Team up two heroes who don't usually work together.

- Write a funny story featuring the Super-Pets.

- Have a sidekick save the day!

- Pick your two favorite Super-Villains. What happens when they join forces?

Published by Capstone Press, an imprint of Capstone.
1710 Roe Crest Drive
North Mankato, Minnesota 56003
capstonepub.com

Library of Congress Cataloging-in-Publication Data
is available on the Library of Congress website.
ISBN: 9781669062172 (paperback)
ISBN: 9781669062189 (ebook PDF)

Summary: Put a new spin on characters from the worlds of Batman,
Superman, Wonder Woman, and DC Super-Pets by learning how to draw
them as dynamic manga characters through easy-to-follow steps.

Editorial Credits
Editor: Abby Huff; Designer: Hilary Wacholz;
Media Researcher: Jo Miller; Production Specialist: Tori Abraham

Image Credits
Photos: Capstone Studio: Karon Dubke, 5 (all), Backgrounds and design elements:
Capstone throughout; Shutterstock: T-flex, cover

Wonder Woman inks by Salvatore Di Marco and Giulia Campobello
Wonder Woman colors by Francesca Ingrassia

Printed and bound in China. 5593